THE
NEW
DEMOCRACIES

THE NEW DEMOCRACIES

GLOBAL CHANGE AND U.S. POLICY

Edited by
Brad Roberts

A *Washington Quarterly* Reader

The MIT Press
Cambridge, Massachusetts
London, England

The contents of this book were first published in *The Washington Quarterly*, (ISSN 0163-660X) a publication of The MIT Press under the sponsorship of The Center for Strategic and International Studies (CSIS). Except as otherwise noted, copyright in each article is owned jointly by the Massachusetts Institute of Technology and CSIS. No article may be reproduced in whole or in part except with the express written permission of The MIT Press.

Carl Gershman, "The United States and the World Democratic Revolution," *TWQ* 12, No. 1 (Winter 1989); George Weigel, "Catholicism and Democracy: The Other Twentieth-Century Revolution," *TWQ* 12, No. 4 (Autumn 1989). Reprinted with permission of Professors World Peace Academy. Zbigniew Brzezinski, "The Crisis of Communism: The Paradox of Political Participation," *TWQ* 10, No. 4 (Autumn 1987); Amos A. Jordan and Richard Grant, "Explosive Change in China and the Soviet Union: Implications for the West," *TWQ* 12, No. 4 (Autumn 1989); Mark Falcoff, "The Democratic Prospect in Latin America," *TWQ* 13, No. 2 (Spring 1990); Colin Legum, "The Coming of Africa's Second Independence," *TWQ* 13, No. 1 (Winter 1990); Hernando de Soto, "The Informals Pose an Answer to Marx," *TWQ* 12, No. 1 (Winter 1989). Reprinted with permission of the Institute for Liberty and Democracy. Ralf Dahrendorf, "Adam Smith Was an Optimist," *TWQ* 10, No. 4 (Autumn 1987); Turgut Ozal, "Turkey's Path to Freedom and Prosperity," *TWQ* 10, No. 4 (Autumn 1987). Reprinted with permission of the Turkish Embassy, Washington D.C. Malcolm Churchill, "Parliaments, Congresses, and the Nurturing of Democracy," *TWQ* 11, No. 2 (Spring 1988); Josef Joffe, "Tocqueville Revisited: Are Good Democracies Bad Players in the Game of Nations?" *TWQ* 11, No. 1 (Winter 1988). Copyright © 1988 Josef Joffe. Reprinted with the permission of the author. Charles Robb, "Developing Democracy at Home and Abroad," *TWQ* 10, No. 4 (Autumn 1987); Paula Dobriansky, "Human Rights and U.S. Foreign Policy," *TWQ* 12, No. 2 (Spring 1989). This article is in the public domain. Enrique Krauze, "England, the United States, and the Export of Democracy," *TWQ* 12, No. 2 (Spring 1989). Copyright © 1989 Enrique Krauze. Reprinted with the permission of the author. Joshua Muravchik, "U.S. Political Parties Abroad," *TWQ* 12, No. 3 (Summer 1989); Marilyn Anne Zak, "Assisting Elections in the Third World," *TWQ* 10, No. 4 (Autumn 1987); Brad Roberts, "Human Rights and International Security," *TWQ* 13, No. 2 (Spring 1990); article is in the public domain. Hans Binnendijk, "Authoritarian Regimes in Transition," *TWQ* 10, No. 2 (Spring 1987); Larry Diamond, "Beyond Authoritarianism and Totalitarianism: Strategies for Democratization," *TWQ* 12, No. 1 (Winter 1989).

Selection, foreword, and introduction, copyright © 1990 by The Center for Strategic and International Studies and the Massachusetts Institute of Technology.

ISBN 0-262-18137-1 (hard)
    0-262-68062-9 (paper)

Library of Congress Cataloging-in-Publication Data

The New democracies : global change and U.S. policy / edited by Brad
  Roberts.
      p. cm.
    "A Washington quarterly reader."
    ISBN 0-262-18137-1. —ISBN 0-262-68062-9 (pbk.)
    1. Democracy—History—20th century. 2. World
  politics—1985–1995. I. Roberts, Brad. II. Washington quarterly.
JC421.N48 1990
321.8'09'04—dc26 —dc20   89-78549
                                                                 CIP

Contents

vii Foreword
     Zbigniew Brzezinski

ix Introduction
    Brad Roberts

I. The Democratic Prospect

3 The United States and the World Democratic Revolution
   Carl Gershman

17 Catholicism and Democracy: The Other Twentieth-Century Revolution
    George Weigel

II. Democracy Abroad

41 The Crisis of Communism: The Paradox of Political Participation
    Zbigniew Brzezinski

49 Explosive Change in China and the Soviet Union: Implications for the West
    Amos A. Jordan and Richard L. Grant

65 The Democratic Prospect in Latin America
    Mark Falcoff

75 The Coming of Africa's Second Independence
    Colin Legum

III. Democracy, Prosperity, and Governance

89 The Informals Pose an Answer to Marx
    Hernando de Soto

97 Adam Smith Was an Optimist
    Ralf Dahrendorf

105 Turkey's Path to Freedom and Prosperity
     Turgut Ozal

111 Parliaments, Congresses, and the Nurturing of Democracy
     Malcolm Churchill

123 Tocqueville Revisited: Are Good Democracies Bad Players in the Game of Nations?
     Josef Joffe

IV. The United States and the Democratic Revolution

137 Developing Democracy at Home and Abroad
     Charles S. Robb

145 Human Rights and U.S. Foreign Policy
     Paula J. Dobriansky

163 England, the United States, and the Export of Democracy
     Enrique Krauze

173 U.S. Political Parties Abroad
     Joshua Muravchik

183 Assisting Elections in the Third World
     Marilyn Anne Zak

203 Human Rights and International Security
     Brad Roberts

215 Authoritarian Regimes in Transition
     Hans Binnendijk

227 Beyond Authoritarianism and Totalitarianism: Strategies for Democratization
     Larry Diamond

Foreword

THE STUDENT OF contemporary international politics, and even more so the policy practitioner, often has a difficult time identifying those long-term historical trends that shape human affairs and national destinies. In an age when so many are seeking technical or bureaucratic solutions to the problems of human organization, it is urgently necessary to stand back and witness the sweep of history unfolding in daily events. The twentieth century embodies, after all, a time of tremendous ferment across the entire spectrum of economic, political, social, technological, and even spiritual matters. In retrospect, it is likely to be seen as that time when the principles and wisdoms first embodied in the liberal democracies around the Atlantic were discovered anew by peoples of quite different traditions. The changes of values and beliefs underlying the turmoil in the Second and Third Worlds will be seen, with the advantage of hindsight, as truly historic.

Despite the potency and breadth of today's democratic revolution, relatively little scholarship has been generated on its dynamics and prospects. What literature exists tends to be parochial or naive, or both. This volume makes an exceptionally valuable contribution to our understanding of democracy in today's world.

The Washington Quarterly rightly has earned for itself in recent years a reputation as a journal of excellence and intellectual leadership in international policy. As a member of its editorial board, I have encouraged its pursuit of those basic forces underlying the contemporary policy debate. Through the CSIS International Leadership Forum, a project in which I also collaborate with *TWQ* Editor Brad Roberts and CSIS Vice Chairman Joe Jordan, we have been able to marshall some of the world's most thoughtful and articulate analysts of the democratic prospect. The Forum has issued a number of reports, two of which are available from CSIS, *The Democratic Revolution* and *Participation: A Pragmatic Agenda for the 1990s*, and the more detailed background analyses have been published in the pages of *The Washington Quarterly*. Additional materials have been commissioned by Brad Roberts and the journal's editorial board in order to develop a comprehensive analysis of the democratic prospect. The resulting product is both insightful and rigorous.

The 20 authors in this volume have succeeded in capturing the essence of a highly complex political phenomenon. No reader can come away from these pages without enhanced historic optimism as well as a better understanding of the difficult path ahead. This book is a challenge to think more creatively about contemporary international politics. It should serve also as a stimulus to both further analysis—and more effective policy.

Zbigniew Brzezinski
Counselor, Center for Strategic and
International Studies

Introduction

THE PRINCIPLES OF democratic governance have emerged with striking potency in the politics of countries around the world. From Argentina to Zimbabwe, political communities the world over today are struggling with the same basic problems of governance and prosperity. In more participatory, democratic forms of governance they seem to be finding pragmatic solutions to political and economic problems. The breadth and depth of this embrace of democracy suggest that it is appropriate to think of a democratic revolution in global politics. Whether this revolution will be sustained and with what import for international affairs are questions that remain unanswered.

Only a few years ago, the democratic prospect did not seem so bright. The tide of history appeared to be moving against democracy in the 1970s. The postcolonial era of democratization in the Third World had ended in a long series of coups and political setbacks. There were few or no hints of the changes to come in the Communist world. Even in the established democracies, fears were voiced about the capacity of democratic institutions to cope with economic decay and the political demands of newly-mobilized groups and of extremists on both ends. Daniel Patrick Moynihan captured the temper of the times in writing that liberal democracy "is where the world was, not where it is going...Increasingly, democracy is seen as an arrangement peculiar to a handful of North Atlantic countries."

The democratic prospect looks entirely different from the vantage of 1990. The large number of democratic transitions in the developing world and particularly in Latin America is a testament to this growing appeal of democracy. Those transitions are a symptom of the bright democratic prospect, however, and not its cause. They reflect a sea change in political attitudes toward and expectations about democracy.

In the past, the appeal of democracy tended to be largely idealistic. If democracy was admired widely as a form of governance consistent with liberty, it also was considered by many to be less effective than other forms of governance at meeting basic social needs. If the various democracies founded in the eighteenth and nineteenth centuries were admired in the twentieth century as progressive and modern, democratic institutions were seen by many to be culturally bound and irrelevant to the needs of other societies.

With the rising public demand around the world for forms of governance that work, democracy has surged ahead. Today, its idealistic appeal has merged with a pragmatic one. Diverse polities seem to have discovered the wisdom of Winston Churchill's observation that, as messy and imperfect as it is, democracy is preferable to all other forms of government.

The practical utility of democracy

relates to keenly perceived contemporary needs. One such need is social justice. The virtues of democracy in this regard have been rediscovered in recent years. No other form of government is so well equipped to cope with the competing legitimate demands of pluralistic societies. Democracy generates the kind of political authority and policy flexibility necessary to cope with fundamental socioeconomic change. Furthermore, it facilitates an open decision-making process that draws on the common sense experience of many actors to make informed policy.

A second need is prosperity. As a generator of short-term bursts of high growth rates or of the rapid redistribution of wealth, democracies have not always done as well as a few—or as badly as most—authoritarian states. Over the long run, however, democracies tend to promote the steady accumulation and distribution of national wealth at a pace that does not tear apart the social fabric.

A third keenly perceived need is a more stable and peaceful international environment. There is not, of course, a strict connection between democracy and peace. History does suggest, however, that there is some connection between domestic political structure and international order. The German philosopher Immanuel Kant, writing in his *Prolegomena to a Perpetual Peace*, provides some careful thinking on this subject that has not been outdated by two centuries of experience. Kant argued that states disposed to respect the rights of individuals would respect the legitimacy of other countries similarly governed and encourage rather than restrict mutually satisfying trade relations, leading to the gradual emergence of a so-called zone of peace. This perspective seems to underlie much of the contemporary sentiment

about democracy and peace. There is no guarantee that democracies will not wage war, but democratic states are likely to be more prudent in their calculations of the national interest and the justification for war than are states dominated by narrow, highly ideological elites.

The fourth need is human dignity. The sense of being robbed of one's dignity is common to people in totalitarian societies, in countries suffering failed development policies, and in states undergoing wrenching modernization. Although political philosophers in these varied countries may not all subscribe to the Western natural right tradition, they seem to share a sense that democracy is the form of governance most consistent with the natural aspirations of humanity in terms of the need to live in a world respectful of the individual's integrity and spiritual identity. An instinctive revulsion to control is a quality common to people of all cultures and defeated by the state only temporarily and with great diligence.

In sum, democracy is more widely understood today not just as an end in itself but as a means to social justice, national prosperity and development, and peace. The democratic revolution has reconnected contemporary political leaders to wider historical experiences and to a rich body of political philosophy in the West and elsewhere that embodies and analyzes the ideals of popular sovereignty—of government "of, by, and for the people."

Of course, in none of these matters is democracy perfect. Any study of democracy and world politics that fails to discuss the problems of democracy would be badly incomplete. Its shortcomings are well known. In fact, democracy can be its own worst enemy. Democracies develop slowly if they are going to have any chance to be authentic and durable; but slowly paced democratic transitions are likely to strain public patience. Democracies are distorted easily as they experiment with institutional forms; the Weimar Republic is a good example of a democracy so excessively consumed with representation in its mathematical form that it lost sight of the broader goal of governability. Democracies sometimes break down when confronted with the problems of governance posed by national and religious minorities. Democracies are also vulnerable to intervention by military authorities grown impatient with the "excesses of democracy." The protection of minority rights is a special problem for democracies. Furthermore, democracies sometimes pursue inconsistent policies. Their policy choices can be rash.

The hard truth is that the adjectives democratic and nondemocratic do not align themselves perfectly in the real political world with the adjectives benign and malign. The fact that mobs can lynch and that kings can rule wisely mean that one's analytical tasks and one's political tasks are complicated. But the point is that, perfect government being beyond the reach of man, no other form of government has so many virtues.

The accomplishments of democracy in providing for pragmatic governance are particularly significant in the context of changing perceptions of authoritarian and totalitarian governance. A certain legitimacy once accrued to authoritarian and totalitarian states—whether of the right or left—as brutal but necessary. Dictators of the right have defended their systems as the only means of achieving economic growth and social peace and justice, while Communists have used much the same defense. But poor economic performance and the total disregard for

social, political, and human needs common to these systems have eroded the perception of legitimacy. The corruption and inefficiency of totalitarian and authoritarian states also have diminished their appeal, underscoring again the pragmatic virtue of a democratic system that provides for government accountability through popular participation in decision making.

However bright the democratic prospect, the speedy and complete democratic transformation of the world is not imminent. Democracy is not uncontested. The evaporation of support for authoritarian solutions of the right or left has proceeded more quickly at the popular level than at the elite level. Furthermore, even as the political power of communism has declined, a new challenger to democracy has emerged—radical religious fundamentalism. The radical Islam of contemporary Iran is perhaps the best but not the only example of this factor. It is wrong-headed to think that all Islam per se is contradictory to the democratic ethic; indeed, certain forms of Islam have facilitated broader political participation in heretofore authoritarian structures. But a radical Islam, such as that in Iran, which plays on xenophobia and blackmail to advance the interests of a narrow elite, is fundamentally contradictory to democracy.

As these essays demonstrate, recent years also have shown that democracy is not just for modern, prosperous, Western, Christian, or racially homogenous societies. Those democracies with their roots in centuries past should look at their own diversity in terms of the genesis of public institutions and the character of constitutional structure to appreciate that democracy must take its own course and result in forms of democratic government that differ in appearance, even function, but not in essential process or purpose. An ethnocentric tendency in established democracies—and the naive belief that democracy can be exported—has done a disservice to the democratic revolution.

It is common to assess the prospects for democracy in terms of the workings of great historical forces and the machinations of great power politics. These factors are certainly relevant. However, they trivialize the principal motor of political change—the decisions and actions of individuals. The external community and environment may help shape choices made by domestic political actors, but ultimately the actions that matter are those of men and women, often acting alone and with great courage. Today's international democratic revolution is the work of thousands of people to build democracy, often one small step at a time. Their commitment to personal sacrifice for the larger good is often exercised largely invisibly to the existing political structure and to democrats abroad.

It is no longer true, if it ever was, that the promotion of democracy is almost solely the foreign policy business of the United States. But the U.S. role remains essential. Promoting democracy abroad is one of the oldest themes of U.S. foreign policy. Many of the country's earliest leaders held the view that the best way to promote democracy abroad was to perfect the American experiment at home while remaining remote from the world, a view that has lingered in U.S. politics ever since.

The obligations of international leadership reluctantly assumed by the United States in the twentieth century have sharpened the conflict between morality and realpolitik, creating an apparent choice between promoting democracy and pursuing ill-defined national security interests. For decades, the shadow of U.S. power and of narrowly defined security interests has diminished the moral leadership that the United States has sought to exercise on behalf of democracy. In many parts of the world, the United States has been considered an obstacle to democracy; unfortunately, this perception has not always been at odds with the facts.

Many observers do not appreciate the extent to which the U.S. approach has matured. A modest but healthy degree of self-criticism of its international role has emerged in the United States. There is a growing appreciation that the ideological competition between freedom and totalitarianism has shifted in the direction of freedom. There is a recognition of the declining utility of conventional military intervention in the resolution of conflicts in the developing world and, concomitantly, of the growing importance of political development. There is a growing confidence, based on experience in the Philippines and elsewhere, of the ability of the United States to exercise diplomatic influence judiciously in the cause of peaceful democratic transitions in key states.

This collection of essays offers a comprehensive review of the themes outlined above. It attempts to convey the drama and potency of the competition over political values in the late twentieth century while shying away from naive or foolish optimism. By probing behind the headlines about political turmoil in Africa, Asia, Europe, and Latin America, this volume offers the reader a realistic assessment of the dimensions of the democratic revolution. Careful consideration is given to the continued role of alternatives to democracy. The essays also explore the meaning of democracy in different regions and cultures, helping to expand thinking about the content of democratic ideals. A key theme cutting across the discussion is the relationship between political participation and economic empowerment, with detailed comparative discussion of different models that put one or the other first. An extended and careful discussion of the role of the United States in promoting democracy is included.

The essays published here are drawn from *The Washington Quarterly*, a journal of international policy issues published by the MIT Press for the Center for Strategic and International Studies (CSIS). The journal has emphasized in recent years the analysis of political change in the Second and Third Worlds and the connection between democracy and peace. Its contributors reflect diverse political views and professional backgrounds. In this collected volume, authors are drawn from seven countries so that the views represented are not just those of scholars or policy makers in the United States.

This volume reflects the enthusiasm and intellectual talents of its 20 contributors, to whom I owe a large debt of gratitude. Thoughtful men and women who can express powerful ideas clearly are what make the journal business rewarding. Special thanks are due Carl Gershman, president of the National Endowment for Democracy and a member of the journal's editorial board, and to George Weigel, president of the Ethics and Public Policy Center, for their special leadership on these issues and their guidance to me in this enterprise. I am grateful for the able assistance of my colleagues at the journal, who over the last three years have included Melinda Amberg, Abby Chack, Linda Crowl, Ousa Sananikone, Sherry Schurhammer, Teresa K. Smith, and Lynn Vega, and, of course, Walter Laqueur, who has helped lead the journal since its inception in 1978. Special thanks are due Stan Burnett, CSIS director of studies, and Joe Jordan and Zbigniew Brzezinski, whose valuable partnership in the CSIS International Leadership Forum has been instrumental to the generation of much of the material in this volume.

The story captured in these pages is one of a new stage of world politics. To be sure, democracy has not triumphed, and the end of history, trumpeted recently by Francis Fukuyama, is not yet upon us. If the experience of the American republic is in any way representative, the democratic experiment is a continuing one engaging the best talents of principled men and women for generations. The years ahead are certain to be rich in democratic successes and failures, in political and philosophical debate, and in triumphs and disasters for U.S. foreign policy. This is the stuff of drama, a drama that inspires, in this observer at least, a sense not only of excitement but also of purpose and promise.

Brad Roberts
Washington, D.C., September 1989

I. The Democratic Prospect

The United States and the World Democratic Revolution

Carl Gershman

IN THE STREETS of Lisbon in 1975, the Portuguese people, led by Mario Soares, defeated a determined drive by the Communist party to impose a totalitarian dictatorship. At the time many observers felt that the Portuguese events represented a decisive moment in the history of postwar Europe and in the evolution of East-West relations. What could not be fully appreciated was the extent to which the Portuguese drama also represented a turning point in the worldwide struggle for freedom and democracy.

Recalling the mood and context of the period is necessary. The spring of 1975 was a desperate moment, a time of deep pessimism with respect to the future of democracy. Indochina had fallen to the Communists in April, putting a bloody and depressing end to a conflict that had sapped the will of the United States to remain actively engaged in the pursuit and defense of freedom in the world. Just two months later Indira Gandhi imposed a dictatorship in India, a country that had been the world's largest democracy and a bastion of pluralist development in the Third World. In Africa, the former Portuguese colonies of Angola and Mozambique were falling under the

control of revolutionary movements tied to the Soviet Union.

These events exemplified what was seen to be a democratic retreat on almost all fronts. Democratic systems in many countries of Latin America broke down, authorities suppressed reform movements in Eastern Europe and the Soviet Union, and China witnessed the Cultural Revolution. A kind of virulent anti-Western nationalism appeared to be ascendant in the Third World. The failure of democracy in the Third World and the triumph of radical, often explicitly pro-Communist forces was commonly viewed as inevitable, a development the democratic world had to accommodate, not to resist. Thus, the democratic retreat was not just political but ideological as well. It was accompanied by a dramatic loss of belief and confidence in the future.

Daniel Patrick Moynihan aptly captured the gloomy temper of the times in the introduction to a collection of essays published on the occasion of the U.S. Bicentennial. The most important fact about the U.S. experiment, Moynihan asserted, was that its institutions were not the type "towards which, as by a law of fate, the rest of civilized mankind are forced to move," as Lord James Bryce had so confidently written almost a century earlier. "To the contrary," Moynihan went on,

Carl Gershman is president of the National Endowment for Democracy, a private non-profit grant-making organization established in 1983 to foster democracy abroad.

liberal democracy on the American model increasingly tends to the condition of monarchy in the 19th century: a holdover form of government, one which persists in isolated or peculiar places here and there, and may even serve well enough for special circumstances, but which has simply no relevance to the future. It is where the world was, not where it is going. . . . Increasingly, democracy is seen as an arrangement peculiar to a handful of North Atlantic countries. . . . [1]

The events in Portugal at first seemed to bear out this gloomy assessment. In the aftermath of the overthrow of fascism on April 25, 1974, the Communists were the most organized and best financed political force in Portugal. They occupied key positions in the government and the armed forces and controlled the Intersindicale labor federation and the media. When the government, backed by the Communists, approved a system of "direct democracy" that would bypass the political parties, it seemed only a matter of time before the nondemocratic left would impose an East European–style political system on Portugal.

However, this was not to be. The turning point came when the government closed the Socialist *Republica,* the last non-Communist newspaper in the country. The democratic forces, led by Soares's Socialist party, took to the streets in protest. Soon there were demonstrations throughout the country, and by August Vasco Goncalves was removed from power and a governing cabinet dominated by non-Communists was established.

The struggle in Portugal during spring and summer 1975 captured the imagination of the world. At a moment when democracy seemed everywhere

to be in retreat, the democratic forces repelled would-be tyrants and established a free and democratic system of government. Like the Battle of Britain more than a generation earlier, the Portuguese struggle checked an expanding totalitarianism and gave hope to democrats around the world.

How much these events in Portugal had to do with the world democratic revival that occurred thereafter is a question that is hard to answer precisely. Suffice to say, they marked a point in history when the momentum that had been running against democracy began to turn in its favor. Since 1975 setbacks to the democratic cause have happened, and undoubtedly setbacks are still to come. But the democratic trend has been broad and strong enough, and sufficiently sustained, to have assumed the character of a historic development—a democratic revolution.

This trend has been most dramatic in Latin America where authoritarian military governments have given way to democratically elected civilian governments in Argentina, Bolivia, Brazil, Ecuador, El Salvador, Guatemala, Honduras, Peru, and Uruguay. The consolidation of democracy in the Dominican Republic and the ouster of dictatorships in Grenada and Haiti are also part of this democratic revival (although, regrettably, a dictatorship has now been reimposed in Haiti). Exceptions to the general democratic trend exist, most notably in Cuba and Nicaragua on the antidemocratic left and in Chile and Paraguay on the antidemocratic right. However, even in these countries, as well as in Panama, the pressures for change have been growing.

The democratic revival has not been limited to Latin America. It is evident in the popular movement for democracy in the Philippines and South Korea, the continued democratic development in Thailand, and the trend toward increased political participation in Taiwan. Even in Africa, where the struggle for survival remains paramount, a recent Freedom House survey noted positive trends in a number of countries, especially Nigeria which "has gradually moved back toward a freer and more consensual society."[2] Despite the conditions of violence and polarization in South Africa, the forces working for a democratic alternative to apartheid have grown stronger over the last decade.

Perhaps most remarkably, a pronounced democratizing trend appears even in the communist world. Although no communist country is on the verge of a democratic transition, reformist leaders in the two largest communist countries, the Soviet Union and China, have taken cautious steps to encourage increased economic pluralism and even a degree of intellectual liberalization. More important, the emergence of a variety of independent social, cultural, and intellectual tendencies signals the revival of civil society. This process is most advanced in Poland, where democratic initiatives have been able to build on the experience of Solidarity's legal existence. The process is underway in other communist countries as well and probably cannot be wiped out.

All this signifies a world in which the democratic idea is growing stronger, not weaker, and where the existence of democratic systems or incipient democratic forms is becoming more, not less, prevalent. But this is not cause for complacency, because democracy is far from being uncontested in the world. In a number of developing countries, especially where sharp ethnic conflict exists as in Lebanon and Sri Lanka, democracy has broken down or become more restricted. Moreover, the rise of Islamic fundamentalism poses a new ideological challenge to democracy when the historic contest between democracy and communism has still not been resolved. According to Samuel P. Huntington, the democratic revolution has been accompanied by a sharp increase in the number of Marxist-Leninist regimes in the Third World—by one count from 6 at the end of the 1960s to 17 by the beginning of the 1980s. Thus, he pointed out, there have really been "two parallel processes of regime transition" underway, suggesting an intensification of political competition in the Third World.[3]

Here, too, the Portuguese struggle is illuminating, for it is a microcosm of the basic political contest that unfolded in the Third World in its aftermath. At issue in Portugal was the kind of system—democratic or totalitarian—that would succeed the collapse of right-wing authoritarianism. The far-reaching implication is that, although traditionalist autocracies may still hold sway in many Third World countries, they do not represent the future. They simply cannot adapt to the pace of change and conflicting political pressures of the modern world. Political observers are confronted, therefore, by a crisis of transition, one that offers the opportunity for the advance of democracy in the world but could also lead to a democratic retreat if the established democracies are not equal to the challenge.

The lesson of the Portuguese experience is that assistance from the established democracies can, indeed, affect the outcome of the transition. Had the European democrats not come to the aid of their Portuguese comrades after the revolution of 1974, the democratic transition might not have succeeded. It certainly would have been far more imperiled than it was even during the darkest days of 1975.

Significantly, the United States was not at the forefront of this exercise in democratic solidarity. Undoubtedly, the United States had many reasons for this, including its preoccupation with Vietnam. At the root of the U.S. paralysis was the absence of a consensus on the need to aid democratic forces, a failure to appreciate the new salience of political competition, and the lack of political experience, contacts, and mechanisms needed to implement a strategy of democratic political assistance even if it had fashioned one.

The United States paid a heavy price for this failing in Nicaragua in 1979. Arguably, it is still paying this price in 1988 if one is to judge from the continuing absence of a political consensus on a policy for Central America. However, the Nicaragua debate in the United States and the larger debate over the doctrine of providing military assistance to resistance forces in Third World communist countries have obscured a growing consensus on the issue of providing assistance for democratic political development.

Ironically, this new consensus can be traced in significant measure to the failure of U.S. policy in Nicaragua. The Nicaragua experience shattered both sides of the argument over U.S. attitudes toward friendly Third World autocrats. On one hand, the conservative view that such regimes are a bulwark against communism seemed a good deal less compelling after the Sandinistas took over from Somoza. The Nicaraguan events seemed to bear out a different analysis, namely, that right-wing authoritarianism is fertile soil for the growth of Marxist-Leninist organizations, which are able to exploit legitimate grievances to seize control of mass-based movements of opposition.

On the other hand, the liberal side of the argument—that policy sufficed in simply seeking the removal of authoritarian dictatorships, as if communist movements could be defeated by denying them this easy target—fared no better. As long as the Communists remained the strongest and most determined alternative to Somoza, the downfall of the dictatorship would enable them to take power.

Thus, in the wake of Nicaragua both conservatives and liberals needed a fresh approach to the question of defending democracy in the Third World. If pro-U.S. authoritarian regimes were not a bulwark against communism and if the removal of such regimes was not a guarantee of democracy, the inevitable conclusion was one on which both sides could agree. Shirley Christian stated in the epilogue to her study of the Nicaraguan revolution:

> Only by promoting democratic political development on a long-term basis can the United States hope to avoid the hard choices between sending troops and accepting a regime that overtly opposes its interests.[4]

Promoting democracy, in other words, is as much a matter of national security as of national conscience. The broad conservative-liberal consensus that emerged on this issue provided the basis on which the National Endowment for Democracy was established in 1983.

This new consensus was reinforced by the democratic revolution itself, which altered the terms of the debate about political change in the Third World. President John F. Kennedy stated the classic U.S. view on this question in 1961 in relation to the Dominican Republic:

> There are three possibilities in descending order of preference: a decent democratic regime, a continuation of the Trujillo regime or a Castro regime. We ought to aim at the first, but we really can't renounce the second until we are sure that we can avoid the third.[5]

By the 1970s, during the period of democratic retreat, the first option was not considered possible, and the policy debate therefore became polarized between two irreconcilable positions—one arguing in favor of accommodating and coopting the forces of change even if they were not particularly democratic or friendly to the United States, the other firmly holding to Kennedy's second option. The democratic revolution revived Kennedy's first option by showing that there were also *democratic* forces of change and that, given the developments in Nicaragua, they needed the support of the established democracies.

A third factor contributing to the new consensus in the United States in favor of democratic political assistance has been the declining utility of conventional military force in the contemporary world. This is due largely to the success of the Western policy of deterrence, which has preserved strategic stability, and to the reluctance in the United States (and apparently, after Afghanistan, in the Soviet Union as well) to become directly engaged militarily in Third World conflicts. In this context, competition is likely to continue to shift from the military to the political realm, and it will become increasingly important for the West to develop a sophisticated and long-term strategy of democratic political assistance.

The outlook for such a strategy is especially auspicious as the communist world—still the principal rival to democracy—is caught up in a systemic crisis of historic proportions. This crisis exists at many levels, the most immediate being the economic stagnation and inefficiency that are the inevitable consequences of a centralized command system. The dilemma confronting Gorbachev and other Communist leaders is that reducing controls will not overcome stagnation as long as the system remains fundamentally monolithic, but piecemeal reforms and greater openness will release pent-up political pressures for change. The combination of economic deterioration and heightened political consciousness presages an extended period of uncertainty and possible instability throughout the communist world.

This economic and political crisis has accelerated the ideological erosion of communism. Unlike traditional authoritarianisms, communism has based its legitimacy primarily on its utopian ideological claims, which the official Soviet press currently questions and sometimes actually refutes. The government now tolerates even criticism of the revered Lenin, including the charge that he bears responsibility for Stalinist terror. It is hard to know where this process will end, but already a breach has been made in the wall of communist orthodoxy that cannot be repaired and may have consequences far beyond those intended by the proponents of *glasnost,* who have wanted to restructure the Soviet system in order to strengthen it.

Indeed, it has now become possible to consider practical measures to support democratic efforts that are already underway in Poland and elsewhere in Eastern Europe, as well as in the Soviet Union itself. The measures will naturally vary, depending on the extent to which democratic movements have developed in different countries. The movement in Poland is still the most advanced, in as much as, in addition to Solidarity, elaborate structures exist to support independent intellectual, cultural, and social activities. Even in Czechoslovakia, citizens produce scores of independent journals—many of a religious nature—where a decade ago there were none; in Hungary, a small but active democratic opposition could play an important role in the event of a larger political opening. The dissident movement in the Soviet Union has expanded into a growing network of independent publications and political clubs. Although these movements are still largely restricted to intellectuals, similar groups in the non-Russian republics have far broader appeal because they speak for the aspirations of repressed nationalities.

Efforts to assist the emergent pluralism in the Soviet Union and Eastern Europe should have as their overriding objective the growth and eventual empowerment of civil society. In the absence of independent institutions, such efforts currently concentrate inevitably on intellectual and cultural activities—the so-called second circulation. The major breakthrough is in the area of new information technology, such as word processors, desk-top publishing, video cassette recorders, and even television satellite dishes. Considering that maintaining a monopoly of information has been one of the principal pillars of Communist party rule, the implications of an information explosion in the Soviet bloc are far-reaching.

It is not unreasonable to assume that, over time, the expression of different points of view could lead to the representation of diverse interests by independent institutions, including unions, business associations, cooperatives, civic and religious organizations, educational institutions, independent media and, not inconceivably, political parties. Such a process may take many years, but it is not unimaginable if the pressure for change is persistent and relentless and if each democratic gain becomes the basis for new efforts and new demands. "The lesson of the democratic opposition movement in Polish postwar history," Leszek Kolakowski wrote, "—and of Solidarity in particular—is that the gradual dismantling of totalitarian institutions by building and enlarging the enclaves of civil society is not impossible. It is a dangerous path, no doubt, but the most promising one."[6] As democratic movements in the Soviet bloc take this path, they should receive moral, material, technical, and political support from their democratic friends in the West.

The economic failure and ideological exhaustion that have made possible the political opening in the Soviet bloc are also creating a new receptivity to democracy in the developing world. The foreign minister of Indonesia reflected a widespread disillusionment with ideological radicalism when he declared in 1985, on the thirtieth anniversary of the Bandung Conference, which gave birth to the Nonaligned Movement, that "The age of 'isms' is over" and that developing countries would now have to struggle by themselves for economic growth.[7] In contrast to the earlier period, greater support currently exists for the view that such a struggle does not require popular mobilization and the centralization of power, but rather greater relaxation of controls and more freedom for the individual.

The accumulating evidence in developing countries that a vigorous private sector is essential for economic growth and that massive government control of the economy has had ruinous consequences has created a much more positive attitude toward systems of economic and political pluralism. As the Chinese dissident, Fang Lizhi, said, "You can't develop a modern economy without democracy."[8] At the same time, there is also evidence that growth itself promotes democracy by increasing the size of the middle class, raising the level of education and political consciousness, and creating pressures for more political participation. South Korea is an excellent example of a growth-induced process of democratization. A young worker stated the matter well in an interview held before last year's presidential election: "In the 1960's, bread was the most important thing. In the 70's, Koreans focused on making more money. But in the 80's, those basic issues have been solved and we need more freedom."[9]

There has also been a popular revulsion over the human suffering caused by dictatorial systems and absolutist ideologies. Peruvian novelist Mario Vargas Llosa noted that the distinctive feature of the democratic trend in Latin America today is that it enjoys massive popular support from people who "have been spurred to turn to democracy by the terrible violence" inflicted on them "by both revolutionary terrorists and political or military counterterrorists." As a result, they "have decided to support that system which they think, intuitively and instinctively, will best be able to defend human rights and social stability, and will attempt to extirpate the pistol, the bomb, and the electric prod from political life."[10]

Their intuition and instincts are sound because democracy offers the most peaceful and effective way for the diverse groups within developing countries to negotiate satisfactory answers to inevitable ethnic and regional cleavages, interest group conflicts, and ideological differences. According to the late Costa Rican intellectual, Luis Burstin, revolutions in Latin America have been provoked not by poverty and social injustice but by rigid, undemocratic systems that block access to political power for emerging groups.[11] The failure of national integration, which is so important for the political stability and development of Third World countries, is explicable in terms of the absence of open, participatory political systems. The president of the Senegalese democratic institute CERDET, Jacques Mariel Nzouankeu, wrote that

> Pluralistic democracy removes most causes for social tensions which clearly delay the achievement of national unity, by respecting all political ideologies and allowing their organization and full expression. By generating cultural pluralism, pluralistic democracy avoids the trappings of cultural contempt, source of frustrations and complexes which are real threats to national unity.[12]

A more open political system, Nzouankeu also pointed out, would help root out pervasive corruption that hurts development and discredits public authority. With democracy, government would have to account for its policies before an ever-demanding public, thus forcing it to elaborate policies more carefully, and "the fear of the press and of the opposition denouncing political scandals, forces government to be more rigorous in its management."[13]

Such statements bespeak a growing understanding within developing countries that democracy is not, as was previously believed, an arrangement peculiar to the West, but is a system that has its own special relevance and practical value for themselves. It offers perhaps the most meaningful framework within which to address such basic concerns as economic development, national integration, clean and efficient government, social peace, and political stability. To be sure, the experience of the industrialized democracies may contain lessons for the developing countries that can be transmitted and learned. However, it is significant that the new understanding of the value of democracy grows out of real, often harsh experience that gives the emergent democratic orientation authenticity, credibility, and, hopefully, durability.

It is important to bear this in mind when considering what can be done to assist democracy in the developing world. There are democratic institutions and organizations throughout the developing world that are led by individuals with imagination, commitment, and courage who are doing important, innovative work. Many associate themselves with the National Endowment for Democracy. They are often isolated and beleaguered, and they certainly need help. However, one should not assume that such help is best offered in the form of custom-made, turn-key projects that are developed in the established democracies for export abroad. It's not necessary to do this, and it won't work. The best programs are those developed locally by democratic activists for whom foreign assistance is not a condition for democratic engagement but a form of practical aid for activites already underway. Such aid should be given in an open, forthright, and nonmanipulative manner, it should be responsive to concrete, practical democratic needs, and it should manifest a con-

sistent, authentic democratic commitment.

Of course, determining what will promote democracy in a particular country or situation is not always a simple matter. The approach described above is not foolproof, but it will minimize error by ensuring that programs are tailored to local needs and do not expose people to more risk than they are prepared to accept. Moreover, knowledge about democratic development is expanding, derived from both practical experience and scholarly inquiry. The study being conducted by Larry Diamond, Seymour Martin Lipset, and Juan Linz is extraordinarily rich with insights about complex democratic processes in developing countries in Africa, Asia, and Latin America.[14] In one sense, the study does not improve on James Madison and Alexis de Tocqueville, for it demonstrates that limited government and civil society are as vital for developing democracies as for the more established ones. However, in so doing, the study affirms the universal applicability of the democratic idea.

Regarding actual programs of support for democratic development, distinguishing between programs to support democratic transitions and those that assist long-term democratic political development is useful. Programs that seek to promote transitions address immediate, often urgent, tactical and political issues that arise when an opportunity develops to move from an undemocratic to a democratic situation. Such a situation existed in Guatemala in 1985 and in the Philippines in 1986, and it exists in Chile in 1988. In these circumstances, the priorities are to assist efforts to promote a broad consensus on a process to establish democracy and to aid those groups (which will be in opposition if the undemocratic government is not committed to a process of real change) that are working for a peaceful democratic transition. Often the focus will be on a particular election or plebiscite where the transfer of power is at issue.

Transitions are special circumstances where timely assistance can open up new possibilities for democratic development. Even if successful, however, they are only an important step toward stable democracy. Without institutions and procedures that enable citizens at all levels to participate responsibly in the life of society and that encourage government efficiency and responsiveness to public concerns, democratic governments could lose support and even legitimacy. Ultimately, the fate of a democracy is the responsibility of its own people and leadership. But external assistance can reinforce democratic groups and strengthen the institutional infrastructure of democracy, thereby increasing the likelihood that pluralistic democracy will succeed and endure.

Such assistance is needed and can be provided in three areas: institutional pluralism, governance, and democratic culture.

Institutional pluralism. Possibly the most important conclusion of the Diamond-Linz-Lipset study is the clear relationship among the strength of voluntary associations, democratic interest groups, and independent media and the chances for stable democracy. A vigorous social pluralism is vital at every stage of democratic development. In authoritarian or one-party states, it provides precious space for autonomous social and intellectual activity that over time could lay the groundwork for political pluralism. In transitional situations, democratic social organizations can marshal support in favor of the establishment of democracy. Thereafter, they provide

channels for citizen participation and a check on the unwarranted extension of government power. They are the first and best line of defense when the survival of democracy is threatened.

The infrastructure of civil society is composed of unions; business and trade associations; intellectual, educational, and religious institutions; an independent media; cooperatives; citizen groups committed to popular civic education and government accountability; and many other types of voluntary institutions. In providing assistance in this area, it is important to ensure that the organizations to be helped have a broad base and an established record of democratic commitment and that the programs funded serve a broad democratic purpose, not a narrow partisan interest. As a general rule, the best initiative in developing the program and in requesting assistance comes from the local group, and assistance should be provided through counterpart private organizations in the established democracies which can offer needed technical help and whose involvement does not compromise the integrity of the recipient organization.

Governance. John Stuart Mill defined the great challenge facing developing countries in the area of governance more than a century ago: "to secure as much of the advantages of centralized power and intelligence as can be had without turning into government channels too great a proportion of the general activity," and to achieve "the greatest dissemination of power consistent with efficiency." How to find the proper balance, Mill added, "is one of the most difficult and complicated questions in the art of government."[15]

The point of balance will vary depending on specific circumstances. The important thing is to have a system of constitutional checks and insti-

11

Carl Gershman

tutional counterbalances that enable government to be strong and efficient while guarding against an overconcentration of power at the center. In this respect, a vigorous and independent judiciary is essential, an area of assistance that has been a high priority for the U.S. Agency for International Development. Also important are constitutional innovations that address specific problems of democratic governance. For example, the Diamond-Linz-Lipset study emphasizes the role of the Supreme Electoral Tribunal in Costa Rica, whose autonomy and constitutional authority have guaranteed the integrity of the electoral process. It also highlights the importance of the rigorous system of accounting controls and audits supervised by the National Assembly in Botswana, which has contained political and administrative corruption. Nongovernmental and nonpartisan policy institutes, which can identify useful constitutional or administrative innovations and secure support for their implementation, are therefore institutions whose development should be encouraged.

Institutes that promote innovative, market-oriented approaches to economic development also should be strengthened. A vigorous private sector helps democracy by balancing government power, dispersing decision making, encouraging individual initiative, and promoting growth and development. Moreover, a strong private sector, by enabling talented and ambitious individuals to find attractive career opportunities outside the government, reduces the premium on political power, thereby fostering a more tolerant political environment.

It is also important to encourage the development of political parties that are able to articulate and represent ef-

fectively the interests of broad sectors of the population. Such assistance should be provided in as balanced and as nonpartisan a manner as possible, and it should try to enhance not only the representational and communicative capabilities of the various parties but also their ability to govern. Parties that are able to define and implement a credible economic policy and that have expertise in areas of defense and security will be prepared to govern and will also be able to instill more confidence in the democratic process in the powerful business and military sectors.

Democratic culture. An area of assistance that is frequently neglected is the promotion of democratic intellectual and political culture. Reasons for this are many, one of the more important being the failure to appreciate the importance of ideas in determining the shape of events and political systems. Ideas, as Mill wrote, are "one of the chief elements of social power," because "what men think . . . determines how they act."[16] It is not enough to buttress democracy by sound institutions and a system of checks and balances, however essential they are. Democracy also requires a strong civic culture and a populace that is committed to the rule of law and the open society. Moreover, the prospects for democracy in the world depend on the ability of people who believe in democracy to argue its case vigorously and cogently against its adversaries.

This is not an area where the democratic world has ever been strong. Perhaps democracy, which instills in its citizens an attitude of tolerance of political differences and a readiness to compromise, is at a permanent disadvantage in competing politically against utopian movements, which satisfy deep psychological needs and promise glorious victories. Still, democracy is in a stronger position now than one would have thought possible only a few years ago, owing to the ideological exhaustion of communism and to the development of a more pragmatic, nonideological temperament in the Third World.

Nonetheless, nondemocratic movements in the Third World remain powerful, and there is a tremendous need to assist what is still, after all, a relatively small band of determined democratic intellectuals. Such a program as Libro Libre in Costa Rica, which is a movement of democratic intellectuals that has produced a new democratic literature for Central America and which represents the first coherent attempt to present an alternative to Marxist ideology in the region, is a model of what needs to be done elsewhere as well.

The program described here is not intended to represent a comprehensive approach to promoting democracy in the world. First, to the extent that such a program has now been launched in the United States through the National Endowment for Democracy, it represents only a small beginning. As Larry Diamond correctly pointed out, a truly serious effort to advance democracy should be funded at a level many times that which is now made available to the endowment.[17] It would still be a modest effort in relation to the overall budget for defense and foreign assistance, but its impact would be of a very great magnitude.

Its impact would be even greater if official government policies to advance democratic trends complemented such a program. The judicious use by governments of political and economic leverage can protect individuals who may be endangered because of their democratic activities, gain vital political space for democratic parties and organizations, and convince authoritarian governments to take steps toward a political transition. International economic policies also should take into account the well-being and survival of democratic governments, especially in cases where they have inherited an economic catastrophe from their authoritarian predecessors. Although democratic governments, like all others, should practice fiscal responsibility, they should be allowed to repay debts in a manner and at a pace that enables them to sustain viable rates of economic growth.

Finally, it is good for the cause of democracy in the developing world for the established democracies to remain militarily and economically strong. Congressman Stephen J. Solarz pointed out correctly that "our global defense posture and policies do create a context for domestic politics around the world."[18] If the United States and its allies are strong and determined, their views and interests will be respected by adversaries as well as by authoritarian rulers who are friendly to the West. According to Juan Linz, "An international environment that makes revolutionary change unlikely, will both make the opposition more moderate and lead sectors in the regime to consider the costs of toleration lower than those of repression."[19]

Although the established democracies can assist and facilitate the process of democratic change, it is the people themselves in the developing countries who will determine whether democratic systems will be established and survive. Once again, it is important to remember when the Portuguese people took events into their own hands to defend their freedom. Speaking in the United States shortly after those events, Soares paid eloquent tribute to their role and courage. When the enemies of democracy

> were on the brink of occupying the whole state machinery, when they controlled the mass media and infiltrated the armed forces in our country, and were in fact on the brink of forming a new political police, it was the spontaneous resistance of the Portuguese people who, as by a miracle, came out into the streets, and in the streets of Portugal, in the factories, in the schools, and in the fields unanimously struggled to defend the threatened freedom.[20]

That same passion for freedom is now beginning to capture the imagination of people throughout the developing world and may ultimately bring down communist tyranny as well. At this point in history, democratic possibilities exist that were unthinkable only a few short years ago. This defines the opportunity. The democracies must now rise to the challenge.

Notes

1. Daniel P. Moynihan, "The American Experiment," *The Public Interest*, Fall 1975, pp. 6–7.

2. Raymond D. Gastil, "The Comparative Survey of Freedom," *Freedom at Issue*, no. 100, January/February 1988, p. 30.

3. Samuel P. Huntington in *The Challenge of Democracy*, a collection of speeches delivered at a conference sponsored by the National Endowment for Democracy, May 1987, p. 105.

4. Shirley Christian, *Nicaragua: Revolution in the Family* (New York: Random House, 1985), p. 310.

5. Quoted in Norman Podhoretz, *Why We Were in Vietnam* (New York: Simon & Schuster, 1982), p. 52.

6. Leszek Kolakowski in *The Challenge of Democracy*, p. 22.

7. *The Wall Street Journal*, April 24, 1985.

8. James R. Schiffman and Adi Ignatius, "Chinese Dissident Urges Democracy, Less Party Control," *The Wall Street Journal*, May 5, 1988.

9. "Days of Democracy," *The New York Times*, July 5, 1987, p. 14.

10. Mario Vargas Llosa, "To Nurture Latin Democracy" excerpted from "Latin America: The Democratic Option," a speech delivered at a meeting of the Trilateral Commission in San Francisco, March 1987, in *Harper's Magazine*, June 1987, pp. 16–17.

11. See Flora Lewis, "A Third World Spring," *The New York Times*, April 8, 1984.

12. "Manifesto," available from the Center for Studies and Research on Pluralistic Democracy in the Third World, BP 12 092 Dakar-Colobane, République du Sénégal.

13. Ibid., p. 15.

14. Larry Diamond, Juan J. Linz, Seymour Martin Lipset, ed., *Democracy in Developing Countries* (Boulder, Colo.: Lynne Rienner Publishers and the National Endowment for Democracy, 1988). The study is in four volumes: a general theoretical introduction and regional volumes on Africa, Asia, and Latin America. The Africa volume, the only one published to date, has just been released.

15. John Stuart Mill, *On Liberty* (New York: The Library of Liberal Arts, 1956), pp. 138–139.

16. Mill, quoted by Gastil, ed., *Freedom in the World: Political Rights and Civil Liberties, 1978* (New York: Freedom House in cooperation with G. K. Hall & Co., 1978), pp. 160–161.

17. Diamond, address to the International Leadership Forum, Lisbon, Portugal, June 19–21, 1988.

18. Stephen J. Solarz, "Democracy in the Third World?", *SAIS Review* 5:2 (Summer/Fall 1985), p. 153.

19. Linz, "The Transition from Authoritarian Regimes to Democratic Political Systems and the Problems of Consolidation of Political Democracy," paper presented to the

International Political Science Association, Tokyo Round Table, March 29–April 1, 1982, p. 21.

20. Mario Soares, "A Spontaneous Movement Against the Communists," *New America* 14:5 (June 1977), p. 8.

Catholicism and Democracy: The Other Twentieth-Century Revolution

George Weigel

IN A CONVERSATION early in the 1980s, Sir Michael Howard, the regius professor of modern history at Oxford, suggested that there had been two great revolutions in the twentieth century. The first took place when Lenin's Bolsheviks expropriated the Russian people's revolution in November 1917. The second was going on even as we spoke: the transformation of the Roman Catholic Church from a bastion of the *ancien régime* into perhaps the world's foremost institutional defender of human rights. It was a fascinating reading of the history of our century. One also sensed, in Sir Michael's story, just the slightest hint of an element of surprise: Fancy that— the Vatican as defender of the rights of man!

There are, to be sure, reasons to be surprised by the contemporary Vatican's aggressive defense of human rights, and by Pope John Paul II's endorsement of democracy as the form of government which best coheres with the Church's vision of "integral

George Weigel is president of the Ethics and Public Policy Center of Washington, D.C. His most recent books include *Catholicism and the Renewal of American Democracy* (New York: Paulist Press, 1989) and *American Interests, American Purposes: Moral Reasoning and U.S. Foreign Policy* (New York: Praeger/Center for Strategic and International Studies, 1989).

human development." In the worlds of political power, those surprised would have to include the late Leonid Brezhnev (puzzled by the concurrent rise of Solidarnosc and the election of a Polish pope), Ferdinand Marcos, Augusto Pinochet, and the leaders of the Czechoslovak Communist party. On the other hand key themes in classic Catholic social ethics—personalism, the common good, and the principle of subsidiarity—seem not merely congruent with democracy, but pointed positively toward the evolution of liberal democratic forms of governance.

That, of course, would come as news indeed to Popes Gregory XVI or Pius IX, whose attitudes in the nineteenth century toward liberal democracy were decidedly chilly. What has happened, between then and now, between the mid-nineteenth and late-twentieth centuries, between an official Catholic skepticism about democracy that bordered on hostility and a Catholic endorsement of democracy that not only threatens tyrants, but actually helps to topple them?

The Mid-Nineteenth Century Argument

The hostility of official Roman Catholicism's papal magisterium to the liberal concepts of the rights of man as defined in the French Revolution's creed, and to the liberal democratic state, is well known to all students of the period and is neatly encapsulated in that last of the condemned propositions in Pius IX's 1864 *Syllabus of Errors, viz.* that "the Roman Pontiff can and should reconcile himself to and agree with progress, liberalism, and modern civilization." What is perhaps less well known is that Pius IX, Giovanni Maria Mastai-Ferretti, was elected in 1846 as a reforming pope with a more tolerant attitude toward modern thought and institutions than his predecessor, Gregory XVI (1831–1846) who, in the 1832 and 1834 encyclicals *Mirari Vos* and *Singulari Nos,* had flatly condemned liberalism (including "this false and absurd maxim, or better this madness, that everyone should have and practice freedom of conscience") as essentially irreligious.[1] In any case, events—particularly the Italian *Risorgimento,* whose liberal anti-clerical leadership made no pretense about its intention to dislodge traditional church authority throughout Italy—hardened Pius IX in his views such that, by the time of the First Vatican Council (1869–1870), the pope who had been elected 23 years earlier as something of a reformer had become, throughout the world, the very symbol of intransigent resistance to the ideas and institutions of modernity.[2]

While there were undoubtedly personal factors involved in the retrenchment strategy of Pius IX, it seems far more fruitful to focus on the substantive reasons why official Catholicism found itself in resistance to the liberal project in the nineteenth century. At least three suggest themselves to this observer.

First, one should not discount the enduring effects of the shock that the French Revolution sent through European Catholicism—a shock of perhaps greater intensity than any the Church had absorbed since the Reformation. There was, to be sure, the crazed bloodiness of the Terror itself. Beyond that, however, and beyond even Napoleon's persecution of Pope Pius VII, the leadership of Roman Catholicism saw the lingering spectre of Jacobinism as an ideological force that threatened the very foundations of European civilization.[3] That civilization, in its public aspects, had been rooted in the notion that states, as well as individual men, were accountable to transcendent moral norms (generally held to be revealed by a God who was sovereign over states as well as over individuals). By its defiant insistence on the autonomous reason of man as the first, and indeed only, principle of political organization, Jacobinism threatened more than the position of the Church as mediator between the sovereign God and his creatures; the anti-clerical laicism imbedded in Jacobinism was a problem, to be sure, but it was not the fundamental threat. In the Church's view, and not without reason, the Jacobin spirit inevitably led to the implosion and consequent collapse of civilization in mobocracy, or what J.R. Talmon has called totalitarian democracy.[4] Thus, a damning equation hardened in the minds of a Church leadership that had long identified, not merely its institutional prerogatives, but civilization itself with the moral understandings that (in however attenuated a form) underlay the structures of the *ancien régime:* liberalism = Jacobinism = (anti-clericalism + The Terror + anarchy). Discriminating or not, fair or not, the brush of Robespierre tarred the revolutionaries of 1848, the leaders of the Italian Risorgimento (Cavour, Mazzini, Garibaldi, etc.), and in fact the entire liberal project in Europe.[5]

The second factor that colored the mid-nineteenth century Church's appraisal of liberalism and democracy was the Church's own internal situation. The answer that Roman Catholicism devised to the political threat posed by the rise of postmonarchical states in Europe and to the advance of liberal ideas was centralization: the radical concentration of effective authority over virtually all matters, great and small, in the person (and, of course, staff) of the Roman Pontiff. The pope would be the sole judge of orthodoxy and orthopraxis; the pope would manage the Church's affairs with sovereign states through an expanding network of papal diplomats, concordat arrangements, and so forth. *Ubi Petrus, ibi ecclesia* ("Where there is Peter, there is the Church") is an ancient theological maxim. But it was given new breadth in the nineteenth century in response to the ideological (and, indeed physical) threats posed by the forces of what the *Syllabus* called "progress, liberalism, and modern civilization."

There is, of course, an irony here: the Church's answer to the threat of "progress, liberalism, and modern civilization" was to adopt a quintessentially modern structure, i.e., one that was highly centralized and bureaucratically controlled. Be that irony as it may, though, the new emphasis on centralized authority, coupled with the traditional understanding of the divinely given prerogatives of the Roman Pontiff, and further complicated by the dependence of the Papal States (pre-1870) on European monarchs for physical security, created a situation in which the Church's leadership was rather unlikely to feel much of a sense of affinity with liberal democracy. In terms of the sociology of knowledge, the conditions-for-the-possibility of a Roman Pontiff looking with much favor on liberal democracy were not, to put it mildly, in place.

In the third place, and as if the above were not enough by way of barriers to rapprochement, liberalism in the latter part of the nineteenth century was widely (and not altogether inaccurately) perceived in Vatican circles as a package deal that included Darwinism (which seemed to threaten the distinctiveness of human beings in creation), "higher criticism" or the "historical-critical method" (which seemed to challenge the integrity of the Bible and its status as the revealed word of God), and socialism (which seemed to threaten the Church's traditional teaching on the right of private property). To these perceived threats in the order of ideas must be added the physical threat of revolutionary Marxism as it showed itself in, say, the 1870 Paris Commune.

The most fundamental reason for the Church's resistance to the liberal democratic project in the nineteenth century should not, though, be located on this institutional/ideological axis. The institutional threats noted above were real, in both corporate and personal terms (ask Pius VII or Pius IX), and those threats did act as a kind of filter through which ideas and events were, in some cases, misperceived. All of that can be conceded. But beneath it all lay, I believe, an evangelical concern.

Rightly or wrongly, the central leadership of nineteenth century Roman Catholicism truly believed that religious liberty—a key plank in the platform of liberal democracy—would inevitably lead to religious indifference and, given the right circumstances, to hostility toward religion on the part of governments. The secularization of Western Europe in the nineteenth century was a complicated business,[6] and it would be a grave historical error to attribute it solely (or even primarily) to the collapse of the old altar-and-throne arrangements that had obtained since the Peace of Westphalia ended the European wars of religion in 1648. On the other hand, and from the Vatican's point of view at that time, secularization proceeded apace with the collapse of those arrangements. Those of us with the luxury of hindsight should be perhaps less quick to dismiss as mindless the inferences that were drawn. As for the breakdown of altar-and-throne eventually leading to hostility toward religion on the part of governments, there was, at the beginning of the nineteenth century, the Napoleonic persecution of the Church; and after 1870 there was the pressing problem of the violently anticlerical Third French Republic: in the face of which, it was all too easy to read the historical record backwards, from the depredations of the Commune and the later anticlericalism of the Third Republic, to the *Declaration des Droits de L'Homme et du Citoyen.*

One cannot, in short, dismiss Roman resistance to the liberal democratic project as merely institutional self-interest. Some liberal democratic states put grave difficulties in the path of the Church's evangelical and sacramental mission, and larger conclusions, appropriate or otherwise, were shortly drawn.

On the other hand, it should also be conceded that the Roman authorities were slow to seize the opportunities presented by what might be called the Catholic Whig tradition, which looks to Thomas Aquinas for its inspiration and which had, in Lord Acton, a powerful spokesman in the mid- and late-

nineteenth century. Given his largely negative views on the utility of the definition of papal infallibility at the First Vatican Council (itself, *inter alia,* an act of defiance against the epistemological spirit of the age), Acton was an unlikely broker of this tradition, which taught the possibility of genuine progress in history when that progress is mediated through rightly-ordered public institutions holding themselves accountable to transcendent moral norms. In any case, the Catholic Whig tradition, a revolutionary liberal tradition in its own right, if in sharp contrast to the Jacobinism with which the Vatican typically associated liberalism, would not have all that long to wait, as history goes, for its moment to arrive.

The Turn Toward Democracy Begins

What accounts for the shift in official Catholic teaching in the period 1864–1965, between the rejection of the modern constitutional state in the *Syllabus of Errors* and the Second Vatican Council's acceptance of the juridical state in the *Declaration on Religious Freedom?* Of the many factors in play, one strikes me as particularly important: and that was the fact of America.

In the United States, the Church was confronted with a liberal society and liberal-democratic state that were good for Roman Catholics. Religious liberty and the constitutional separation of church and state had led not to religious indifference but to a vibrant Catholicism that still, unlike its European counterparts, held the allegiance of the working class. Moreover, while anti-Catholicism was a fact of life in the United States,[7] the U.S. government had never come close to conducting an overt program of persecution on the basis of religious conviction.

This was, as can be imagined, somewhat difficult to handle for those in Rome who were still committed to a restoration of the *ancien régime,* or even those who were simply skeptical about the American experiment. A bold, public attempt to press the argument for religious liberty and liberal democracy in Rome itself took place on March 25, 1887, when the newly created Cardinal James Gibbons of Baltimore took possession of his titular Church of Santa Maria in Trastevere, and preached to his Roman congregation in these terms:

... Scarcely were the United States formed when Pius VI, of happy memory, established there the Catholic hierarchy and appointed the illustrious John Carroll first Bishop of Baltimore. This event, so important to us, occurred less than a hundred years ago. . . . Our Catholic community in those days numbered only a few thousand souls . . . and were served by the merest handful of priests. Thanks to the fructifying grace of God, the grain of mustard seed then planted has grown to be a large tree, spreading its branches over the length and width of our fair land. . . . For their great progress under God and the fostering care of the Holy See *we are indebted in no small degree to the civil liberty we enjoy in our enlightened republic.*

Our Holy Father, Leo XIII, in his luminous encyclical on the constitution of Christian States, declares that the Church is not committed to any particular form of civil government. She adapts to all; she leavens all with the sacred leaven of the Gospel. She has lived under absolute empires; she thrives under constitutional monarchies; she grows and ex-

pands under the free republic. She has often, indeed, been hampered in her divine mission and has had to struggle for a footing wherever despotism has cast its dark shadow . . . but in the genial air of liberty she blossoms like the rose!

For myself, as a citizen of the United States, and without closing my eyes to our defects as a nation, I proclaim, with a deep sense of pride and gratitude, and in this great capital of Christendom, that I belong to a country where the civil government holds over us the aegis of its protection without interfering in the legitimate exercise of our sublime mission as ministers of the Gospel of Jesus Christ.

Our country has liberty without license, authority with despotism. . . . But, while we are acknowledged to have a free government, we do not, perhaps, receive due credit for possessing also a strong government. Yes, our nation is strong, and her strength lies, under Providence, in the majesty and supremacy of the law, in the loyalty of her citizens to that law, and in the affection of our people for their free institutions. . . . [8]

Gibbons's proud assertions sound mild to our ears, but in their own day they were intended as a manifesto and a challenge, and were understood as such, by contemporary celebrants and detractors alike. As Gerald Fogarty, SJ, puts it, "Here was the gauntlet of the benefit of American religious liberty thrown down by the new world to the old. . . . "[9]

Pope Leo XIII (1878–1903) was happy to acknowledge the practical benefits of the American arrangement in the American circumstance, but he was not yet prepared to concede the moral superiority of the liberal (i.e., confessionally neutral) state over the

George Weigel

classic European arrangements. In his 1895 encyclical letter to the American hierarchy, *Longinqua Oceani,* Leo cautioned against any temptation to universalize the American experience and experiment:

> . . . the Church amongst you, unopposed by the Constitution and government of your nation, fettered by no hostile legislation, protected against violence by the common laws and the impartiality of the tribunals, is free to live and act without hindrance. Yet, though all this is true, it would be very erroneous to draw the conclusion that in America is to be sought the type of the most desirable status of the Church, or that it would be universally lawful or expedient for State and Church to be, as in America, dissevered and divorced. The fact that Catholicity with you is in good condition, nay, is even enjoying a prosperous growth, is by all means to be attributed to the fecundity with which God has endowed his Church, in virtue of which unless men or circumstances interfere, she spontaneously expands and propagates herself; but she would bring forth more abundant fruits if, in addition to liberty, she enjoyed the favor of the laws and the patronage of the public authority.[10]

Thus, the situation in the late nineteenth century—the American arrangement and the liberal democratic, confessionally-neutral state it represented—*tolerari potest* (could be tolerated). Indeed, the accomplishments of the Church under such a new arrangement could be forthrightly and gratefully acknowledged. This was quite a step ahead of the rejectionist posture of Pius IX and the *Syllabus.* We have yet to reach the stage, however, at which the confessionally neutral state

that acknowledges the right of religious liberty as an inalienable right of human beings as such, prior to their status as citizens, is preferred to a benign altar-and-throne (or altar-and-desk) arrangement.

The path to that more developed position, which is the basis of the contemporary Catholic rapprochement with liberal democracy, would be traversed over the next sixty years. The vigor of American Catholicism continued to play a role, by way of example, in ensuring that the issue remained alive. One would also have to take due account of the effect of the providential loss of the Papal States. Absent this direct political responsibility, popes from Leo XIII on were in a more advantageous position to consider, from a far less encumbered theological and practical position, the relative merits of various forms of modern governance.

As the nineteenth century gave way to the twentieth, other realities of modern life began to influence the Church's perspective. Among the most significant were the following:

The rise of totalitarianism, in both its Leninist and fascist forms, and the threat posed to Roman Catholicism by both of these demonic modern political movements, led the Church not only to look toward the democracies for protection, but to look toward democracy itself as an antidote to the totalitarian temptation. This was particularly true in the immediate post-World War II period, when Vatican diplomacy, often working closely with U.S. diplomats and occupation forces, worked to strengthen Christian Democratic parties in Germany and Italy. In the Italian case, this represented a shift indeed, for Pope Pius XI (1922–1939) had summarily ended the proto-Christian Democratic experiment led by Don Luigi Sturzo in the early twentieth century—with most unfortunate results.[11] In any event, Christian Democracy, in theory and in practice, seemed to many Vatican minds (including that of Giovanni Battista Montini, later Pope Paul VI) as the best available alternative to either Leninist or fascist totalitarianism, in a world where even constitutional monarchy was clearly on the wane. Montini was influenced in this judgment by his regard for the philosophical work of the French neo-Thomist Jacques Maritain, whose *Christianity and Democracy,* written during the summer of 1942, became a kind of theoretical manifesto for the Christian Democratic movement.[12]

The Church's turn toward Christian Democracy was also facilitated by the decline of anticlericalist bias among European liberals, and by the horrible clarification of the difference-in-kind between liberals and radicals that totalitarian persecution made plain. The Vatican may still have had its differences with liberals, but after the ruthless persecution of Christianity under Lenin and Stalin, the Ukrainian terror famine, and the Holocaust, it was no longer possible even to suggest that modern radical dictators such as Stalin and Hitler were but exceptionally virulent forms of a general liberal virus. In the French situation, cooperative efforts during World War II between Catholic intellectuals and a few religious leaders, and the wider Resistance movement (with its secularist and Marxist leaderships), helped break down some of the stereotypes that had plagued life under the Third Republic.[13] In Italy, the tradition of Don Sturzo, incarnated in such major postwar figures as de Gasperi and Moro, could be reclaimed, just as in Germany Konrad Adenauer was able to tap the Christian Democratic tradition of the old Catholic Center party.[14]

In the post-World War II period, then, there were new facts of national and international life that validated Gibbons's thesis beyond the borders of the United States and that created the sociological conditions for the possibility of retrieving Pius VII's views on the compatability of Catholicism and democracy.

Finally, and perhaps most significantly in terms of the history of ideas, the evolution of Catholic social teaching itself pushed the Church toward a more positive appraisal of liberal democracy. The key development here was Pius XI's emphasis on the principle of subsidiarity, a principle that was central to the pope's teaching in *Quadragesimo Anno,* issued in 1931 for the fortieth anniversary of Leo XIII's groundbreaking social encyclical *Rerum Novarum.* The key passage in Pius XI's letter was the following:

It is true, as history clearly shows, that because of changed circumstances much that formerly was performed by small associations can now be accomplished only by larger ones. Nevertheless, it is a fixed and unchangeable principle, most basic in social philosophy, immoveable and unalterable, that, just as it is wrong to take away from individuals what they can accomplish by their own ability and effort and entrust it to a community, so it is an injury and at the same time both a serious evil and a disturbance of right order to assign to a larger and higher society what can be performed successfully by smaller and lower communities. The reason is that all social activity, of its very power and nature, should supply help [*subsidium*] to the members of the social body, but may never destroy or absorb them.

The state, then, should leave to these smaller groups the settlement of business and problems of minor importance, which would otherwise greatly distract it. Thus it will carry out with greater freedom, power, and success the tasks belonging to it alone, because it alone is qualified to perform them: directing, watching, stimulating, and restraining, as circumstances suggest or necessity demands. Let those in power, therefore, be convinced that the more faithfully this principle of subsidiary function is followed and a graded hierarchical order exists among the various associations, the greater also will be both social authority and social efficiency, and the happier and more prosperous too will be the condition of the commonwealth.[15]

As it has worked itself out in subsequent Catholic social teaching, the principle of subsidiarity has consisted of the following substantive elements:

(1) The individual human person is both the source and the end of society: *civitas propter cives, non cives propter civitatem* ("The city exists for the benefit of its citizens, not vice versa.").

(2) Yet, the human person is "naturally" social, and can only achieve the fullness of human development in human communities; this is sometimes referred to, particularly in analyses of the writings of John Paul II, as the principle of solidarity.

(3) The purpose of social relationships and human communities is to give help [*subsidium*] to individuals as they pursue, freely, their obligation to work for their own human development. Thus, the state or society should not, save in exceptional circumstances, replace or displace this individual self-responsibility; the society and the state provide, as it were, conditions for the possibility of the exercise of self-responsibility.

(4) There is a hierarchy of commu-

nities in human society; larger, "higher" communities are to provide help [*subsidium*], in the manner noted above, to smaller or "lower" communities.

(5) *Positively,* the principle of subsidiarity means that all communities should encourage and enable (not merely permit) individuals to exercise their self-responsibility, and larger communities should do this for smaller communities. Put another way, decision-making responsibility in society should rest at the "lowest" possible level, commensurate with the effective pursuit of the common good.[16]

(6) *Negatively,* the principle means that communities must not deprive individuals, nor larger communities deprive smaller communities, of the opportunity to do what they can for themselves.

Subsidiarity, in other words, is a formal principle "by which to regulate competencies between individual and communities and between smaller and larger communities." Because it is a formal principle, its precise meaning "on the ground" will differ according to circumstances; because it is rooted in "the metaphysics of the person, it applies to the life of every society."[17]

There is both a historical and a substantive connection between the identification of the principle of subsidiarity and the Roman Catholic Church's increasingly positive appraisal of democracy in the mid-twentieth century. Historically, the very concept of subsidiarity was developed in the German Koenigswinterer Kreis, a group of Catholic intellectuals interested in questions of political economy who deeply influenced both the author of *Quadragesimo Anno,* the Jesuit Oswald von Nell-Breuning, and the evolution of Christian Democracy in pre- and postwar Germany.[18]

The substantive connection was

closely related to the historical connection. *Quadragesimo Anno* was written under the lengthening shadow of totalitarianism. If its predecessor encyclical, *Rerum Novarum,* had been written, at least in part, to warn against the dangers inherent in Manchesterian liberalism, *Quadragesimo Anno* was written in response to the threat posed by the overweening pretensions of the modern state:[19] thus, the importance of the principle of subsidiarity, which tried, *inter alia,* to set clear boundaries to state power. The question then arises: under modern circumstances, what form of governance is most likely to acknowledge, in practice as well as in principle or rhetoric, the limited role of the state, the moral and social importance of what Burke called the "small platoons," and the principle of *civitas propter cives?*

A number of theoretical possibilities come to mind, but in actual historical practice, it is liberal democracies that best meet the test of these moral criteria. That was not precisely what Pius XI, with his corporatist vision, had in mind in 1931, but it was certainly what Pope Pius XII (1939–1958) had in mind by the mid-1940s. Pius XII was not a "global democrat," as a later generation of U.S. paleo-conservatives would say. He did seem to think, however, that democracy provided the best available modern form of government in the developed world.

Vatican II on Church and State

The proximate origins of what I have termed elsewhere the "Catholic human rights revolution,"[20] which led in turn to the Church's new appreciation for, and overt support of, the democratic revolution in world politics, should be located in the Second Vatican Council's *Declaration on Religious Freedom* (so aptly styled, in its Latin title, *Dignitatis Humanae Personae* [hereinafter *DHP*]), issued by the Council in 1965. The *Declaration* was itself a child of the American experience and experiment, and a brief sketch of that background is in order.

The chief intellectual architect of *DHP* was the U.S. Jesuit theologian John Courtney Murray. Beginning in the late 1940s, Murray conceived and orchestrated a creative extension of Catholic church/state theory. The official Roman position, when Murray first took up the topic, was precisely where Leo XIII had left it in *Longinqua Oceani:* the "thesis," or preferred arrangement, was the legal establishment of Catholicism on either the classic altar-and-throne, or modern Francoist, models; the American arrangement, i.e., religious liberty for all in a confessionally neutral state, was a tolerable "hypothesis." Moreover, in a confessionally neutral state, the Church ought (according to the official position) to work for the day when it, too, would enjoy the benefits of state support. The "thesis" arrangement, with its rejection of religious liberty as a fundamental human right, was grounded on the moral-theological maxim that "error has no rights," which meant, in public terms, that "erroneous" religious communities (such as the sundry forms of Protestantism in America) should not, under "ideal" circumstances, receive the tolerant (if tacit) blessing of the state. This view was defended by prominent American Catholic theologians like Joseph Clifford Fenton and Francis Connell, C.SS.R. of the Catholic University of America and the *American Ecclesiastical Review.*[21]

Murray's challenge to this position, and his creative extension of Catholic church/state theory, involved a classically Murrayesque maneuver, i.e., the retrieval and development of an older

25

and largely forgotten current in Catholic thought that antedated the altar-and-throne model. Murray found the *locus classicus* of this forgotten current in a letter sent by Pope Gelasius I to the Byzantine emperor Anastasius in 494, in which the pope had written, "Two there are, august emperor, by which this world is ruled on title of original and sovereign right—the consecrated authority of the priesthood and the royal power." As I have written elsewhere about this modest but crucial statement,

> This was not a radical 'two kingdoms' construct so much as a declaration of independence for both Church and state. The Church's freedom to exercise its ministry of truth and charity was a limit on the powers of government; the state's lack of authority in matters spiritual 'desacralized' politics and, by doing so, opened up the possibility of a politics of consent, in place of the politics of divine right or the politics of coercion. The Gelasian tradition frowned on a unitary Church/state system for the sake of the integrity of both religion and politics.[22]

After considerable theological and ecclesiastical-political maneuvering, Murray's Gelasian retrieval prevailed at Vatican II and, enriched by a personalist philosophical approach which taught that persons had rights, even if their opinions were erroneous, was incorporated into *DHP*, with a palpable effect on the Church's subsequent stance toward democracy.

The connection here—between the definition of religious freedom as a fundamental human right and the affirmation of democratic forms of governance—has to do with the very nature of religious freedom itself, for religious freedom has both an "interior" meaning and a "public" meaning.

The interior meaning of religious freedom can be stated in these terms: Because human beings, as persons, have an innate capacity for thinking, doing, and choosing and an innate drive for meaning and value, freedom to pursue that quest for meaning and value, without coercion, is a fundamental requisite for a truly human life. This innate quest for meaning and value, which is the basic dynamic of what John Paul II has called the interior freedom of the human person, is the object or end of that human right which we call the right of religious freedom; the right of religious freedom, in other words, is the juridical expression of this basic claim about the constitutive elements and dynamic of human beings in the world. One can argue, then, that religious freedom—as the Council put it, the claim that "all men are to be immune from coercion on the part of individuals or of social groups and of any human power, in such wise that in matters religious no one is to be forced to act in a manner contrary to his beliefs"[23]—is the most fundamental of human rights, because it is the claim that corresponds to the most radically human dimension of human being in the world.

This brings us, in short order, to the public meaning of religious freedom. On the personalist analysis above, religious freedom can be considered a prepolitical human right: it is the condition for the possibility of a *polis* structured in accordance with the inherent human dignity of the persons who are its citizens. Thus, the right of religious freedom establishes a fundamental barrier between the person and the state that is essential to a just *polis*. The state is not omni-competent, and one of the reasons we know that is that the right of religious freedom is the juridical expression of the prepolitical fact that there is a *sanctum sanctorum* within every human person wherein coercive power (most especially including coercive state power) may not tread.

The right of religious freedom—which includes, as the Council taught, the claim that "No one is to be restrained from acting in accordance with his own beliefs, whether privately *or publicly*, whether alone *or in association with others*, within due limits"[24]—is also helpful in establishing that distinction between society and the state which is fundamental to the liberal democratic project. Democracy, in theory and in practice, rests upon the understandings that society is prior to the state, and that the state exists to serve society, not the other way around. Social institutions[25] have a logical, historical, and one might even say ontological priority over institutions of government; among the many social institutions that have persistently claimed this distinctive priority are religious institutions and, in the Gelasian tradition, the Christian Church.

Thus the public dimension of the right of religious freedom is a crucial barrier against the totalitarian temptation, in either its Leninist or its mobocracy forms. Some things in a democracy—indeed, the very things that are the building blocks of democracy, i.e., basic human rights—are not up for a vote. Democratic politics is not merely procedural politics; democracies are substantive experiments whose successful working-out requires certain habits (virtues) and attitudes, in addition to the usual democratic procedures. The public meaning of the right of religious freedom reminds us of this, in and out of season. And thus the importance of the right of religious freedom for unbelievers as well as believers, for the secularized U.S. new class elite as well as for the 90 percent of the U.S. people who remain stubbornly religious.[26]

In short, and as Murray himself put it, at Vatican II and in the *Declaration on Religious Freedom*, Roman Catholicism embraced "the political doctrine of . . . the juridical state . . . [i.e.] government as constitutional and limited in function—its primary function being juridical, namely, the protection and promotion of the rights of man and the facilitation of the performance of man's native duties."[27] The juridical or constitutional state is ruled by consent, not by coercion or by claims of divine right. The state itself stands under the judgment of moral norms that transcend it, moral norms whose constitutional and/or legal expression can be found in bills of rights. Moreover, religious liberty, constitutionally and legally protected, desacralizes politics and thereby opens up the possibility of a politics of consent. Where, in the modern world, could such constitutionally regulated, limited, consensual states be found? The question, posed, seemed to answer itself: in liberal democratic states.

Thus the path to an official Roman Catholic affirmation of democracy had been cleared, and indeed the obligatory ends of a morally worthy democratic *polis* specified, in this American-shaped development of doctrine on the matter of the fundamental human right of religious freedom.

The Contemporary Discussion

Pope John Paul II has deepened and intellectually extended the Catholic human rights revolution during his pontificate, not least by explicitly connecting it to the democratic revolution in world politics.

This extension undoubtedly reflects the pope's personal experience in Poland, where the "parchment barriers" (as Madison would have called them) of communist constitutions and other forms of political flim-flam have illustrated precisely how important it is that rights be secured by the structure of governmental institutions, as well as by the habits and attitudes of a people. Here, again, we see how the totalitarian project in the twentieth century has been, paradoxically, a prod to the extension and evolution of Catholic social teaching.

John Paul II has also had to contend with the phenomenon of the various theologies of liberation. While liberation theology is a reality vastly more complex (and, just possibly, of considerably less long-term importance) than has typically been presented in the U.S. secular media, the sundry theologies of liberation share a pronounced skepticism, at times verging on hostility, to what they often term the bourgeois formalism of liberal democracy. Whether liberation theology represents a genuinely distinctive phenomenon in Catholic history, or whether it is the old Iberian fondness for altar-and-throne arrangements in a unitary state moved from right to left on the political spectrum, is an intriguing question, the full exploration of which is beyond the scope of this paper. What is clear is that, by the early 1980s, the theologies of liberation had evolved, in this matter of Catholicism and democracy, along a rather different path than that taken by the Roman magisterium.

Closing the widening breach between official Catholic social teaching and the theologies of liberation, and challenging the currents in the latter which were most out-of-phase with

the developments sketched above, was the task undertaken by the Congregation for the Doctrine of the Faith in its two Instructions on liberation theology, the first published in 1984 and the second in 1986.

The 1984 "Instruction on Certain Aspects of the 'Theology of Liberation,'" issued by the Congregation with the pope's personal authority, acknowledged that liberation was an important theme in Christian theology. It frankly faced the overwhelming facts of poverty and degradation in much of Latin America and argued that the Church indeed has a special love for, and responsibility to, the poor. On the other hand, the Instruction rejected a number of themes which had been key teachings of the various theologies of liberation. Among these the Instruction cited the primary location of sin in social, economic, and political structures; the class struggle model of society and history and related analyses of structural violence; the subordination of the individual to the collectivity; the transformation of the concepts of good and evil into strictly political categories, and the subsequent loss of a sense of transcendent dimension to the moral life; the concept of a partisan Church; and an "exclusively political interpretation" of the death of Christ.[28]

For our purposes here, the most crucial passage in the 1984 Instruction was the following:

> One needs to be on guard against the politicization of existence, which, misunderstanding the entire meaning of the Kingdom of God and the transcendence of the person, begins to sacralize politics and betray the religion of the people in favor of the projects of the revolution.[29]

Against the core dynamic of the Catholic human rights revolution, the theologies of liberation were proposing a return to the altar-and-throne arrangements of the past—this time buttressed by the allegedly scientific accomplishments of Marxist social analysis. With this new monism came, inevitably, the use of coercive state power against individuals and against the Church. The politics of consent was, again, being threatened by the politics of coercion. In short, the theologies of liberation had broken with the modern retrieval of the Gelasian tradition as it had evolved in the teaching of the Second Vatican Council and the social teaching of John Paul II.

The 1986 "Instruction on Christian Freedom and Liberation" pushed the official Roman discussion even further toward an open endorsement of the moral superiority of democratic politics in this passage:

. . . [T]here can only be authentic development in a social and political system which respects freedoms and fosters them through the participation of everyone. This participation can take different forms; it is necessary in order to guarantee a proper pluralism in institutions and in social initiatives. It ensures, notably by a real separation between the powers of the State, the exercise of human rights, also protecting them against possible abuses on the part of the public powers. No one can be excluded from this participation in social and political life for reasons of sex, race, colour, social condition, language, or religion. . . .

When the political authorities regulate the exercise of freedoms, they cannot use the pretext of the demands of public order and security in order to curtail those freedoms systematically. Nor can the alleged principle of national security, or a narrowly economic outlook, or a totalitarian conception of social life, prevail over the value of freedom and its rights.[30]

The politicization of the Gospel—its reduction to a partisan, mundane program—and the resacralization of politics were decisively rejected by the 1984 Instruction. The 1986 Instruction taught that participatory politics were morally superior to the politics of vanguards, whether aristocratic or Marxist-Leninist. The linkage between these themes and the positive task of democracy-building was made in late 1987 by the encyclical *Sollicitudo Rei Socialis*.

Sollicitudo's portrait of the grim situation of Third World countries was based on a more complex analysis than could be found in the encyclical it was written to commemorate, Paul VI's *Populorum Progressio* (1968). Where Paul tended to locate primary (some would say, virtually exclusive) responsibility for underdevelopment in the developed world, John Paul II argued that responsibility for the world's underclass was not unilinear, and involved "undoubtedly grave instances of omissions on the part of the developing countries themselves, and especially on the part of those holding economic and political power."[31] In a more positive vein (and here extending the Catholic human rights revolution in explicitly structural/political terms), John Paul II taught that economic development would be impossible without the evolution of what would be called, in Western terms, the civil society: or in the pope's own words, "the developing nations themselves should favor the self-affirmation of each citizen, through access to a wider culture and a free flow of information."[32]

Yet, the enhanced moral and cultural skills of a people were not enough, the pope continued. Important as they were, they would not yield "integral human development" if the peoples in question remained the vassals or victims of inept, hidebound, ideologically rigid, and/or kleptocratic dictatorships. Thus, true development requires that Third World countries "reform certain unjust structures, and in particular their political institutions, in order to replace corrupt, dictatorial, and authoritarian forms of government by democratic and participatory ones."[33]

In short, in *Sollicitudo Rei Socialis*, the formal leadership of the Roman Catholic Church reconfirmed its support for the democratic revolution in world politics. As John Paul II said of this striking phenomenon of the 1980s,

> This is a process which we hope will spread and grow stronger. For the health of a political community—as expressed in the free and responsible participation of all citizens in public affairs, in the rule of law, and in respect for and promotion of human rights—is the necessary condition and sure guarantee of the development of the whole individual and of all people.[34]

Sollicitudo in fact brought Catholic social theory into congruence with Catholic social practice during the pontificate of John Paul II. Whether the locale has been El Salvador, Chile, Nicaragua, Paraguay, Poland, the Philippines, South Korea, or sub-Saharan Africa, John Paul II's has been a consistent voice of support (and, in Poland, rather more than that) on behalf of the replacement of "corrupt, dicta-

toral and authoritarian forms of government" by "democratic and participatory ones." As for criticism that his preaching on behalf of human rights and democracy constituted an unbecoming interference in politics, the pope had this to say to a reporter who asked him about such carping, while pope and press were en route to Chile and Paraguay in 1987: "Yes, yes, I am not the evangelizer of democracy, I am the evangelizer of the Gospel. To the Gospel message, of course, belongs all the problems of human rights, and if democracy means human rights it also belongs to the message of the Church."[35] From religious conversion, to moral norms, to institutions and patterns of governance, the pope's sense of priorities is clear, but so too is the connection between Catholic social teaching and the democratic revolution.

None of this should be taken to suggest, of course, that the Church of the 1990s and beyond will be an uncritical or naive celebrant of the democratic possibility. As John Paul II made clear during his pastoral visit to the United States in 1987, democratic polities must always remind themselves of the transcendent norms of judgment to which they hold themselves open. Most particularly, today, this means deepening the democracies' understanding of human freedom. As the pope put it in 1987, speaking of the United States,

> Among the many admirable values of this country there is one that stands out in particular. It is freedom. The concept of freedom is part of the very fabric of this nation as a political community of free people. Freedom is a great gift, a blessing of God.
> From the beginning of America, freedom was directed to forming a well-ordered society

and to promoting its peaceful life. Freedom was channelled to the fullness of human life, to the preservation of human dignity, and to the safeguarding of human rights. An experience of ordered freedom is truly part of the history of this land.

This is the freedom that America is called upon to live and guard and transmit. She is called to exercise it in such a way that it will also benefit the cause of freedom in other nations and among other peoples.[36]

Thus did the Bishop of Rome endorse the moral intention of the American experiment in the categories of the Catholic Whig tradition, as exemplified by Acton and his postulate that freedom is not a matter of doing what you want, but of having the right to do what you ought.

Cardinal Joseph Ratzinger, chief intellectual architect of the two Instructions on Christian freedom and liberation, has been another challenging critic of the gap between intention and performance in the established democracies. Ratzinger, like John Courtney Murray, is particularly concerned that democracy not be reduced to what the American Jesuit would have called "an ensemble of procedures" with no substantive foundation. As the cardinal put it in a 1979 essay,

. . . democracy is by its nature linked to *eunomia*, to the validity of good law, and can only remain democracy in such a relationship. Democracy in this way is never the mere domination of majorities, and the mechanism whereby majorities are provided must be guided by the common rule of *nomos*, of what internally is law, that is under the rule of values that form a binding presupposition for the majority too. . . . democracy is only capable of functioning when conscience is functioning, and . . . this latter has nothing to say if it is not guided and influenced by the fundamental moral values of Christianity, values which are capable of realization even in the absence of any specific acknowledgement of Christianity and indeed in the context of non-Christian religion.[37]

These developments in Catholic social teaching and the Church's theology have had significant effects "on the ground," as papal teaching and Catholic reformist practice have, in a variety of locales, become a powerful support for the democratic revolution—and a means for keeping that revolution from spilling over into anarchy. Catholic lay organizations, supported by their local bishops and by the Holy See, have proven an indispensable part of the democratic transitions in Spain and Portugal. The Church is clearly aligned on the side of democracy in Latin America, to the discomfort of caudillos right and left. In Poland, Czechoslovakia, and Lithuania, the Church is at the forefront of the democratic churnings in the world's last empire. In East Asia, the Church was the chief domestic institutional support for the democratic insurgency that toppled Ferdinand Marcos and installed Corazon Aquino, and Church leaders and laity played important roles in the transition to democracy in South Korea. This complex pattern of activism was buttressed by, even as it influenced, the Church's moral case for the democratic alternative—a case that combined idealism and realism in an impressively sophisticated mix.

Thus, Sir Michael Howard's identification of the "other twentieth century revolution" seems, by the end of the 1980s, not quite so surprising after all, and in fact remarkably prescient.

George Weigel

Issues for the Future

The dialectic between the evolution of Catholic social teaching and the democratic revolution can be expected to continue. Among the issues that may rise to the front of the intellectual agenda are the following.

(1) Catholic social teaching, in the United States and in Rome, should more fully integrate the experience of the American Founding—including the Founders' and Framers' philosophical justification for their revolutionary activity—into its reflection on the quest for human freedom. There remains a tendency in Rome to view the modern history of that quest through primarily Continental filters. Thus, the seminal 1986 "Instruction on Christian Freedom and Liberation" could argue that "it was above all . . . at the French Revolution that the call to freedom rang out with full force. Since that time, many have regarded future history as an irresistible process of liberation inevitably leading to an age in which man, totally free at last, will enjoy happiness on this earth."[38]

Yet, there was another revolutionary tradition in the late eighteenth century. Contrary to the revolution of 1789, the American revolution of 1776 and 1787 was a deliberate extension rather than a repudiation of the central political tradition of the West. Beginning with its declaration of inalienable rights given by "Nature, and Nature's God," the American Revolution was channelled into the process of constitution-making, not into the sanguinary excesses of Jacobinism.

The current historiography of the American Founding stresses that the Founders and Framers, far from being the radical Lockean individualists and libertarian Smithite merchants portrayed by Vernon Louis Parrington and Charles Beard, were in fact thoroughly convinced that the success of the American experiment required a citizenry that would live the life of " . . . public virtue, public liberty, [the] public happiness of republicanism, the humane sociability of the Scottish Enlightenment." For the American Founders and Framers, in other words, "the concept of public virtue stood at or near the center of 'republicanism.'" The American Founders and Framers were moral realists, not antinomians; knowing that all men were sinners, they tried to devise "republican institutions which could preserve liberty in virtue's absence."[39]

This moral realism of the Founders and Framers is, of course, not identical with the Catholic social ethical tradition of moderate realism as developed by Augustine and Aquinas.[40] There would seem to be important points of connection between the two, however—a point emphasized by such giants of the American Church as John Carroll, John England, James Gibbons, John Ireland, and John Courtney Murray. Thus, an intense conversation with the leadership of the universal Church, as it continues to reflect on the political/institutional implications of the Catholic human rights revolution, needs to take place, and ought to focus at least some of its attention on the dialectic between the American experience of democratic republicanism and the public philosophy undergirding (or failing to undergird) the experiment launched in 1776 and 1787.

If that point is not particularly well understood in Rome today, the problem may lie not primarily with Rome, but with the successors of Carroll and Gibbons in the American episcopate, and the successors of Murray among American Catholic intellectuals. In both quarters, today, one finds a disturbing phenomenon: men and women who insist on being *American* Catholics, but who, deep down, are profoundly skeptical about, indeed in some cases overtly hostile to, the American experiment.[41] In short, the current episcopal and intellectual leadership of the Church in the United States has not completed the task begun by Gibbons in his 1887 sermon at Santa Maria in Trastevere. It is time to take that task up again—for the sake of the moral deepening of the American experiment, and for the sake of the evolution of Catholic social teaching.

(2) The argument with the various theologies of liberation must continue. The Vatican Instructions of 1984 and 1986—and the democratic revolution itself in Latin America—have had a beneficial impact on this front. In an interview with the *New York Times* in the summer of 1988, for example, Father Gustavo Gutierrez of Peru, widely recognized as the father of liberation theology, distanced himself from those of his brethren who deprecate the accomplishments of Latin America's nascent democracies as but bougeois formalism. "Experience with dictatorship," Father Gutierrez said, "has made liberation theologians more appreciative of political rights." So, too, have the "changes in Marxist and socialist thinking" in Eastern Europe.[42] So, too, one suspects, have the Vatican Instructions of 1984 and 1986, and the social teaching of John Paul II, in his encyclicals and during his pastoral visits to Latin America.

In short, it is now possible to imagine a second-phase or third-phase liberation theology that supports, rather than deprecates, the democratic revolution and the possibilities it holds out for the empowerment of the poor. To imagine such a development and to find it are, of course, two different things. Today, a liberation theology of

democracy is a possibility, not a reality.[43] And so a continued conversation, which is sure to be brisk, remains in order.

(3) Problems of religious liberty—and thus of the right-ordering of political communities—are showing up more frequently in the Church's interface with other world religions. Militant Hindus in Nepal and India, and above all Islamic fundamentalists throughout Africa and Asia, are now impeding, with various degrees of persecutorial vigor, the evangelical and sacramental mission of the Church.

These confrontations raise intriguing new questions for the Catholic human rights revolution and the Church's support for democratic transitions. In many Asian and African locales, or even in a quasi-Western nation such as Haiti, the cultural roots of democracy seem scanty, at best. The Church, like democrats throughout the world, has to explore a number of questions here:

What are the cultural prerequisites for successful transitions to democracy? Can these cultural building-blocks of the politics of participation and consent be enhanced or strengthened by the intervention (the term is used neutrally) of external religious forces?

Islam and Hinduism are complex bodies of religious thought: What currents within them are supportive of democratic politics? What currents are opposed? What is the correlation of forces, to borrow from the Marxists, between supporters and opponents?

Catholicism is now formally committed to a strategy of inculturation in its missionary work.[44] What is the relationship, if any, between the inculturation of the Gospel and the inculturation of human rights norms and political institutions generally perceived in Third World arenas to be

Western—and thus suspect? How, in other words, does the Church concretely give expression to John Paul II's comment cited earlier that "To the Gospel message belongs all the problems of human rights, and if democracy means human rights it also belongs to the message of the Church"— and do so without appearing to be the agent of Western cultural imperialism?

In sum, then, the new official Roman Catholic support for the democratic revolution in world politics raises at least as many questions as it answers, for both theology and political theory, for evangelization and political action. The "other revolution" will, it seems, be an ongoing one.

Acknowledgment: This paper was prepared for a conference on "Liberal Democratic Societies: Their Present State and Their Future Prospects" in London on August 25–29, 1989 and is reprinted by permission of the Professors' World Peace Academy.

Notes

1. From *Mirari Vos,* as cited and discussed in Roger Aubert *et al., History of the Church VIII: The Church Between Revolution and Restoration* (New York: Crossroad, 1981), pp. 286–292. The historical and sociological context of Gregory XVI's condemnation is well summarized by Rodger Charles, SJ.: "Gregory XVI was a temporal ruler faced with a revolt in his own dominions, a revolt which was in the name of a liberalism which . . . was in practice anti-clerical and anti-Christian . . . The Pope could not accept state indifferentism in matters of religion, nor grant liberty of conscience while these implied positive anti-clerical and anti-Christian attitudes. Liberty of the press and separation of the Church and the state were likewise rejected absolutely because of their secularist implications. *This was the essence of the papal dilemma: popes, as vicars of Christ, could hardly recommend policies which, if put into practice in their own states, would link them [i.e., the popes] with men and ideas both anti-clerical and anti-religious.* Only when the question of temporal power of the papacy had been solved

. . . could the situation satisfactorily be resolved." *The Social Teaching of Vatican II* (San Francisco: Ignatius Press, 1982), p. 239 (emphasis added).

2. For a portrait of Pius IX that usefully complexifies many of the regnant stereotypes, cf. E.E.Y. Hales, *Pio Nono: A Study in European Politics and Religion in the Nineteenth Century* (London: Eyre & Spottiswoode, 1954).

3. The Holy See was not, of course, alone in this judgment, although the logic of concern varied from institution to institution. Cf. Henry A. Kissinger, *A World Restored: Metternich, Castlereagh and the Problems of Peace, 1812–1822* (Boston: Houghton Mifflin, 1973).

4. For a discussion of this point, see John Courtney Murray, *We Hold These Truths: Catholic Reflections on the American Proposition* (New York: Doubleday Image Books, 1964), pp. 40 ff. The danger in question was encapsulated in the Abbe Sieyes' defense of the replacement of the old States-General by the revolutionary National Assembly: "The nation exists before all, it is the origin of everything, it is the law itself." Cited in Conor Cruise O'Brien, "A Lost Chance to Save the Jews?" *New York Review of Books,* April 27, 1989, p. 27. O'Brien correctly identifies the Jacobin current as the forerunner of twentieth century totalitarianism, and chillingly cites the German theologian Gerhard Kittel [a "moderate"] who wrote in 1933, in *Die Judenfrage,* that "'Justice' is not an abstraction but something which grows out of the blood and soil and history of a *Volk.*" O'Brien could, of course, have cited any number of Leninist *mots* to this effect, too.

5. Pope Pius VII (1800–1823) was an interesting countercase. Despite his personal suffering at the hands of Napoleon, Pius VII was not so thoroughly soured on the liberal project as his successors Leo XII, Gregory XVI, and Pius IX. As Cardinal Luigi Barnaba Chiaramonti, Pius VII was a compromise candidate at the conclave of 1800, but one who had shown his moderate colors at Christmas 1797, when he shocked his conservative congregants with a sermon in which he declared there to be no necessary conflict between Christianity and democracy. As pope, Pius VII and his secretary of state, the brilliant Cardinal Ercole Consalvi, tried to "blend administrative,

judicial, and financial reforms on the liberal French model with the antiquated papal system"—an effort at cross-breeding that "exasperated reactionaries and progressives alike, and led to serious revolts." (J.N.D. Kelly, *The Oxford Dictionary of Popes* [Oxford: Oxford University Press, 1986], pp. 302–304.) Pius VII's modest reforms were rolled back by his successor Leo XII (1823–1829), who also took up again the rhetorical cudgels against liberalism. Thus ended what might be called the Chiaramonti/Consalvi experiment in rapprochement between Roman Catholicism and the liberalizing reforms of the day. For the next fifty years, conservative retrenchment would dominate Vatican policy and the notion of conservative reform pioneered by Pius VII and Consalvi would fall by the wayside.

6. See Owen Chadwick, *The Secularization of the European Mind in the 19th Century* (Cambridge: Cambridge University Press, 1975).

7. Arthur Schlesinger, Sr. once told the dean of American Catholic historians, John Tracy Ellis, that "I regard the prejudice against your Church as the deepest bias in the history of the American people." Cited in John Tracy Ellis, *American Catholicism*, 2nd edition, revised (Chicago: University of Chicago Press, 1969), p. 151.

8. "Cardinal Gibbons on Church and State," #129 in *Documents of American Catholic History*, volume 2, John Tracy Ellis, ed., (Wilmington: Michael Glazier, 1987), pp. 462–463 (emphasis added).

9. Gerald P. Fogarty, SJ, *The Vatican and the American Hierarchy from 1870 to 1965* (Wilmington: Michael Glazier, 1985), p. 41.

10. *Longinqua Oceani*, in Ellis, *Documents of American Catholic History*, volume 2, p. 502.

11. See Anthony Rhodes, *The Vatican in the Age of the Dictators, 1922–1945* (New York: Holt, Rinehart and Winston, 1973), pp. 14–15.

12. See Jacques Maritain, *Christianity and Democracy* (San Francisco: Ignatius Press, 1986). Maritain had an interesting historical perspective on the events through which he was living, in exile in the United States: "We are looking on at the liquidation of what is known as the 'modern world' which ceased to be modern a quarter of a century ago when the First World War marked its entry into the past. The question is: in what will this liquidation result? . . . [T]he tremendous historical fund of energy and truth accumulated for centuries is still available to human freedom, the forces of renewal are on the alert and it is still up to us to make sure that this catastrophe of the modern world is not a regression to a perverted aping of the Ancient Regime or of the Middle Ages and that it does not wind up in the totalitarian putrefaction of the German New Order. It is up to us rather to see that it emerges in a new and truly creative age, where man, in suffering and hope, will resume his journey toward the conquest of freedom." (pp. 11, 17).

13. The divisions in prewar French society are well captured, in fictional form, in Piers Paul Read, *The Free Frenchman* (New York: Ivy Books, 1986).

14. One should also note, with an eye to 1992, the connection between these national Christian democratic movements and the movement for West European integration that led to the Common Market and the European Parliament.

15. Cited in Joseph A. Komonchak, "Subsidiarity in the Church: The State of the Question," *The Jurist* 48 (1988), p. 299.

16. Is there a connection between the principle of subsidiarity and the American concept of federalism here? It would be going considerably out of bounds to suggest that Madison's concept of federalism, as suggested in *Federalist 10* and *Federalist 51*, was informed by that classic Catholic social theory that eventually evolved the principle of subsidiarity; Madison should not be taken as a kind of proto-Pius XI. Indeed, *Federalist 10* and *Federalist 51* endorse decentralized decision making not as an expression of human possibility, but as a remedy for human defects (the defect of faction). On the other hand, one can argue that federal arrangements (irrespective of their political-philosophical rationale) are one possible expression, in history, of the principle of subsidiarity. One could possibly go further and suggest that the principle of subsidiarity establishes a firmer moral-cultural and indeed philosophical foundation for federal arrangements than Madison's "let a thousand factions bloom," so to speak, that no one of them may become oppressively dominant. Grounded as

it is in an ontology of the person that links *being* and *acting,* and that regards human community as rooted in the social nature of the human person, the principle of subsidiarity might provide a more satisfactory basis for federalism than the voluntarism with which Madison is (wrongfully, in my view) often charged, but of which some of his successors in American political theory (principally the "progressivist" historians of the Parrington/Beard school) are surely guilty.

17. These definitions, as well as the schema above, are adapted from Komonchak, "Subsidiarity in the Church."

18. On the Koenigswinterer Kreis, see Franz H. Mueller, *The Church and the Social Question* (Washington: American Enterprise Institute, 1984), pp. 116–117.

19. On this distinction between the two encyclicals, cf. Mueller, *The Church and the Social Question,* p. 114.

20. See George Weigel, "John Courtney Murray and the Catholic Human Rights Revolution," *This World* 15 (Fall 1986), pp. 14–27.

21. For a detailed examination of the Murray/Fenton/Connell controversy, see Donald Pelotte, *John Courtney Murray: Theologian in Conflict* (New York: Paulist Press, 1975).

22. *Catholicism and the Renewal of American Democracy* (New York: Paulist Press, 1989), p. 86.

23. *Dignitatis Humanae Personae,* p. 2.

24. *Ibid.* (emphasis added).

25. Chief among these "prior" social institutions and the fundamental values they incarnate are what Murray called the *res sacrae in temporalibus,* those "sacred things in man's secular life" of which the Church had been the traditional guardian:
". . . man's relation to God and to the Church, the inner unity of human personality as citizen and Christian but one man, the integrity of the human body, the husband-wife relationship, the political obligation, the moral values inherent in economic and cultural activity as aspects of human life, the works of justice and charity which are the necessary expressions of the Christian and human spirit, and finally that patrimony of ideas which are the basis of civilized life—the ideas of law and

right, of political power and the obligations of citizenship, of property, etc." (John Courtney Murray, "Paul Blanshard and the New Nativism," *The Month* [new series] 5:4 [April 1951], p. 224.)

26. For a fuller discussion of the interior and public meanings of religious freedom, see my essay, "Religious Freedom: The First Human Right," in *This World* 21 (Spring 1988), pp. 31–58.

27. John Courtney Murray, SJ, "The Issue of Church and State at Vatican Council II, *Theological Studies* 27:4 (December 1966), p. 586.

28. For a fuller discussion of the Instruction, and references, see my *Tranquillitas Ordinis: The Present Failure and Future Promise of American Catholic Thought on War and Peace* (New York: Oxford University Press, 1987), pp. 291ff.

29. Instruction on Certain Aspects of the "Theology of Liberation," p. 17.

30. Instruction on Christian Freedom and Liberation, p. 95.

31. *Sollicitudo Rei Socialis,* p. 16.

32. *Ibid.,* p. 44.

33. *Ibid.,* p. 44.

34. *Ibid.*

35. Quoted in The *New York Times,* April 6, 1987.

36. Cited in *Origins* 17, no. 15 (25 September 1987).

37. Joseph Ratzinger, "Europe: A Heritage with Obligations for Christians," in *Church, Ecumenism and Politics* (New York: Crossroad, 1988), pp. 228–229, 234.

38. Instruction on Christian Freedom and Liberation, p. 6.

39. William Lee Miller, *The First Liberty: Religion and the American Republic* (New York: Knopf, 1986), pp. 145–146.

40. For the Catholic tradition of "moderate realism" in social ethics, see my *Tranquillitas Ordinis,* pp. 25–45.

41. See my chapter "The Jacobin Temptation in American Catholicism—The Worlds of the *National Catholic Reporter,*" in *Catholicism and the Renewal of American Democracy,* pp. 47–69.

42. *New York Times*, July 27, 1988.

43. Such a second- or third-phase liberation theology would also have to address the liberation of Latin American economies, and individual Latin Americans, from the crushing weight of mercantilist regulation and bureaucracy. One important test of the reality of a second- or third-phase liberation theology will be its openness to the analysis and prescriptions of, say, Hernando de Soto in *The Other Path* (New York: Harper & Row, 1989). One point of connection between de Soto's empirical studies on entrepreneurship and the evolution of Catholic social teaching may be found in *Sollicitudo Rei Socialis*, where John Paul II defends the "right of economic initiative" as an essential component of integral human development.

44. "Inculturation . . . refers to the central and dynamic principle governing the Christian missionary outreach to peoples not yet evangelized, or among whom the church is not yet rooted firmly and indigenously. More commonly, this is known as the principle of catholicity, or accommodation, or adaptation, or indigenization, or contextualization . . . [T]he principle of inculturation may be traced to its earliest articulation in St. Paul's great debate with the Jewish Christians [who]. . . . erroneously confused their new faith with their own ethnic conventions, cultural practices and local laws which they wished to impose upon all non-Jewish converts to Christianity. . . . [In contemporary terms, the principle means that if the Church] is to become a universally visible and intelligible sign of humankind's unity and salvation . . . [it] must learn to experience and express itself through the cultural riches not only of Western peoples but of all peoples." [Eugene Hillman, "Inculturation," in Joseph A. Komonchak, Mary Collins, and Dermot A. Lane, eds., *The New Dictionary of Theology* (Wilmington: Michael Glazier, 1987), pp. 510–512.]

II. Democracy Abroad

The Crisis of Communism: The Paradox of Political Participation

Zbigniew Brzezinski

WITHIN THE CONTEXT of the new scientific-technological competition between the East and the advanced West, I would like to address the key issue that every ruling Communist party will have to address in the remaining years of the twentieth century: the problem of political participation.

I would first like to set forth the central impulses prompting the Communist governments to focus on the need to engage the citizenry in the political, economic, and social dimensions of national life. I would then like to examine how three Communist states—the Soviet Union, China, and Poland—have chosen to grapple with this dilemma and what problems have arisen from each approach. Finally, I would like to make some observations about the prospects for the resolution of the crisis of communism.

The problem of participation is paradoxical in nature. By participation I mean real participation in shaping the national and local decisions that are of consequential importance to the citizen. In its origins, the ideology and political movement of communism represented an attempt to create a ba-

sis for a fuller participation both in the social system and in the political system of the early industrial age.

Yet, when its proponents have succeeded in seizing state power, communism has become an institutionalized system of highly regimented, disciplined, and bureaucratized nonparticipation. It is, moreover, very difficult for Communist states to break out of this mold. None has been capable of transforming itself from a system in which an elite exerted top-down control over society into one in which society participated in shaping its future from the bottom up, through indirection, choice, and freedom of information.

The original idea of communism was essentially Utopian in nature. It called for the working class to govern itself. Leninism then superimposed the party as a political formula for elite control, first over the workers' movement and then over the revolutionary government of the workers and peasants. Stalinism in turn institutionalized the supremacy of the party through the *nomenklatura*, thereby creating the hierarchical control mechanism which has become known as twentieth-century totalitarian communism. Yet, as successful as ruling Communist parties have been in controlling society, they have failed in

---

Former national security adviser Zbigniew Brzezinski is a counselor to CSIS.

mobilizing those same societies to achieve desired social objectives.

Therein lies the contemporary problem of participation under communism. Marxism-Leninism-Stalinism has proven itself capable of social mobilization for rapid industrialization, even though comparative data show that non-Communist countries have been able to achieve higher rates of growth and higher standards of living while incurring far lower social costs. Nonetheless, it is undeniable that rapid industrialization was achieved by Stalinist-type mobilization. The real failure of the Communist system, however, lies in its inability to transcend the phase of industrialization, to move from the industrial era into the post-industrial world.

We must recognize that this transformation will reshape the world as much as industrialization did. It involves three interrelated revolutions: a political revolution, a social revolution, and an economic revolution. Each revolution is independent of the others but, at the same time, feeds into the others. National success in the remaining years of this century and beyond will depend on the facility with which each nation harnesses these revolutionary forces.

The political revolution is animated by the idea of democracy. Human rights, self-government, and pluralism have become the universal aspirations of mankind. This was evident in Spain and Portugal, where one-party fascist regimes did not succeed in perpetuating themselves. It is also apparent in Latin America, where a proliferation of democratic governments has taken place in the last 10 years, and in the Far East, where the Filipino people ousted a dictator and where pressures have risen for a more democratic order in South Korea. It is no exaggeration to assert that human rights and individual liberty have become the historical inevitability of our times.

New techniques of communication and information processing have spawned the social revolution. Advances in computer and communications technology have transformed the way people interact in modern society and have on balance tended to break down the ability of a centralized state to control the flow of information through dogmatic censorship. These new technologies have also opened the way for vast increases in social productivity and, over time, will have the effect of increasing the gap between those societies which adapt to the new environment and those which do not.

The economic revolution involves the globalization of economic activity. Autarchy, even for the world's largest economies, is a fetter on efficiency. A country that seeks to develop solely within itself is likely to fall behind in development. The great national economic success stories of the last 10 years—Japan, South Korea, Hong Kong, Singapore—all were based on capitalizing on the growth of world trade. Full exploitation of the potential of the world market in the decades ahead will be a precondition for continuing national prosperity—but that means sensitivity to the global market and hence flexibility and risk-taking in prompt and responsive economic decision making.

We can expect the countries that lead economically in the years ahead to be those whose political, social, and economic systems maximize individual and collective innovation. That requires that individuals participate in the system. Thus, for Communist countries, transcending the industrial phase requires a solution to the problem of participation.

Effective participation requires self-motivation. A system can motivate its members by ideas, threats, or incentives. Under Lenin, the idea of communism had a genuine appeal and impact. Under Stalin, the application of mass terror compelled obedience. Today, the idea of communism as a motivating force is dead beyond resurrection, and no one even in ruling Communist parties wants to resurrect the mechanism of mass terror. Thus, incentives remain the only means to induce participation on the part of citizens in Communist countries—but Communist regimes have been singularly incapable of providing and structuring such incentives.

As they confront the crisis of communism, the Soviet Union, China, and Poland have a common point of departure: the heritage of Marxism-Leninism-Stalinism. In the political sphere, this involves the exclusive rule of the Communist party, with democratic centralism and a prohibition of horizontal communication imposing strict control over party members by the upper-most elite. In the economic sphere, it involves state control of all productive resources, with allocation based on central planning and with the price mechanism exerting minimal influence on economic decisions. In the social sphere, it involves a state-directed cultural and intellectual life and a strict prohibition on independent social organizations.

In the Soviet Union, Mikhail Gorbachev's three initiatives—openness, democratization, and economic restructuring—represent an effort to address the question of participation. In a recent address before the Soviet trade unions, he declared that

The more democracy we have, the faster we will progress along the path of restructuring, socialist renovation, and the more order and discipline there will be . . .

So the question today is this: Either we have democratization or we have social inertness and conservatism. There is no third way here.[1]

One must at least give Gorbachev credit for having put his finger on the critical problem.

Solutions, given the Soviet system, are more difficult to identify, however. On the political front, while Gorbachev has never questioned the importance of total party control, he has been grappling to find a way to make the Communist party more dynamic and to overcome the hide-bound party bureaucracy. He has used his campaign for *glasnost* to remove political adversaries, create more participation at the lowest levels of the party, and stimulate a higher degree of individual motivation. We should not, however, overestimate the significance of Gorbachev's glasnost. French political observer Michel Tatu has correctly noted that the campaign's concentration on the spheres of culture and information reveals its weakness and fragility: "It is not a sign of a leader's strength, because if a leader were very strong he would do big things inside the apparatus."[2]

There is a joke circulating in Moscow which captures in an amusing way the superficiality of the glasnost campaign. A man visits his doctor and says, "Doctor, I have a problem, but I need two specialists: one for the ears, nose, and throat, and one for the eye." The specialists then arrive and inquire about the man's condition. He answers, "Gentlemen, I hope very much that you will be able to help me. It's a very worrying state I'm in: I don't see what I hear."

The fact is that reformist rhetoric is not the same thing as a concrete reform program. On the economic front,

Gorbachev has so far announced reforms which at best nudge the country away from central planning, particularly in foreign trade, but which in no sense promote widespread market-based pricing or allocation of resources. Central planning will still prescribe production quotas, but factory managers will have increased latitude in determining their production and in marketing their products. Gorbachev has sought not to overturn the system but to rationalize it, with East Germany, not Hungary or China, as his model.

It is too early to know how thorough a reform of the Soviet economy Gorbachev is seeking. Will collectivized agriculture be abandoned? We do not have the answer to the key question: How systemic, in the eyes of the Kremlin leadership, is the internal economic crisis? Related to this is the question of how far reaching a cultural revolution the Soviet leadership is prepared to promote both within the Soviet labor force and within Soviet management. After 70 years of the Soviet system, neither Soviet workers nor Soviet managers are predisposed toward self-motivation and risk-taking. The engrained habits of work emphasize conformity, laxness, bureaucratic security, and camouflaged privilege. The simple fact is that Soviet Russians are not Communist Prussians.

Beyond that, there is an enormous divide beyond economic decentralization from above and economic participation from below, between economic dispersal and political participation. Where to draw the line between the former and the latter is likely to be the major preoccupation of the Soviet leaders for years to come. This is the case not just because of the conservative nature of bureaucracy. A more important cause is the multinational character of the modern-

day Great Russian Empire. The Soviet Union is the last surviving multinational empire in the world. The Great Russian people dominate a dozen major nations and scores of lesser nations. The national diversity ultimately represents the Achilles' heel of the system. A program of reforms for genuine participation could easily devolve into general national conflict between the Great Russians and the non-Russian nations of the Soviet Union.

Moreover, one must anticipate that Gorbachev's initial reforms may produce considerable confusion and almost inevitably some rise in consumer prices. A drop in the standard of living is thus likely, and that could trigger dangerous unrest. As Soviet citizens become more accustomed to even modestly enhanced participation, they will become emboldened in venting their dissatisfaction. One should not be surprised to see at that stage open manifestations of student unrest, of demonstrations by housewives, and even of strikes in the factories. The litmus test will be how the Soviet leadership then reacts to such unprecedented forms of participation from below.

In China, Deng Xiaoping's reforms have focused on economic decentralization. He has disbanded collectivized agriculture and introduced other reforms which, when completed, will remove 65 to 70 percent of production from state control by the year 2000. This will make profitability, not political pliability, the test of economic management. These reforms are not superficial—they are consequential. They change the way the system works because they shift the locus and method of decision making.

The central dilemma is whether economic reform will produce irresistible pressures for political reform. As evident in the recent student demonstrations for greater democracy, there is a link between the two. Fang Lizhi, the intellectual leader of the Shanghai student movement, addressed this question in a speech before his expulsion from the Chinese Communist Party:

> Socialism is at a low ebb. There is no getting around the fact that no socialist state in the post-World War II era has been successful, and neither has our own thirty-odd-year-long socialist experiment.

He later added: "I feel that the first step toward democratization should be recognition of human rights."[3]

It was inevitable that the question of political reform would be posed, especially as the Chinese Communist Party itself has formally diluted the importance of Marxist dogma. Deng Xiaoping's slogan calling on China to "seek truth from facts" casts doubt on the notion of ideological dogma itself. That made the rise of some kind of political challenges to the leading role of the party a matter of time. If truth lies in examining facts, anyone can deduce the truth, and competing interpretations of the facts will certainly arise. If no single truth exists and if others beside the party can divine this truth, no rationale exists for dictatorial rule by the party.

Last year I discussed the issue of political reform with Hu Yaobang, then general secretary of the Chinese Communist Party, several months before the student protests that led to his ouster. In the course of a five-hour-long conversation, Hu told me that the reform program was far from finished and that future reforms would have to involve a restructuring of the Chinese political system. He said that initial discussions on this issue had taken place within the Politburo and that a party document on the subject would be finished in 1987. He explained that the fundamental nature of the party would not change and that the party would remain the leadership core of China. He added that the central party bureaucracy would be streamlined, that there would be considerable reform in the relationship between subordinates and superiors within the party, and that other political parties within China—the so-called democratic parties—would be given greater autonomy.

But the Chinese party leaders are clearly reluctant to take that giant step leading from economic decentralization to political decentralization. In recent months, if anything, a reverse trend has manifested itself. A number of key Chinese political leaders have become alarmed that economic decentralization will spill over into the political realm, creating something which might be called a more liberalized political system. They have been quite explicit in their denunciations, and Hu Yaobang has fallen from power. Reflecting the ruling elite's anxiety, Hu Sheng, the chairman of the Academy of Social Sciences, said:

> Some people have used the open policy and situation of letting 'one hundred schools contend' to preach bourgeois liberalism, refute socialism, advocate total Westernization and lash out at party leadership.[4]

Most likely, the catalyst for China's political future will be the succession struggle after Deng passes from the scene. Given China's mass scale, one is entitled to expect a protracted conflict between the political imperatives of the Communist system and the economic requirements of the modernization program. My own expectation is

45

that eventually the latter will prevail over the former, but only after a few zig-zags in domestic policy and after intense conflicts on the political level.

In Poland, communism has essentially broken down. Formally, the Communist Party still rules the country. But in reality a combined military-police clique holds power in the name of the party, the church is a significant force, and the leadership of Solidarity has become in effect an organized, if unofficial, political opposition.

What is significant is that Polish society has in a very real sense emancipated itself. The Communist Party has been unable to retain its monopoly on social organization and had to accommodate itself to pressures from below to an unprecedented degree. When I travelled through Poland recently, I was genuinely impressed by the extent to which the opposition functions as a parallel social leadership. Its underground press published hundreds of newspapers, which are widely available and easily accessible. It even has managed to break the state's monopoly on the electronic media through the use of video-cassette recorders. Whenever I arrived for meetings with opposition figures, it was always amidst a battery of video cameras and cassette tape recorders. While freedoms are not as great as they were at the peak of the Solidarity movement, it is significant to note that the opposition to the Communist regime feels so confident that it can hold "photo opportunities" for its own news media.

I was also impressed by the extent to which the confidence of the Polish Communist regime has been broken. As a result of state mismanagement of the economy, Poland is an economic calamity, and its Communist leaders know it. Even to begin the process of economic renewal, the state needs to persuade the people to participate in the process. Since the imposition of martial law, however, Polish society has essentially adopted a strategy of passive resistance. To overcome this willful inertia, all the Polish Communist leaders with whom I met accepted the fact that they needed in some fashion to engage or coopt the opposition leadership. But a political gridlock has developed over the question of how such accommodations might proceed. The government demands that the opposition operate in government organs such as the official trade unions or the new advisory commission, but the opposition will not let itself be seduced into such subordinate status.

There seem to be basically three prospects for communism in Poland, with the precipitating catalyst for change being Poland's deepening economic crisis and the need for Western credits. The first is a continuation of the current political stalemate, with the growing risk of an eventual explosion from below. The second is a progressive return to repression, leading to a renewal of central control and administration. The third is a continuing transformation of the sociopolitical structure, leading eventually perhaps to formalized coparticipation and even in the long term to a system that, for geopolitical reasons, remains Communist in name only.

The bottom line is that genuine participation is incompatible with the rule of a Leninist-type party. In Poland, such a party no longer rules, but a new system of overt participation has not replaced it. The situation is one of an unstable stalemate. In the Soviet Union, political experimentation is confined to the lower political-social level, while the present economic reforms, to be truly successful, require a monumental change in the culture and working habits of both labor and

Participation in Communist Systems

	Marxism-Leninism-Stalinism	Soviet Union	China	Poland
Political Participation	Total party control. Centralized party discipline. Prohibition on horizontal communication. Nomenklatura	Efforts to energize party bureaucracy. Minimal experimentation with low-level multi-candidate elections.	Official dilution of Marxist dogma. Party recruitment of technical expertise. Experimentation with municipal electoral choice.	Military-party symbiosis. Church represents a political force. Solidarity leadership acts as organized but unofficial opposition which is excluded from policy participation.
Economic Participation	State ownership of productive resources. Collectivized agriculture. Centralized command economy. No role for price mechanism.	Proposed limited exposure to international prices and to price mechanism beyond state-fixed quota. Proposed elections for workplace managers.	Retrenchment in central planning. Decollectivization of agriculture. Widespread influence of price mechanism. Integration into capitalist world economy.	Private land ownership. Local trade unions, often run by former Solidarity members, influential in some industries. Stalemate between state and society over economic future.
Social Participation	Prohibition on independent social organizations. State-directed intellectual and cultural life. Communication tightly controlled.	More openness about problems within the Soviet Union. More cultural and artistic freedom.	Nascent consumerism. More cultural and intellectual freedom, but suppression of "bourgeois liberalism."	Self-emancipated society. Party monopoly on independent social organization broken. Effectively free underground press. Independent cultural and intellectual life.
Key Issue	---	Scope and implementation of reform program.	Balance between economic and political reform.	Interaction between economic recovery, social austerity, and political participation.
Alternative Prospects	---	Slowdown of reforms. National unrest leading to reversal of reforms. Systemic reform.	Political retrenchment. Political decentralization. Collision between political and economic imperatives.	Continued stalemate, with the risk of political explosion. Progressive repression. Formalized co-participation.
Precipitating Catalyst	---	A politically activating and polarizing drop in the standard of living.	Succession struggle linked to programmatic debates.	Deepening economic crisis and realization of unavailability of Western aid.

management. In China, economic decentralization is in collision with continued political centralization, though China's commercial culture favors the progressive emancipation of the economic sector.

In conclusion, what is common to these three countries is that their Communist-type systems are encountering great difficulties in evolving beyond the phase of development associated with rapid industrialization. All have so far been unable to solve the problem of participation. At the core of the problem is the concept of an elitist party with a dogmatic conception of the truth. Such a ruling party is, very simply, incompatible with the notion of genuinely spontaneous social participation in the political, economic, and social spheres of a more modern, complex society. Until the nature of the party is changed or the party disappears, the issue of participation will continue to be a source of conflict both within the party and between the party and society.

Ultimately, the inability to resolve that conflict and to provide for genuine participation may prove to be the undoing of modern communism. There

is considerable evidence that modern communism is becoming an increasingly sterile system in which the ruling party is viewed by society at large as the principal obstacle to social progress and to societal well-being. If one is correct in stating that the quest for genuine political participation is today's universal imperative, one is also correct in surmising that it augurs the approaching historical demise of the Communist system of social mobilization and political nonparticipation. Indeed, in many respects, the mood within large portions of the public in the Communist world is today reminiscent of the mood within capitalist states almost six decades ago, during the Great Depression: there is a sense that a fatal flaw exists in the system itself. That flaw is called the Communist Party.

Notes

1. *TASS*, February 2, 1987.
2. *Soviet-Eastern Europe Report*, June 10, 1987.
3. *China Spring Digest*, March-April 1987.
4. *The New York Times*, January 17, 1987.

Explosive Change in China and the Soviet Union: Implications for the West

Amos A. Jordan and Richard L. Grant

Massive student unrest and violent repression, widespread ethnic demonstrations and riots, electoral rejection of party leaders, growing economic woes—these dramatic events of the past few months in the Peoples Republic of China and the Soviet Union force the question of whether their leaders can manage the accelerating pace of change in those nations. Indeed, the drama of Tiananmen Square from April to June of 1989 indicates that China's leadership has for the time being lost control of the process.

Clearly, the ice of totalitarianism is breaking up in much of the Communist world. Indeed, the fundamental transformations underway in China and the Soviet Union amount to "second revolutions"—which may well change their societies and international affairs as much in the twenty-first century as their predecessor revolutions did in the twentieth century. To gauge the depth and character of these transformations—and their meaning for the West—it is useful to examine their origins and dynamics.

Amos A. Jordan is president emeritus of the Center for Strategic and International Studies and holder of the Henry Kissinger chair in national security policy. Richard L. Grant is a fellow in national security studies at CSIS.

The Roots and Character of Reform

Just as battlefield retreat before a skilled enemy is the most complex and dangerous maneuver in the art of war, so strategic withdrawal in the wake of systemic failure is the most difficult task of governance. By the end of the 1970s, leaders in Beijing and Moscow were hunting for a way out from a common, urgent, overriding problem—their economic systems were manifestly failing and reform was essential. Yet, as de Tocqueville pointed out, rulers are most vulnerable precisely when they begin to reform.

In the case of the Chinese, the massive upheavals of Mao's Cultural Revolution from 1966 to 1976 had produced virtual chaos. As Deng Xiaoping expressed it later, "We lost 20 years from 1957 to 1976 in the Great Leap Forward, the commune system, and the Cultural Revolution. We moved backward while the rest of the world made great economic progress during those years."[1] When Deng came to power in 1978, despite isolated pockets of progress, China's one billion people were mired in deep poverty and unable to meet the country's basic requirements for food, shelter, and other necessities. In 1980, per capita gross national product (GNP) was only $250. As a result of Mao Ze-dong's preference for "red," rather than "expert," the stagnating Chinese economy was in the hands of ideologues and bureaucrats; traditional Chinese entrepreneurial strengths were being invested in getting around the system, or getting by despite the system.

In the Soviet Union, events were not so tumultuous nor was the decline so dramatic. Nevertheless, the signs of mounting economic trouble were increasingly clear. From 1965 to 1970 the Soviet economy grew at an average rate of about 5.1 percent; in the period 1971–1975, the growth rate fell to 3.0 percent, in 1976–1982 to 2.1 percent; in 1983–1984, it bumped up slightly to 2.3 percent, and then in 1985–1988 it fell to 2.0 percent. (The 1987 rate was less than 1 percent!)[2] By the latter 1970s, Brezhnev and his countrymen were increasingly floundering in a Stalinist model of a rigid, centrally planned economy, marked by an emphasis on heavy industry, priority to defense, and consumer neglect. So deep and pervasive were the difficulties that many Western experts were convinced that only root and branch reform, not tinkering or changes at the margin, could provide a cure.[3] Neither Brezhnev nor his immediate successors, Andropov and Chernenko, however, could muster the resolve and energy needed to clean the Augean stables. In Gorbachev's words, "a pre-crisis situation" had developed.

Under Deng's skillful and determined leadership, China moved first on the reform front. The guiding principle of these reforms was to create incentives rather than to depend on Mao's "mass mobilization" approach. Stimulated by the success of the peasantry in taking matters into its own hands in Anwhei, Sichuan, and other provinces, Deng launched a series of nationwide agricultural reforms in the latter 1970s.[4] Agriculture was the natural place to start, for 80 percent of the population was rural and China was barely able to meet its food and fiber needs in good years—and there was very little foreign exchange available to buy imports to buffer crop shortfalls.

At the heart of Deng's initiatives was the "household responsibility" system, under which the farmer and his family replaced the commune as the unit of production; long-term (15–year) leasing of land to the peasant and free marketing of part of his crop—beyond obligatory quotas required by the state—provided the needed incentives. The results were electrifying; rural production (including village industry) soared 10.5 percent annually between 1978 and 1986, with galvanizing spillover effects into the urban sector.[5]

In an effort to enlist the energies of city workers in a comparable way, Deng and his colleagues next launched a counterpart "management responsibility" system for urban enterprises, based on either leasing or contracts. In effect, factory managers of some state enterprises took responsibility for their units' productivity, wages, profits and losses; they agreed to deliver to the state a quota of goods at predetermined prices—then production beyond the quota could be sold on the free market and the proceeds distributed as bonuses or used to expand or modernize facilities, etc.

Alongside the state-owned enterprises, China permitted individually or cooperatively owned private enterprises. Originally limited in size to ten workers, this particular part of the economy proved so dynamic that the limitation on the number of workers was subsequently removed. As a consequence, some private firms have grown quite large. Stone Enterprises, for example, which is a computer manufacturing firm, provides a Chinese version of the Hewlett-Packard story. Begun with a few workers in 1983, by 1988 it had grown considerably, producing the highest quality computers in the PRC, using no state funds, and paying several times the wages of state-run computer factories.

Indeed, one of the most intractable problems the Chinese have faced lies in these kinds of imbalances between the market and nonmarket sectors of the economy. Not only Stone computer employees, but also taxi drivers, merchants, and a host of other entrepreneurs earn several times the wages of those employed in universities, government, or state-controlled companies. Even the peasants are in many cases far better off than the workers in typical state enterprises. Unfortunately, this dual economy—with two sets of prices for the same or related commodities—has given rise not only to glaring inequities but also to gross corruption.

Imbalances have grown sharply, too, between interior provinces and coastal areas where the government established, in the early 1980s, special economic zones in which preferential tax rates and exemptions are given to foreign companies investing in export projects and where the forces of the market are allowed greater play than in the rest of the country. Beijing views these zones as laboratories where experimental economic policies can be tested before being applied to the country as a whole. The Chinese also hope that the special economic zones will develop into high technology centers and as effective channels to Hong Kong, Macao, and Taiwan.[6]

By the summer of 1988, the combination of structural reforms and economic progress had produced a Chinese economy on a knife's edge. By the Chinese leaders' own reckoning, the economy was more than 50 percent market-determined. To use Deng's metaphor, "We are in the middle of the river and must choose whether to go forward or backward." Recognizing the impossibility of remaining midstream and the high cost of retreating, Deng and his key colleagues (Zhao Zijang, in particular) were determined to push forward. Acknowledging that further economic deregulation and price reform would be painful, Deng observed that "a short pain is better than a long pain."[7]

As Deng sought to open China economically, he also opened it somewhat in terms of internal politics. His maxim, "It does not matter whether the cat is black or white; if it catches mice, it is a good cat," reflected his basic pragmatism in matters political as well as economic. In his repudiation of the Cultural Revolution and all its consequences, Deng attempted to deemphasize ideology and curtail the party's intrusion into all aspects of political, social, and cultural life—even as he consistently insisted on the continued primacy of the Communist party in the nation's life.

In the latter 1970s and 1980s, China's leaders pursued a number of political goals: first, to decentralize from Beijing to the provinces a measure of economic and political power; second, to move many economic decisions from the Party's hands to those of enterprise managers, bankers, farmers, and local government officials; third, to revitalize the Party by bringing in younger, better educated members who would focus on vanguard political roles; and, fourth, to energize the Party and the political system by permitting somewhat broader participation in both Party and state decision making. However, in politics even more clearly than in economic matters, Deng insisted on continuing Party primacy.

Political controls on social life were lessened after 1978, too, with the exception of family planning. Checks on freedoms of belief and expression were eased, and discriminatory class labels were lifted. Competitive elections were actually permitted, both at the grass-roots and enterprise level—though local cadres were often able to subvert the election processes. (Although the Communist Party constitution provides for competitive elections at all levels, apparently there has been little true competition.)

In the post-Mao era, the role of the various people's congresses, particularly of the National People's Congress, has been strengthened somewhat, and frank discussions have sometimes occurred on salient issues—with negative votes actually cast in some cases. There has also been revision of the legal system to institute new procedural rights and to guarantee a fair trial, but the notions of equality before the law or judicial independence are hard to implant in a state where the Party itself is firmly in charge and largely outside the law.

Alongside these measures of internal economic and political liberalization, Deng and his colleagues, reversing the autarky of the Maoist era, opened China to the West. Deng warned "any country that closes its door to the outside world cannot achieve progress."[8] In particular, Beijing welcomed foreign investment, accepting loans and credits from multilateral lending institutions and commercial banks. Thousands of foreign corporations set up joint ventures and subsidiaries in China, which, unlike the Soviet Union, set no limit on the percentage of foreign ownership.

Over 40,000 students were sent abroad—20,000 to the United States alone.

The grudging way that the post-Mao leaders accepted the idea that some political liberalization was essential if economic progress were to be achieved undoubtedly stemmed in part from the national trauma produced by the Cultural Revolution. Deng and his colleagues had come to view disorder as a social and political pathology that they (and most of their generation) were determined to avoid. Political freedoms were metered out cautiously, as might be expected in a society where authority, Confucian or Communist, has always descended from above.

As might also be expected in the midst of such fundamental changes, not all the cats caught mice. Experiments went awry, incompetence surfaced, intellectuals "pushed freedom too far," and rectification campaigns became necessary. The campaign against "spiritual pollution" in 1983–1984 was typical: the too-zealous modernizers were attacked; the mass media were enlisted in the assault; an education and disciplinary program was carried out in party circles, and a clampdown, including arrests, was ordered against the most ardent. The pattern was repeated in the 1987 campaign against "bourgeois liberalization." Until 1989, however, each of these "rectifications" proved to be relatively short-lived and mild, and in their wake each seemed to leave a somewhat widened range of political discourse and involvement. Throughout the period, Deng and his colleagues watched Eastern Europe and the Soviet Union carefully, and General Secretary Zhao expressed their consensus, "the Russians have let political reform run ahead of economic reform, creating unrealistic expectations, while we are carefully keeping the two in tandem."[9]

As Zhao implied, the Soviet Union chose a different path of reform. Soon after Mikhail Gorbachev came to power in 1985, it became clear that he intended to cure the economic mess he inherited. He began by emphasizing greater discipline and by attacking corruption and incompetence, as his immediate predecessor Andropov had done during his brief tenure.

It was quickly apparent, however, that emphasis on the "human factor" was producing only pallid results. Not only was the stagnant economy creating a lag between people's rising expectations and performance, with continuing damage to public morale and Party credibility, but it was also threatening the Soviet Union's future status as a superpower. Falling behind in science and technology and incapable of producing industrial goods which could be sold for hard currency anywhere in the world, the Soviet Union was indeed, as some of its internal critics put it, "in danger of descending to the status of a Third World power." Gorbachev and his reform-minded colleagues were determined to do whatever was necessary to make the economy work.

Although following the successful Chinese example with the agricultural sector might have seemed a logical place to start, given the perennial difficulties in that part of the Soviet economy and its stubborn unresponsiveness to disproportionately large investments in the past, Gorbachev chose to begin his restructuring efforts more broadly. Perhaps his own earlier experience when he had responsibility in the Politburo for overseeing agriculture had convinced him of the special difficulties in that sector; or, perhaps, the political sensitivities attached to the painful, bloody past of farm collectivization deterred him.

In any case, Gorbachev chose to start with a series of broad administrative and economic reforms, with emphasis on industry rather than agriculture. Up to 1988, these included such measures as wholesale trade and banking reforms, decentralization of decision making to the enterprise level in such matters as financing and wages and bonuses, reorganization and downgrading of the central planning apparatus, selective but limited price reforms, foreign trade reform, priority emphasis on quality control, and encouragement of small-scale cooperatives.[10]

These reforms were introduced hurriedly, piecemeal, and selectively, however, and they were piled on top of the existing five-year plan. Managers were not released from their obligation to meet plan targets, even though they were receiving inconsistent reform directives. Not surprisingly, the resulting confusion and dislocations (plus bad weather, low oil prices, bureaucratic footdragging, and various other troubles) produced poor results.[11] By 1988 the Soviet GNP was increasing at or less than the Brezhnev era's stagnation rates.

Gorbachev's problem lay in part with the fact that he had to wrestle a Party bureaucracy that had been entrenched for 70 years and had never undergone the wrenching of a cultural revolution. (The Cultural Revolution in China had resulted in the grave weakening and discrediting of the Communist party organization, which, in turn, meant that Party bureaucrats were often unable to frustrate reformers' initiatives.) To create his own cultural revolution, to counter bureausclerosis, and to put pressure on the

Party apparatchiks from the bottom as well as the top, Gorbachev turned to *glasnost* or openness, as well as *perestroika* or restructuring. Through *glasnost's* revelations of the depth of the problems confronting the Soviet Union and the inadequacies of past measures to deal with them, the reformers hoped to enlist the energies and enthusiasm of the intelligentsia and later the workers and the masses. *Perestroika's* reform measures were aimed at overcoming those problems.

In his book, *Perestroika*, Gorbachev provides a formidable list of the kinds of problems that gave rise to his restructuring and renewal initiatives. These problems include economic stagnation, wasteful or inefficient use of materials, the gradual erosion of ideological and moral values, a governmental credibility gap, and "disrespect for the law and encouragement of eyewash and bribery, servility and glorification," etc.[12] Confronted with these ills, Gorbachev appears to have become convinced that only a thoroughgoing transformation of Soviet society and its politics could provide the preconditions for revitalizing the economy. Accordingly, he has piled political reforms on top of each other and deepened and broadened the scope of economic reforms.

Central to Gorbachev's plans for economic revitalization has been a reduction of the claim of defense resources on GNP. In recent years, various foreign experts have generally estimated these claims to be about 15–16 percent. Within a year of taking power, Gorbachev made it plain that resources had to be diverted from defense to consumption. Although the Soviet military-industrial complex continued to spew out tanks, artillery, aircraft, and other sinews of war at an undiminished pace from 1986 to 1989, General Sergei Akhromeyev told senior U.S. officials that plans for the cuts in Soviet forces, announced by Gorbachev at the United Nations in December 1988 and to be implemented starting the summer of 1989, were more than two years in the planning stages. Moreover, in this same 1986–1988 period, Gorbachev also directed a number of "military factories" to initiate the manufacture of such consumer items as tractors, refrigerators, and television sets.

Although the data are still incomplete, it is widely agreed in the West that the 12 percent figure that Premier Ryzhkov announced on June 7, 1989, considerably understates the true burden of defense spending on the Soviet economy. Achieving arms reduction agreements with the West and reducing international tension, as well as unilateral measures to prune the inflated level of military expenditures, could result in a substantial diversion of these of resources to the civilian economy. Tension reduction has also led to an enhanced flow of credits, investment, technology transfer, and trade as well; in 1988 alone, the surge of Western commitments of credits and investment totalled over $8 billion.

Whether he was merely making a virtue of the economic necessity of reducing the level of military confrontation, or whether he was convinced by the evidence of growing world interdependence, Gorbachev in 1987 set forth his new thinking about the world, as well as about internal Soviet problems. One key to the new thinking about the international situation has been rejection of war as an instrument of policy and recognition that "security is indivisible." The traditional formulation of security policy under Stalin held that the USSR could only be secure if it were stronger than its enemies combined. Under Brezhnev, the axiom was changed such that the Soviet Union must have parity with its combined potential enemies. Gorbachev articulated yet another version: "It's either equal security for all or none at all. . . . Adversaries must become partners and start looking jointly for a way to achieve universal security."[13]

Further principles of the new thinking include not only arms reduction measures, but also stabilization of the nuclear balance at greatly reduced levels, increased international contacts and dialogue, a common European home, an enhanced role for the United Nations, cooperation to defuse regional conflicts, and a shift from offensive to defensive military deployments, armaments, and doctrine.

Accompanying these signs of decreased Soviet bellicosity and adventurism have been skillful diplomatic efforts to exploit the increasingly peaceful image of the Soviet Union and the new thinking behind it. In particular, Gorbachev has sought to diminish the sense of threat in Western Europe and to undercut NATO and the U.S. presence that underwrites it. Soviet diplomatic efforts have not been restricted to Europe; in Asia, Gorbachev held out olive branches in his 1986 Vladivostok and 1987 Krasnoyarsk speeches to U.S. allies and friends. Invariably, these formal presentations of the Soviet "reasonable" positions have been accompanied by Soviet propaganda designed to blame the United States for whatever problems exist in the region.

Prospects for Success

Up until the early summer of 1988, China's reforms seemed to be succeeding, though painfully, unevenly, and somewhat fitfully. At that point Deng and Zhao still appeared ready to press forward with wage and price reform and the further development of the principle that the "state is to regulate the market and the market is to lead the enterprise." In Zhao's words "we have met the two preconditions of a further thrust forward: a healthy economy with adequate public consumption of the essentials and a good international economic position which will cushion any shocks." Even so, Zhao went on to observe, "the course is risky, but if we can hold to it for the next three to five years, the frictions of the transition will disappear and a new era will boom."[14]

The stalling of the economic reforms and the quickening of the pace of inflation in the summer of 1988, however, together with instances of panic food buying and riots during that period, caused Deng, Zhao, and Premier Li Peng (an increasingly important actor) "to consolidate" rather than press forward. Zhao's pragmatic approach of "groping for the stepping stones" to cross the river was being questioned as the water deepened; indeed, some critics were beginning to observe that his strategy was appropriate to crossing a mountain stream but would not work in the Yangtze where China was finding itself. Price reform was halted; indeed, controls were reinforced in some areas and even joint ventures were hit with new constraints.

These deepening problems in making the unprecedented transition to an increasingly free, "socialist market economy" were related to another deeply serious malaise, namely, a growing sense of purposelessness. The lack of a vision of the future—beyond materialism, that is—affected all sectors of Chinese society, but particularly the youth. The void left by the eclipse of Confucianism earlier in the century had been filled for a time with "Mao Zedong thought" and its accompanying certitudes. However, with the dashed hopes of the Great Leap Forward and the Cultural Revolution's excesses, and with the denigration of Marxist-Maoist verities which followed, where were the principles to guide individual behavior and provide the social harmony so prized in Sinic cultures?[15]

Perhaps Deng Xiaoping's formulation expressed the new era's paucity of vision: "Our goal is to have relative prosperity for the Chinese people. Just to extricate one-fifth of the human race from poverty would be a major achievement."[16] While his statement undoubtedly reflects one of the verities upon which all leadership elements could agree, it hardly provides an all-embracing system of thought, such as Confucianism and Maoism had done.

The replacement of Mao's failed effort to create a "new socialist man" by Deng's "acquisitive man" led inevitably to a feeling on the part of many Chinese that their society no longer provided them a satisfactory sense of identity. Intensifying this difficulty was growing, rampant corruption—especially prominent in the special economic zones—which necessitated payoffs or special connections in order to get even the simplest things accomplished. All this combined with growing inflation (by mid-1988 unofficially estimated by World Bank officials at 30 percent annually in urban areas) and gradually escalating demands for greater freedom and political participation, particularly by students.

Demonstrations by students and then by students and workers began in mid-April 1989 with the death of former Party leader Hu Yaobang, who had been ousted in early 1987 for his failure to clamp down on student demonstrations. The demonstrators, who were extraordinarily peaceful, disciplined, and modest in their initial demands, met a totally unyielding Leninist wall—until June 4, that is, when the wall crashed down upon them in the form of brutal military assault that caused many hundreds, perhaps thousands, of casualties among the demonstrators and a much smaller but significant number of police and military casualties as well.

Beijing's bloody days of June represent a profound tragedy at many levels and in many ways. In the first instance, of course, there is the tragedy of the thousands killed and wounded and of their bereaved families. There is the concomitant tragedy of the shattered hopes and bitterness of the millions who demonstrated for freedom and democracy—goals that were often only vaguely defined and understood but deeply felt.[17] Although not a direct part of the events unfolding in Beijing and provincial cities across the country, the tens of thousands of Chinese students studying overseas are part of that same tragedy.

There is the larger national disaster as well. The reformers, with Deng at the lead, had succeeded over the previous decade in putting the country on the course of economic development and in the process opened internal freedoms and external contacts that were unthinkable in Maoist days. In addition to political progress, this opening had brought trade, investment, and technology transfers that were indispensable elements of the economic modernization process. In the decade after 1978, billions of dollars of direct foreign investment poured into the country, with accompanying technological and managerial skills. Thousands of joint and cooperative ventures and technology transfers were arranged. Tens of billions of dollars worth of machinery, electronics equipment, computers, and other items essential to development were imported.

It will be years before the damage of the June days in Tiananmen Square is recouped. In part this is a simple function of the fact that a secure and stable business environment is essential to attract foreign investors. There are other reasons, however. It will take years to restore the belief that modernization and economic liberalization have become irreversible or that the long-standing volatility of Chinese internal politics has ended, even if reform elements regain the ascendancy in the government in a relatively short time. Deng's assurances, a week after the bloodshed, that China's policy of economic reforms and its opening to the West will not change are not likely to reassure skeptics.[18]

The promised reversion of Hong Kong to China in 1997 was already producing a worrisome drain of talent and resources from the colony. (In 1988, 45,800 people left, more than twice the average number from 1981 to 1986.)[19] Convincing arguments that China will respect the freedoms promised Hong Kong for at least 50 years will be hard to find in view of the television images from Beijing. The rising stream of emigrants will likely become a flood. The 22 percent drop in the Hong Kong stock index immediately following the repression is indicative of the impact on local business confidence; investment, both by Hong Kong residents and through Hong Kong by overseas Chinese, will likely disappear too. Although there is no prospect that Britain will break the 1984 agreement to relinquish Hong Kong, China will receive in 1997 a far weaker, less valuable asset than the one for which it had bargained.

Investments from Taiwan, which had become very substantial through Hong Kong and were beginning to be felt directly, are drying up, along with other foreign investment. Moreover, the political impact in Taiwan is also highly negative. The prospects for rapprochement and eventual reunification were growing with the image of a modernizing, democratizing China successfully incorporating Hong Kong; but they have now been set back for years or, more likely, decades.

In a variety of other ways, China's place in the community of nations has been damaged. Its pending membership in GATT will no doubt be delayed, as will further loans from the Asian Development Bank and the World Bank. The worldwide readiness to give China special consideration as the largest less developed country (LDC) also will suffer.

With regard to the relationship with the United States, where there has long been a reservoir of goodwill for China, the readiness to make various special exceptions, for example, in permitting larger than normal import quotas under the Multi-Fiber Agreement (MFA), will give way to coldness instead, if not to outright retaliation.

Clearly, with its act of repression, China has dealt a grievous blow to its political and economic prospects. How they will cope with this self-inflicted wound is unclear. The conservatives, including Li Peng and, ironically, Deng (who opted during the June crisis to scuttle the reforms he had so long and arduously promoted), must realize that economic modernization is essential to govern their vast country and to its participation in the modern world in the twenty-first century. They probably believe that modernization can be managed in a more planned and controlled manner. They no doubt also believe that some political reforms are essential to accompany economic development, but they probably intend to gear those to strengthening party control rather than weakening it.

Li's education in the Soviet Union, his background as an engineer with professional experience on large-scale, centrally planned state projects, and his more cautious approach to modernization than Zhao in the period from 1987 to 1989 suggest at least a partial reversion to the Stalinist-Leninist model of development that Mao had earlier discarded and that Gorbachev and his colleagues are in the process of jettisoning. It remains to be seen whether this particular approach, or some other centrally directed model, will be adopted by the conservatives. It is clear, however, that the relatively open, pragmatic approach backed earlier by Deng has been discredited and will not again be pursued as long as the conservatives are in control. China's aging conservatives, Moscow-trained bureaucrats, and lower-level party functionaries throughout the country seem resolutely determined to take a "Great Leap Backward."

Politically and socially, too, repression will likely continue for some time and probably intensify as reformers and democratizers are hunted down. The gradually expanding freedom of speech, thought, and travel enjoyed up until June 1989 will surely be reversed. Since any totalitarian system requires control of information, the media will be a special target of the ideologues and conservatives who orchestrated the June crackdown.

In sum, China's future is in jeopardy. Repression and stagnation are likely in the short and medium term. As a minimum, the ground gained from 1978 to 1988 will have to be regained before the nation can again begin the difficult processes of modernizing and adapting to the growing interdependence of the rest of the world. Since it is improbable that the conservatives will be able to both govern and modernize effectively, a rebirth of economic and political reform is likely sometime in the middle or late 1990s. Given the likely scale of the problems by then, it is unclear whether reform at that late date will succeed.

While the Chinese leaders flinched in the summer of 1988 in the face of mounting problems and drew back "to consolidate before moving forward again"—and then abruptly reversed course in the bloody repression of the summer of 1989, Gorbachev pressed forward. Indeed, rather than reacting with caution to new obstacles, he seems to prefer to raise the ante and redouble the effort.

The problems of reforming the USSR have proven to be at least as formidable as those of China, despite important differences between the two. As suggested above, it was clear by 1987 that Gorbachev's economic reform program was in dire straits. Performance against the targets of the twelfth five-year plan was so poor that the goals were completely out of reach. Various analysts were suggesting that not until the fourteenth plan of the late 1990s would there be significant productivity gains and improvements in the standard of living.

The drop in international oil prices in 1987 and 1988 was a particularly sharp blow, for oil and natural gas provide the bulk of the country's foreign exchange earnings. (At his June 8, 1989, report to the Congress of National People's Deputies, Premier Ryzhkov complained that, given depressed prices on the international market, the Soviet Union was not able to cover the service on its foreign debt from energy revenues, as it had in the past.) Lack of experience and drive, arbitrary and unrealistic pricing, and the difficulties of operating in a partly free and partly controlled environment meant that few factory managers proved able to take advantage of new flexibility in the economy. A budget deficit amounting to over six percent of GNP (or about three times as great a relative burden as the combined U.S. federal-state deficit) presented constant inflationary pressure. The combination of inflation and structural problems resulted in the promised price reform being delayed into the indefinite future.

In the face of these assorted economic disappointments and catastrophes, Gorbachev again moved forward. He took steps to further economic liberalization (such as 50-year leases on land for private farming), to redouble his efforts to open up the political system, to reduce the military's drain on resources, and to secure foreign loans and investment.

To consolidate his political position and to press *glastnost* and *perestroika*, Gorbachev called the Nineteenth Party Conference in the summer of 1988—the first conference since World War II. It introduced the Soviet people to an entirely new style of politics. Issues were seriously and vociferously debated and abuses and shortcomings frankly revealed before television audiences numbered in the tens of millions. Onlookers, commentators, and many of the conferees clearly found the experience contagious. When relatively free elections for a new legislative body, the Congress of Peoples' Deputies, were held in early 1989, Communist Party nominees—even key Party secretaries—were frequently defeated wherever there were multicandidate races, despite official favoritism.

It is not yet clear just how effective the new Congress will prove to be, for it is too large (with 2,250 members) and it is scheduled to meet only briefly each spring and autumn. One of its key functions is that of an electoral assembly; it chooses the national president and—from its own ranks—the full-time, 540-member Supreme Soviet. Presumably this latter body will wield most of the legislative power while the Congress performs its electoral functions and airs national issues. (In its first session in May and June 1989, the Congress performed both tasks with élan, electing Gorbachev president, as expected, choosing a heavily conservative Supreme Soviet, and providing high drama for perhaps 150 million nationwide television viewers, as delegates debated issues with unprecedented frankness and vigor.) The claims of various non-Russian republics and ethnic groups—which the Congress and *glasnost* generally highlighted—were particularly evident at the Congress and pose a major future challenge to the central government.

Ethnic problems may slow the progress of reform. Decentralization of some power to the regions and of state enterprises is a key element of Gorbachev's reforms; this is, however, a much tougher nut to crack in the Soviet Union than in China. In China, 94 percent of the people are Han and only 6 percent are minorities, while in the Soviet Union, 52 percent are Russian and 48 percent are minorities. There is a strong tradition of autonomy lingering in the Baltic states, the Transcaucasian republics, and central Asia. We have seen the problems in Azerbaijan with the Armenian minority exploding in defiance of the Kremlin, forcing Gorbachev to declare: "It is a gross error for people to believe that decentralization can be exploited on behalf of the nationalities." Decentralization in the Soviet Union clearly has definite limits; its impact on the progress of reform has yet to be defined.

For some time, however, political reform in the Soviet Union will outrun economic reform—perhaps as far as economic reform in China outpaced political reform. It is clear that the economic measures Gorbachev and his colleagues have instituted thus far are wholly inadequate to revive the economy, though they may yield marginal improvements over time. Indeed, a Damoclean set of questions continues to hang over Gorbachev: will vitalization of the economy require such far-reaching economic reforms that the political system cannot handle them? Relatedly, have the political reforms undertaken thus far generated expectations which the economic system cannot deliver? Or, key to the long-run success of both political and economic reform, have democratization and the strengthening of the rule of law so revolutionized Soviet society and politics that the gains have become irreversible?

Clearly, the bulk of the difficult task of making the Soviet economy work still lies ahead. Gorbachev has succeeded in creating a political constituency for hard economic choices—he has replaced something like two-thirds of the senior government and Party leaders with supporters and has won over the intelligentsia and a sizeable fraction of the public—but he still faces a vast bureaucratic machine with an almost infinite capacity to delay, confuse, and obstruct. Moreover,

. . . workers are disgruntled. The reforms tie wages and bonuses directly to performance, even though productivity often hinges on factors beyond an individual worker's control. Workers see the reforms as demanding more discipline, while providing less job security, slower wage increases and only the promise of an eventual pay off in consumer goods and services.[20]

Even if razor blades, television sets, or pantyhose are produced or imported in numbers large enough to satisfy consumer demand, the central problem that defeated China's modernizers will remain—namely, price reform. With an enormous budget deficit, a large foreign debt to service ($56 billion, according to Premier Ryzhkov's first report to the new Supreme Soviet), and already serious suppressed inflation, President Gorbachev will have no prospect—and likely no stomach—for serious price reform in the next few years.

The possibilities of shifting resources from the military to civilian investment and consumption are much brighter. Through his various arms reduction and control proposals to the West and by converting half a million soldiers into civilian workers, Gorbachev can expect realistically to redeploy approximately five percent of the nation's resources, as well as help meet an emerging labor shortage. Moreover, the accompanying and intensifying effort to use military production facilities for civilian purposes should improve somewhat both the flow and the quality of producer and consumer goods.

In sum, it is not yet clear what degree of success the Gorbachev reforms will achieve. It is highly unlikely they will be either an unalloyed success or an utter failure. Given the Soviet approach, it seems probable that many of the reforms will continue, irrespective of the degree of overall success. In his book, *Perestroika*, Gorbachev observes that "democratization will make *perestroika* irreversible." While the theory behind this thought may be correct, and the trends are promising, it is not certain that either democratization or *perestroika* is yet irreversible.

Implications for the West

Any assessment of the implications of China's reforms for the West must start with the bloody days of June and gauge what is likely to follow. Humpty Dumpty cannot be put back together again, and if political repression deepens and economic stagnation ensues, even trade will take years to repair. Through five administrations, U.S. leaders have acted upon the assumption that China's internal and external interests were consonant with those of the United States. Clearly in the U.S. interest is a China economically modernizing and liberalizing at home, focussing on internal development rather than adventures abroad, and providing a check on Soviet power. A weak, politically repressive, and unstable China is a far less desirable partner for the United States and a poor business partner for Japan and Western Europe as well. The West also seems to have lost an asset in certain Asian regional security problems—a China preoccupied with internal strain and strife will be less able to help resolve the Cambodian tangle or ease tensions on the Korean peninsula.

Despite the martial law repression for which he is responsible, Deng will continue to be the preeminent leader as long as his health and vigor hold out. However, his efforts to establish a settled line of succession have failed twice, and he is unlikely at this late date to establish an enduring one. The succession problem is part of the larger reform problem. As Henry Kissinger has written,

Hu Yaobang and Zhao Ziyang were consumed by the processes they had been installed to institutionalize and by the inability of the great reformer to face the proposition that economic reform creates not short-term gratitude, but momentum toward political pluralism.[21]

If Deng has the will and physical strength to restart the modernization program, the otherwise predictable course of repression, stagnation, and isolation can be reversed, although only after a considerable time. Only in that circumstance can the West again count on China to play a constructive role in its region and the world. If Deng's health fails, or if he proves unable or unwilling to reverse the course taken in June 1989, Stalinist-Leninist elements in the Party or the People's Liberation Army may well turn back the clock even further, and with it the once promising partnership with the West.

If Gorbachev's political course succeeds, the implications for the West are essentially positive, even though East–West rivalries and dangers will continue. It will be no easy task, however, to convince Western public opinion of these dangers. Gorbachev's new political thinking in foreign policy has already decreased threat perceptions in Western Europe and the United States. If this policy continues to be pursued aggressively, existing difficulties in maintaining alliance political cohesion and in justifying substantial defense expenditures to allied publics will increase.

If Moscow's economic reforms also succeed, Soviet relations with the West will further strengthen. If the political reforms fail, so will the economic ones. Theoretically the Soviet economic reforms could succeed while its political reforms fail—confronting the West with an invigorated, economically more powerful, and closed authoritarian state with few brakes on central authority. Fortunately, economic success in the face of political failure is such an improbable outcome that it need not cause much concern. Even so, the West needs to be cautious about helping the Soviet Union economically until its political reforms are proceeding and democratization, openness, and respect for human rights are advancing.

Robert Gates, deputy assistant to the president for national security affairs, summed up the kind of Soviet state that would be in the interest of the West as follows,

> What we seek is a Soviet Union that is pluralistic internally, non-interventionist externally, observes basic human rights, contributes to international stability and tranquility, and a Soviet Union where these changes are more than an edict from the top and are independent of the views, power and durability of a single individual. We can hope for such change but all of Russian and Soviet history tells us to be skeptical and cautious.[22]

Considering the baggage of the past and the difficult challenges ahead, the evolution of such a Gatesian state will surely take decades, and its path of development will surely not be as straight as the Nevsky Prospekt. The required changes to Soviet society and political and economic life will be so fundamental that a zig-zag course with setbacks, false trails, and disappointments is certain.

Nevertheless, in the words of President Bush, it is in the long-term interest of the United States and of the West as a whole that reform in the Soviet Union succeed and that the USSR increasingly be integrated into the community of nations. Further, as Zbigniew Brzezinski has expressed it, it is in our interest

> . . . to exploit the current phase of internal Soviet travail to stabilize the external geostrategic relationship between our two countries while encouraging a more wide-ranging transformation of the Soviet system itself. Obviously, American leverage is much greater in regard to the former than to the latter, but our policy must take both dimensions into account.[23]

If Gorbachev succeeds in his new thinking, at home and abroad, the Soviet Union will inevitably become a much more significant actor in international affairs. It should be, however, a much less threatening actor, as it practices greater political pluralism at home, tolerates greater pluralism in Eastern Europe, reduces its military forces, and increasingly opens its economy and society to the West. In these circumstances, its integration with the rest of Europe should prove to be stabilizing.

Unfortunately, at this point, too much depends on the continuation of one man's vigor and vision. Still, the processes of reform and revitalization are building constituencies for constructive change which over time will be increasingly difficult to turn back, even if Gorbachev falters or disappears. While the reversal of Gorbachev's reforms over the next few years is possible, and while the prospects for major economic success are dim and distant, the implications of the Soviet reform efforts currently underway are positive for the West.

Notes

1. Author's conversation with Deng, June 1988.

2. CIA data quoted in "The Soviet Union: The Gorbachev Reforms Preparing for the 13th Party Plan" *Bulletin of the Foreign Service Institute* No. 4 (January 1989), Center for the Study of Foreign Affairs, U.S. Department of State, p. 7.

3. Robert F. Byrnes, "Critical Choices in the 1980s," *After Brezhnev*, Robert F. Byrnes, ed., (Bloomington: Indiana University Press, 1983), pp. 423–440.

4. Marshall and Merle Goldman, "Soviet and Chinese Economic Reform," *Foreign Affairs* "America and the World 1987/88," 68:1, pp. 554–555.

5. Harry Harding, *China's Second Revolution: Reform After Mao* (Washington, D.C.: Brookings Institution, 1987), p. 105.

6. *Ibid.*, pp. 164–167.

7. Conversation with Deng, June 1988.

8. Harding, *China's Second Revolution*, p. 133.

9. Author's conversation with Zhao, June 1988.

10. *Bulletin of the Foreign Service Institute*, p. 7.

11. *Ibid.*, p. 8.

12. Mikhail Gorbachev, *Perestroika* (New York: Harper & Row, 1987), pp. 19–25.

13. *Ibid.*, p. 142.

14. Conversation with Zhao, June 1988.

15. John Woodruff, *China in Search of its Future* (Seattle: University of Washington Press, 1989), pp. 157–159.

16. *Ibid.*, p. 158.

17. *Ibid.*, p. 164.

18. "China's Deng Reappears as Fear of Arrests Mount," *The Washington Post*, June 10, 1989, p. 1.

19. "For Hong Kong, All Bets on China are Off," *The Wall Street Journal*, June 8, 1989, p. A16.

20. *Bulletin of the Foreign Service Institute*, p. 8.

21. Henry Kissinger, "The Drama in Beijing," *The Washington Post*, June 11, 1989.

22. Robert Gates, "Ending the Cold War," a speech to a conference in Brussels, Belgium on transatlantic relations in the 1990s sponsored by the Center for Strategic and International Studies and the Centre for European Policy Studies, April 1, 1989.

23. Zbigniew Brzezinski, "The Brink of a New Grand Strategy," *The Washington Post*, June 11, 1989.

The Democratic Prospect in Latin America

Mark Falcoff

A MERE TEN years ago, it was impossible to write about the political prospect in Latin America without exposing oneself to an enveloping sentiment of despair. Argentina, Bolivia, Chile, Uruguay, Guatemala, Honduras, El Salvador, and Nicaragua all languished under military dictatorships of one kind or another. Paraguay and Mexico—neither of which had ever known democracy—seemed further from any kind of political opening than ever before. Although Brazil, Ecuador, and Peru were traversing the first steps toward democratic transition, in no case was the outcome certain. The radically different picture today should serve to remind us of the region's remarkable capacity for political renewal.

Not since the end of World War II has the notion of democracy enjoyed more prestige in Latin America, and never before have so many countries been ruled by elected, civilian governments. This is true not only of countries with a tradition of representative institutions, like Colombia, Uruguay, or Costa Rica, but also in countries with deeply troubled civic histories, like the Dominican Republic, Argentina, Bolivia, El Salvador, Guatemala, and Honduras. Although Western commentators are prone to emphasize the fragility and tentative quality of

Mark Falcoff is a resident scholar in foreign policy at the American Enterprise Institute.

democratic institutions in such countries, they often forget that one has to start somewhere. Venezuela, for example, although arguably the firmest democracy in the region, knew nothing but authoritarian rule until little more than a generation ago.

Of course, there are still laggard cases. These include Cuba, Nicaragua (which has moved from one form of dictatorship to another), Chile, Paraguay, Haiti, and Panama, as well as Mexico, which finally may be emerging from a bureaucratic dictatorship of civilian machine politicians. Nonetheless, the winds of change are being felt almost everywhere. In Chile, long-time dictator Augusto Pinochet, defeated in a plebiscite in October 1988, has stepped aside to permit competitive elections in December 1989. In Nicaragua, the Sandinistas have promised, for whatever that may be worth, the same in February of 1990. Even in Mexico, where presidential races normally are more a plebiscite than an election, the most recent contest of June 1988 was characterized by unprecedented challenges to the anointed candidate of the dominant PRI party by opposition candidates on the left and the right.

Moreover, several countries have moved beyond new or rejuvenated electoral exercises to genuinely competitive politics. The beneficiaries have been leaders and forces from all points on the political spectrum. In the May 1989 Argentine elections, an opposition party (the Peronist Party led by Carlos Menem) defeated a sitting government (led by Raúl Alfonsín of the Radical party) for the first time since 1916. Unprecedented democratic transitions already had occurred in Bolivia, Ecuador, Peru, and El Salvador and had just been repeated in Bolivia. Such an unprecedented transition seems likely to occur again in Peru next year. In Chile, the combined Christian Democratic-Left opposition shows every sign of besting Hernán Buchi, a man who represents Pinochet's constituency, if not precisely his political model. In Brazil, a conservative outsider is leading in the polls at the time of this writing against his populist–leftist rivals, one of whom represents the incumbent administration.

The growing participation of those forces which, for one reason or another, have chosen historically to remain outside the framework of electoral politics is especially heartening. The exclusion or self-exclusion of the right typically has led to military coups; of the left, to guerrilla warfare and urban terrorism. In Argentina, the conservative community is now represented by the Union of the Democratic Center. In El Salvador, the ARENA party has managed not only to articulate the concerns of the business community and middle class, but actually to win power at the ballot box. In Chile, a National Renewal party, imaginatively led by younger personalities more presentable than the aging dictator and also vastly more attuned temperamentally to the give-and-take of democratic politics, stands ready to represent the nearly four out of ten voters who expressed their support of the government in the October 1988 plebiscite. Even if the conservative alternative in Brazil is unsuccessful in the short term, its very emergence marks a qualitative change in that country's political scene, and in the relationship between its business and political communities.

The political engagement of the left has been slower to evolve. In Venezuela, ex-guerrillas now sit in parliament as members of the MAS party. In Uruguay, the former Tupamaros form part of the leftist Broad Front electoral coalition. An encouraging development has taken place in El Salvador, with the participation of Guillermo Ungo, Rubén Zamora, and other civilian allies of the Farabundo Martí National Liberation army (FMLN) in the recent presidential and congressional elections. Whatever their motives, the leaders of El Salvador's Democratic Convergence (civilian politicians with links to the violent left) have done much to advance the cause of "bourgeois democracy," and also to undermine the argument of the guerrillas that they alone represent the downtrodden masses.

To be sure, democracy is something more than elections or jousting among political parties and leaders. It also presupposes greater participation at all levels of public life by people of varying social and economic resources, as well as a judicial system which ratifies the concept of equality before the law. In that sense, perhaps no country in Latin America is fully democratic, although the cumulative effect of several generations of civic practice is bound to improve the texture of public life at all levels. As discussed below, economic growth and the diffusion of property remain, of course, the strongest guarantees of the political enfranchisement of ordinary citizens, and also the biggest challenge facing Latin American democracies in the immediate future.

The Sources of Democracy's Renaissance

If this picture of the democratic prospect is encouraging, history teaches that the roots of democracy must be deep as well as broad if it is to survive. Democracy has flowed and ebbed in Latin America. What is different this time is that it has a solid foundation in unprecedented social, economic, and political change.

Foremost among these is a kind of sea change on the part of Latin American intellectuals. Although Marxism and other authoritarian ideologies still exercise a residual hold, writers, artists, teachers, and other cultural workers no longer speak so disdainfully of "formal democracy" or of "bourgeois democracy." The military dictatorships in the 1970s taught many of Latin America's intellectuals powerful lessons about democracy's merits, however limited from their perspective. Moreover, some of the region's leading men of letters now espouse frankly the cause of democratic liberalism and even of democratic capitalism—most notably Mario Vargas Llosa in Peru and Octavio Paz in Mexico. The environment, in short, is more favorable for pluralism and the civilized exchange of ideas than ever before.

Some of the reasons for Latin America's democratic renaissance are purely negative. Principal among these is a backlash against the military regimes that ruled most of the continent throughout the 1970s, and perpetrated horrendous violations of human rights, particularly in Argentina, Chile, Uruguay, El Salvador, and Guatemala. Governments in uniform also drastically mismanaged local resources, eventually turning over countries like Argentina, Guatemala, and Peru to civilian authorities in a state of virtual bankruptcy. The notion that the military knows how to do things well has suffered a stunning blow throughout the hemisphere, and the prestige of the armed forces in most countries has fallen dramatically. Since losing the war for the Falkland (Malvinas) Islands to Great Britain, even the competence of Argentina's military to perform its narrow professional mission is in doubt.

The democratic prospect also has benefited from a decline in the attraction of nondemocratic ideologies and models, particularly Marxism–Leninism. The collapse of the socialist idea in its Soviet homeland, and the outpouring of criticism and self-criticism there, have had a devastating effect on the Latin American left, even, or perhaps especially, that part of it which is not strictly speaking Communist or Communist-inspired. Moreover, almost nowhere is the Cuba of Fidel Castro regarded as worthy of emulation; after 30 years of revolution, there simply is too little to show for the sacrifices of its people. While Castro's alleged achievements in education and health continue to justify his regime to the occasional American or West European, no democratic Latin American government, including some which advertise themselves as solidly left of center, has found the Cuban model to be worthy of emulation, even on a selective basis.

There are some positive reasons, too, for the widespread embrace of the democratic idea. The successful transition to democracy in Spain and Portugal, and their economic and cultural renaissance under social-democratic leadership, has had a powerful demonstration effect, particularly among those Latin Americans who have spent time in the Iberian peninsula during the last 10 years. As one Argentine academic put it to me recently, "to

Mark Falcoff

replicate the United States is something we could never reasonably be expected to do, but to resemble Spain is quite another matter." Probably no international figure commands as much attention and respect in the region today as Spanish Prime Minister Felipe González, whose quiet, firm statesmanship appeals to both the left (for his social-democratic values and connections) and the right (for his championing of pragmatic, performance-minded economic policies).

The more fluid contact between the United States and Latin America has done much to persuade a new generation of the virtues of democratic capitalism and an open society. Television, jet travel, and educational exchanges have done much to diminish the historic suspicion and resentment of U.S. culture and life, as well as to lead to a greater understanding of its institutions and values. The U.S. National Endowment for Democracy (NED) and the AFL–CIO have been particularly valuable in nourishing the proliferation of interest groups and intermediating structures in many Latin American countries, helping individuals and social groups historically excluded from power to assert demands and establish their legitimacy as participants in the social process.

The international context also has changed. In the past, the major foreign powers in Latin America, including the United States, tended to treat the area with an ice-cold pragmatism. There was a tendency to extend diplomatic recognition to whatever government could control the national territory, and to ask few if any questions about what went on below the level of diplomatic and business exchange. This certainly is no longer the case. Latin America today is perpetually criss-crossed by junketing members of the U.S. Congress and other parlia-

ments, human rights and other church groups, investigative reporters, and officials of the United Nations. Although nondemocratic governments deeply resent this intrusion into their internal affairs, they are powerless to avoid it and cannot fail to be influenced by it. Furthermore, those who would move against an elected government now know, in a way they have never known in the past, that the economic and political costs of coup-making will be high, perhaps prohibitively so.

This changed international context is the legacy of the human rights revolution in foreign policy. Begun in the U.S. Congress during the administration of President Gerald Ford, this human rights revolution reached something of a controversial high tide under the Carter administration. It then attained a bipartisan synthesis during the Reagan years. That synthesis holds that democratic values are indivisible in the region—if elections are the order of the day in El Salvador and Nicaragua, so should they be in Chile, and vice-versa. Evidently, the human rights conundrum has not been wholly solved. Considerable differences of opinion remain about the facts of individual cases, about appropriate policy instruments, and about how and when human rights can be balanced against other priorities. But given the relatively low geopolitical weight assigned to Latin America by policymakers in the United States, a more coherent human rights policy has been possible there than in many other areas of the world.

It is at least arguable that the Reagan administration's somewhat unexpected decision to appropriate for its own purposes one of the principal leitmotifs of the Carter years actually advanced human rights in the region more than otherwise might have been the case. Certainly, General Pinochet and the colonels in Guatemala were bound to take more seriously—if not act upon—U.S. concerns when voiced by Ronald Reagan, whom they admired, rather than those of his predecessor, whom they did not. It is difficult to imagine that elections would have been held as expeditiously in El Salvador, Guatemala, and Honduras, or that the conditions of the plebiscite in Chile would have been as fair, were it not for the unambiguous signal from Washington that such was a precondition for an improvement in political relations, the resumption of arms sales and military training, and the appropriation of economic aid packages. Cynics may argue that this was the only way the Reagan administration could obtain the military aid it wanted to prop up the then-faltering government of El Salvador or for the Nicaraguan resistance fighters; realists can respond that in the end results, not motives, are what count.

Democracy and Debt

None of this means that the new democracies of Latin America, or the old ones for that matter, face no serious problems ahead. These problems may not be, however, the ones which Latin American leaders prefer to discuss. One hears frequently from the region warnings that the burden of foreign debt is somehow threatening the future of democracy. As former presidents Alfonsín of Argentina and Sarney of Brazil have both said on repeated occasions, if people cannot identify democracy with economic improvement, they will look back nostalgically to earlier, less salutary periods in their nations' history. Therefore, they claim, it is incumbent upon all nations who favor the advance of democracy in Latin America to pro-

vide adequate debt relief to these beleaguered governments and peoples.

With all due respect to both gentlemen, the argument is self-serving to a fault. In fact, there is no simple and direct relationship between a country's debt burden and its economic performance. Two of the most dynamic economies in the Third World, those of Chile and the Republic of Korea, have an extraordinarily high ratio of per capita debt. What these countries possess that most Latin American republics do not is business confidence, i.e., that quality of their political economy which attracts sufficient local and foreign capital to make its debt burden manageable. The Argentine case illustrates the problem well—if it were able to bring home the resources its past policies have chased into foreign banks, it probably would have no foreign debt at all.

Nor does there appear to be a necessary connection between authoritarian regimes and economic performance. While military governments in Brazil and Chile can take credit for unprecedented stretches of economic growth, there is no particular reason for voters in Argentina, Peru, Honduras, Uruguay, or Guatemala to associate past military governments with economic prosperity. In the case of Argentina, living standards consistently dropped under every military government since 1955, and Peru's self-styled socialist military regime (1968–1979) actually destroyed that country's productive system.

Moreover, the historic cause of military governments in Latin America has not been economic failure, but the breakdown of the political system, of authority, or of both. Certainly, the coups in Argentina, Chile, and Uruguay between 1973 and 1976 were inspired more by chaos, terrorist violence, and the fear of Marxist dictatorship than by the economic failings of the regimes they disposed. A fear of political revolution rather than poor economic performance led the armed forces in Brazil to seize power. The recurrence of military governments in El Salvador and Honduras has much more to do with rivalries between the landowners and the political class than with poverty as such, although the lack of economic opportunity makes possible an environment in which politics is the plaything of nonrepresentative elites. The point again is that Latin American governments are made and broken by politics not economics, and that very specifically includes democratic governments.

This is a difficult lesson for the Latin American political class to put into practice, given its historic preference for statist–populist economic policies, typically financed by heavy foreign borrowing. Such policies have been successful for many years in their own narrow terms; that is, they have delivered goods, services, credits, and jobs for deserving supporters of the party in power. The cost, however, has been to the overall economic efficiency of the society. As Hernando de Soto has pointed out in his vitally important book *The Other Path*,[1] the trends toward statism so profoundly have impoverished Peru that economic needs and entrepreneurial energies are forced into what he calls the informal sector, i.e., perfectly honorable services and activities which are, nonetheless, technically illegal. Even in much wealthier Argentina, the costs of this approach finally have become prohibitive, as even the state oil company runs a deficit this year of $1.03 billion, making it the only petroleum enterprise in the world to lose money.[2] Inflation in that country recently was running at 300 percent per month, more than cancelling out whatever benefits in terms of employment or artificially low prices for basic services the system conferred upon ordinary Argentines.

What makes the present economic moment particularly difficult for all Latin American governments is the bunching of foreign obligations contracted in the 1970s, when Western banks were awash in liquidity as a result of the sudden flow of dollars to the oil-exporting countries. What Latin leaders really are referring to when they talk about the debt crisis is their inability to borrow new money to finance deficit-producing economic policies, when compounded interest payments on old loans have soared beyond their reach. (They are not lying when they insist that the debt problem is a political issue, since for them it really is.) Under these circumstances, they have been forced to reshape their own domestic economic systems to make them more productive. This explains the liberalization policies currently afoot in Venezuela, Costa Rica, Bolivia, and Argentina, and the prospect of political victories by free market candidates in Brazil and Peru. Put rather undiplomatically, lacking any other alternative, the governments and parties concerned finally have decided to do the right thing.

The success of these economic reforms eventually will determine an important qualitative dimension of democracy in the region. The model citizen of the statist–populist regime is utterly dependent upon the political authorities for his basic means of subsistence; independence is a luxury he cannot begin to afford. In such societies, a narrow political logic dominates economic life, and limits its capacity for growth. (Indeed, as the cases of Peru and Argentina demonstrate, over the long term such systems tend to devour their own sources of subsistence.) One of the many reasons why the Latin American political class has been so reluctant to adopt free market mechanisms is that such reforms tend to diffuse both property and authority, thereby enfranchising citizens who otherwise would be wholly dependent upon the state or its ruling party. The profession of politics becomes less important, and also less productive economically for its practitioners, as entrepreneurs, shopkeepers, scientists, managers, and others emerge to assume a more important role in society. The extent to which this process continues through the 1990s will determine the degree to which the Latin countries make the transition to democracy in the fullest sense.

The Democratic Failure of Latin Foreign Policy

From a foreign policy point of view, the Latin republics still have a long way to go on the path of democratic solidarity. The two values which long have dominated Latin American diplomatic practices are nonintervention and ideological pluralism. Whatever it may be in theory, in practice nonintervention means the absence of intervention by the United States; it does not in substance refer to the involvement of extra-hemispheric powers such as the Soviet Union, their allies like East Germany or Bulgaria, or their local proxies, like Cuba. Ideological pluralism is a shorthand term for the notion that all regimes should be accorded the same legitimacy *prima facie,* whether they are the consequence of elections, revolutions, or coups d'état, and also that they should be given equal moral weight whether they rule by force or by reason and consultation. Probably very few Latin American politicians would admit to so

bald-faced a definition. The record speaks for itself.

Thanks to the cult of nonintervention and rigid adherence to ideological pluralism, the United States has been unable to mobilize support within the Organization of American States (OAS) with regard to basic goals. The OAS has done little or nothing about the involvement of Cuba, the Soviet Union, and other Eastern bloc countries in Nicaragua and El Salvador. Nor has it exerted pressures to force the Sandinistas to keep their own promises to the organization when, in an abrupt reversal of its own commitment to nonintervention, it withdrew recognition of the Somoza regime in 1979. More surprising still, the United States also has found it impossible to move the other American republics in the direction of sanctions against Panamanian strongman Manuel Noriega, whose theft of the most recent elections in that country occurred quite literally before the eyes of the entire hemisphere.

In fact, the thrust of practically all Latin American diplomatic initiatives in the Central American crisis has been to avoid defining the central problem in such a way as to seem to be taking sides. For example, the Contadora group's 21–point program for a settlement in the isthmus amounted to nothing more than an undifferentiated laundry list of all good things, in no particular order, with some, such as democracy, cancelling out others, such as nonintervention.

The failure to make crucial distinctions between regimes and to practice a bit of democratic militance tends to encourage cynicism and undermine the growth of a genuinely democratic political culture throughout the region. If the Latin American consensus, country by country, is that democracy is best for oneself but dictatorship elsewhere is a matter of local taste, then the United States will find itself pushed into the curious position of being asked to care more about democracy for the Latins than they care about it themselves. This surely is not a viable basis for a long-term policy. It is also a dangerous precedent. If Guatemala's response to the lack of democracy in Nicaragua is, to use President Cerezo's term, "active neutrality," then what is to prevent others, including the United States, from exercising the same sort of insouciance in the event of, say, a right-wing military coup in Guatemala?

The Latin American political and diplomatic establishment has yet to arrive at the point where its positions are based on substantive principles, rather than a felt need to avoid convergence, however incidentally, with those of the United States. The point here most emphatically is not that the United States is always right and that Latins must prove that they are democratic by agreeing with it; rather, that when the United States *is* right, by failing to support it, the Latin Americans are undermining the cause of democracy in their own countries as well as throughout the hemisphere. The peoples of the American republics deserve governments which are capable of making clear distinctions between right and wrong, letting the chips fall where they may, and until they do have them, their political systems cannot be said to have reached democratic fruition.

The United States and Latin Militaries

A new cycle of Latin military regimes is taken by many as just around the corner. Indeed, over the past two years, credible rumors have circulated in Washington and elsewhere of im-

minent military coups in Peru and Brazil. For reasons already set forth, the old-fashioned military junta is probably a thing of the past. Military politics—and the military in politics—surely is not. In almost no Latin American country have the armed forces accepted fully the supremacy of civilian authorities, and many civilian political forces are not committed fully to a nonpolitical army. In Cuba and Nicaragua, for example, there is no separation between army, state, and party, nor is there likely to be. The process of demilitarizing Latin American politics may take some time, even in the happy event of a long and uninterrupted succession of elected governments. During this period policymakers and members of the U.S. Congress will be weighing the merits and drawbacks of military exchanges between individual countries and the United States, and also the thornier problem of approving police assistance for countries with serious problems of civil order.

In the past these decisions have been somewhat easier to make, either because the Cold War required a pragmatic acceptance of those forces willing to enlist in the U.S. political camp, or subsequently, because military and police forces in Latin America had behaved so atrociously to their own people that the best prescription for the moral hygiene of the United States was to cut off all relations with them. In the 1990s the political and moral horizon will be somewhat more murky. The Soviet threat presumably will have receded. Nonalignment will be the order of the day in almost all of the republics, rendering the Rio Treaty and other security agreements with the United States anachronistic.[3] At the same time, elected governments will struggle with a new set of judicial and moral questions: how to address past human rights abuses involving the armed forces and the police, and also how to appease and how much to punish the institutions themselves (or at any rate, individual members thereof). These are judgments from which the United States must, perforce, recuse itself.

One of the longest-running debates between the political and military establishments in the Untied States has been the degree to which military training of Latin American military officers in the United States (or at the School of the Americas, formerly in Panama and now at Fort Benning, Georgia) has influenced the political outlook of the Latin American military. At its extremes, the United States is seen either as a training ground for fascism or as a place where future Latin American generals absorb democratic values and learn the virtues of civic action. Most studies, supported by much anecdotal evidence, suggest that U.S. training is basically irrelevant to the values and subsequent conduct of Latin American military officers, although exposure to U.S. doctrine and weaponry sometimes has helped to promote the sale and use of U.S. military technology.[4] The era of big-ticket arms purchases probably is gone for most countries, although military training programs probably will continue until eventually it dawns on the Departments of State and Defense that these countries are no longer allies, but neutrals. Police training probably will remain a relatively explosive issue on Capitol Hill, one in which a Bush administration studiously avoiding confrontation with the Congress is unlikely to invest much political capital. In either case, the impact on local political life probably will be marginal, since most Latin American countries no longer rely exclusively or even principally upon the United States as a source of arms, military training, or police assistance.

Latin America After the Cold War

Frank Fukuyama's carefully reasoned essay in *The National Interest*[5] predicting the end of the Cold War and the replacement of the great ideological struggles of the past by technical discussions on trade and tourism points indirectly to the long-term future of U.S. relations with Latin America. If he is right, the United States will be much less involved in Third World areas such as Latin America, and also less concerned about their health and direction. There are many indications that the Latin American republics themselves have yet to take notice of this development, much less make provision for it. Although the United States may have abandoned what Abraham Lowenthal once called the "hegemonic presumption," the Latin countries—particularly the Central American republics, including Nicaragua—have not. That is, they continue to expect the United States to be interested in their stability and well-being, even as they turn elsewhere, such as Japan, Western Europe, and even the Soviet Union.

This suggests an important discontinuity between political development and international relations. At the very time when democracy is becoming the order of the day, the Latin countries are declining in importance to the great powers. Although this means a loss of the leverage which in the past allowed them to extract concessions and resources from them, it actually may be a blessing in disguise, since it will force decisions which should be taken anyway, and which might not otherwise occur. Democratic regimes will be forced to stand on their own to an unprecedented degree—to develop more productive societies, and to do so within the framework of greater political openness, a more effective pluralism, and a clearer posing of critical choices. Most of the countries already have made a start at this quiet but important revolution; if they continue in that direction, the notion of democracy in Latin America will be transformed from a utopian project to a casual reality of everyday life. If they do not, there is nothing the United States or anyone else can do to make up the difference for them.

Notes

1. Hernando de Soto, *The Other Path* (New York: Harper and Row, 1988). See also "The Informals Pose an Answer to Marx," *Washington Quarterly* 12:1 (Winter 1989), pp. 165–172.

2. *New York Times*, September 11, 1989.

3. This is not to suggest that these security agreements will not be needed. Rather, there will be a crucial incoherence in the military and foreign policies of the major Latin American states.

4. See for example Alain Roughié, *The Military and the State in Latin America* (tr. Paul Sigmund), (Berkeley: University of California Press, 1987).

5. Francis Fukuyama, "The End of History," *The National Interest* 16 (Summer 1989).

The Coming of Africa's Second Independence

Colin Legum

SIGNS OF MOUNTING discontent across the entire African continent are reminiscent of the anticolonial storm that gathered after World War II and bear some resemblance to the current movement of dissent in Eastern Europe. Whereas the anticolonial movement spearheaded a revolt against alien rule, the present targets are the postindependence African ruling classes and, especially, the political systems they built and now defend. Although challenges to rulers and regimes have been endemic ever since the first army coup d'état in Togo against President Sylvanus Olympio in January 1963, the significant difference now is the thrust of opposition against the existing *political systems* and not just against a particular ruler or regime.

During the first 30 years of postcolonial independence, the overthrow of rulers and regimes seldom produced fundamental change, despite outward changes in the style of government and an often temporary rearrangement of priorities. In 28 of the continent's 51 states civilian governments were overthrown by military coups d'état

Colin Legum has been analyzing political developments in Africa for nearly 50 years. Former associate editor of the *Observer* (London), he is consultant editor of the annual *Africa Contemporary Record* and editor of *Third World Reports*. His latest book is *The Battlefronts of Southern Africa* (New York: Holmes & Meier, 1988).

that were primarily bloodless; but military regimes were composed more of co-opted civil servants than soldiers. The military used its power to exercise authority but, with few exceptions such as Niger under Lieutenant Colonel Seyni Kountche, military governments had little influence, mostly because they lacked the consent of an electorate. Even the initial popularity that often greeted the overthrow of an unpopular regime quickly evaporated because of the harshness and general ineffectiveness of military rule.

With only three notable exceptions—Burkina Faso under Thomas Sankara, Ghana under Jerry Rawlings, and Ethiopia under Mengistu Haile Mariam—no serious attempt was made to create new institutions with political and economic programs that differed radically from those of their predecessors. Sankara survived for less than four years, and his assassination ended his radical reform policies. Rawlings has lasted for 10 years, but he has shifted away from his Nkrumaist socialist ideas, becoming one of the favorites of the International Monetary Fund (IMF).[1] In Ethiopia—the only African country where a serious attempt has been made to build a structured Marxist state—the revolution has been obstructed, probably permanently, by the obdurate resistance of nationalist forces in Eritrea, Tigre, and Oromo-inhabited regions. Of all the states beyond the borders of sub-Saharan Africa, only Libya so far has succeeded in creating a wholly different system—the *Jamahiriya*—that has existed since 1977; but this theoretically decentralized system of power exercised by people's committees actually is dependent on the leadership of the idiosyncratic Colonel Mu'ammar Qadhafi, and it is unlikely to survive his personal rule.

Military coups also produced relatively brief tyrannical dictatorships in Uganda under Idi Amin, the Central African Empire (now the Central African Republic) under Emperor Jean-Bedel Bokassa, and Equatorial Guinea under Francisco Macias Nguema. These three nasty regimes, relatively short-lived, were aberrations both in their brutality and in the fact of their being the only properly classified dictatorships to have emerged in sub-Saharan Africa. These three exceptions gave rise to the popular Western misconception of Africa as a whole being under despotic rule.

The first 30 years of African independence witnessed two major political phenomena: the rise of the single-party state and army coups d'état. The latter have occurred with the breakdown in postcolonial institutions, when internal conflicts, economic failure, corruption, nepotism, and repressive laws paralyzed governments and provoked varying degrees of popular discontent. The rise of the single-party state, on the other hand, was a response to the political, economic, and security problems that faced postindependence leaders.

The Political Phenomenon of the Single-Party State

Upon independence, the former colonies that had achieved independence without a violent struggle against the metropolitan power adopted a multiparty parliamentary system fashioned along Western democratic lines. One notable exception was Tanganyika (now Tanzania), whose ruling party won over 95 percent of the vote in preindependence elections supervised by the colonial power; this gave some legitimacy to its decision to turn the country into a single-party state. Only six countries have maintained multiparty parliamentary systems with regular and, more or less, free elections: Botswana, The Gambia, Djibouti, Mauritius, Tunisia, and (arguably) Morocco. These exceptions suggest that multiparty political systems can be maintained, even in societies as culturally cleaved as Mauritius and Djibouti, and perform at least as well as, if not better than, most single-party states.

Although it is convenient to speak of the "single-party state," there are substantial differences among the states. Some countries with one-party rule, like Tanzania, provide for a reasonable level of genuine democratic participation in the election and deselection of members of parliament, while others such as Uganda, Burundi, Zaïre, and Somalia lack any democratic pretensions.

Protagonists of the single-party state advance several reasons for its advantage over multiparty democracies in developing societies. Former president Julius Nyerere of Tanzania and others have argued that consensus politics is the traditional form of government in precolonial African societies. This is a myth.[2] Some claim that democracy is a luxury that developing societies cannot afford because of the curbs on policy-making imposed by often ethnically centered oppositional politics. Others claim that the task of nation-building in new states—themselves not yet nation states—is retarded by allowing free play to political parties that, in the nature of most Third World countries, are ethnically or regionally based. A combination of these three reasons provides the rationale for the claim that new states in their formative stage of becoming nation-states, during a period of rapid modernization and in urgent need of economic growth, demand single-party rule. Accordingly, the one-party governments will allow for as large an element of democracy as is thought will not obstruct the objectives of national unity and economic growth.

Without, for the moment, examining the merits of single-party rule over a multiparty democracy, it must be conceded that some of the more fragile, young sovereign states would have fallen prey to civil war or violent conflicts, might have risked splitting up into one or more separate states, or might have been consumed by ethnically charged politics. One example of an arguably justified decision to move toward single-party rule was the agreement by Zimbabwe's two major leaders, Robert Mugabe of the ruling Zimbabwe African National Union (ZANU) and Joshua Nkomo of the Zimbabwe African People's Union (ZAPU), to merge their parties as a means of healing the breach between the Shona and Ndebele people. Their decision certainly has helped to ease one major problem, but it has exacerbated others. For example, the merger led to the breakaway of one of ZANU's founding leaders, Edgar Tekere, who formed his own left-wing opposition party.

With only few exceptions, crises occured in the new African states within months of their independence and at a time when the new governments still were struggling to establish themselves. The origin of these postindependence crises was the political composition of the anticolonial liberation movement. In the majority of cases, there were coalitions between left-wing and right-wing parties and of different ethnic and regional groups. Once the colonial rule was driven out, the interests of the different groups that formed the new government diverged. This resulted in the breakup of most independence movements, made for serious and often ethnically based conflict, and destabilized the new state. Therefore, the rapid shift of many African governments from the parliamentary system inherited from the colonial period to a single-party system is understandable. In many cases, however, this move was made not because of any serious danger to the state, but simply in order to entrench the power of a particular ruling group.

Single party states diverge from each other not only in different levels of their democratic content, but also in their choice of economic systems. For example, Côte d'Ivoire, Gabon, Cameroon, and Kenya opted for private enterprise, the free market, and foreign capital and entrepreneurial assistance; other states, including Algeria and Tanzania, opted for non-Marxist socialism; a few countries nailed their flag to the Marxist mast. This last group, confined to small francophone countries like Benin and the Congo, used Marxist rhetoric but made no serious attempt to create the structures of a Marxist state. Ethiopia, as already mentioned, was the exception. Although the liberation movements of Angola and Mozambique were committed to Marxism, the civil wars and economic collapse the two countries have faced since independence have impeded the implementation of such ideology.

Irrespective of whether the ruling parties were pro-capitalist or pro-socialist, they created parastatal corporations to take control of their principal resources and financial institutions. A basic reason for this continental pattern was the perceived need to replace the former colonial control over major economic sectors with an economic instrument of the state in order to achieve effective control over the policies and revenues of the major wealth-earning crops, minerals, and enterprises, thereby establishing national priorities for both economic and social development. Unfortunately, these parastatals mushroomed into large, centralized bureaucracies that were quite often corrupt and in many, if not most, cases inefficient. In some countries, these parastatals became so powerful that they were virtual states within the state. Because of their inflexible bureaucracies and particular priorities for investment and development, instead of being the motor to drive the economy forward, the parastatals had become a major obstacle to development.

Those governments that had opted for the socialist path of development saw the parastatals as the means of gaining control over the major components of the economy—a lesson learned from the Labour Party in Great Britain and the Socialist Party in France. In spite of whatever benefits there may be to nationalized industries in the West European countries, the developing countries mostly lacked the expertise to manage large corporations and the governmental institutions to monitor and control them. Thus, instead of building socialist institutions, most African countries succeeded only in establishing state capitalism, in an inefficient version more appropriately named unfree capitalism. The expensive failure of the parastatal policy was one major cause of economic decline and helped to discredit governments. In a speech delivered to the University of Zimbabwe in Harare, Julius Nyerere admitted that if there were a parliamentary opposition in Tanzania, many of the malpractices and inefficiencies of parastatals might have been avoided, but he added that the disadvantages of oppositional politics outweighed the advantage of having a watchdog to prevent the slackness, nepotism, and corruption of single-party rule.[3]

All African governments currently are engaged in either privatizing their parastatals, substantially reducing their number, or turning them into joint state–private sector enterprises as part of the IMF structural adjustment programs. Africa's experience with parastatals is one expensive lesson about the advantages of an open society, where a parliament, political parties, professional and other associations, and the media are free to criticize government policies. Now that most African governments increasingly are adopting free enterprise or market economy systems, the logical question is whether it is feasible to open up the economy without also opening up the political system. Mikhail Gorbachev's twin policies of *glasnost* and *perestroika* demonstrate an understanding of the reality that one cannot be accomplished without the other, whereas the Chinese leaders' attempt to open up the economy while maintaining a party dictatorship led to the disaster of Tiananmen Square.

Two major claims were made for the advantages of a single-party state in a developing society. First, the one-party state system was claimed to be the most effective way of integrating a large variety of ethnic communities and of harmonizing the interests of the modern urban sector with the traditional rural sector. Second, the system was deemed to offer the quickest way of promoting balanced economic development. After the experience of 30 years, both of these claims appear to be seriously flawed. There is no evidence that the half-dozen African states that have retained multiparty parliamentary systems have fared worse in the promotion of national unity or economic development than those governed by a single ruling party. Botswana with its nine ethnic groups and Mauritius with its dynamic heterogeneous society are, in many respects, prospering more than most other countries. The experience of other countries has been like that of Kenya, which today is more ethnically divided than before the government of President Daniel T. arap Moi turned the country into a single-party state.

It might be argued that it is easier to maintain a democratic system in small countries such as Botswana and Mauritius rather than in larger ones. If this were the case, if tiny Djibouti can be democratic, then why not the minuscule Comoros; and if in The Gambia why not in Gabon? If a country the size of Senegal with its acute cultural and sectarian diversities is now democratic then why not the other smaller countries in the region, Sierra Leone and Liberia, for example? Size and the degree of cultural cleavage in societies are undoubtedly important factors that determine the governability of states. Yet, India, one of the world's largest and most culturally divided countries has managed to retain a multiparty parliamentary system for almost 40 years. Explanations other than just

size and cultural diversities must be sought to justify the single-party state. Its protagonists have been put on the defensive over their failure to justify the claim that the suppression of opposition parties is necessary in order to achieve rapid economic growth.

Nevertheless, the fact that most sub-Saharan African countries are worse off today than they were a decade ago cannot be ascribed simply to their political systems. Adverse international factors affecting commodity prices, an inequitable world trading system, the quadrupling of oil and fertilizer prices, drought, locust plagues, and other deleterious climatic conditions have all contributed to the grave decline in most African countries.[4] Still, these negative factors, although beyond the control of local governments, need not have been so severe were it not for the failure of governmental policies, and the unresponsiveness of state bureaucracies to popular opinion, especially from the peasantry that constitutes over 70 percent of the population of most sub-Saharan countries. Ethiopia, to cite but one example, is in desperate economic straits not just because of drought and eroded land, but because a tiny elite of soldiers and intellectuals have remained determined to nail down an unpopular Marxist system on an unwilling population, instead of tackling the fundamental problem of establishing a viable constitution acceptable to a majority of Ethiopians and Eritreans. Sudan is wallowing in war, misery, and economic hardship because a section of the community is intent on imposing the *Shari'a* (Islamic law) on both the sizable non-Muslim minority in the south and on the influential secularists in the Muslim north.

Wars are now being fought in several parts of the continent—not for revolutionary ideologies, but in the name of democracy. Today, the advent of the end of the first period of African liberation—from colonial or other forms of alien rule or domination—is heralding the beginning of a second period of liberation from unpopular, unsuccessful, and undemocratic governments. It is a time of turbulence and uncertainty. What will result from this transitional period is still unclear. It is clear, however, that the tide is turning against the political systems devised to cope with the difficult problems of the immediate postcolonial era.

The Democratic Tide

The evidence that Africa has reached a watershed between the first and second periods of its liberation is to be found in five developments: the breakdown of political and economic institutions; the growing number of countries abandoning the experiment in single-party states; the establishment of centers for the promotion of pluralist political systems in the continent; the growing chorus of outspoken dissent from single-party rule; and the spread of a human rights movement initiated by Africans themselves. Each of these developments merits separate consideration, although they are directly interconnected.

Over the last three years, the number of countries with a multiparty political system has increased from six to eight, with a ninth, Nigeria, now poised to return to parliamentary democracy. In two of the six countries that previously had maintained a framework of parliamentary democracy, Morocco and Tunisia, the scope for broader political security has been enlarged. The two countries that have abandoned single-party rule are Senegal and Algeria. The Algerian change

is particularly significant because following the country's emergence from a long and bitter independence struggle as a single-party state in 1962, it rigorously had repressed any sign of serious political dissent. The extent of the existence of clandestine opposition was revealed when no fewer than 20 political parties surfaced after the ban against them was lifted. With the transformation of Algeria's political system, the entire North African littoral (except for Libya), now possesses the rudiments of parliamentary democracy.

Senegal, which had a brief flirtation with single-party rule, now displays a vibrant, open political system with no fewer than 17 competing parties (seven of them Marxist factions). This new system already has stood the test of two elections. Nigeria—the continent's most populous state with almost 100 million people, 4 distinct national groups, and over 20 sizable minority groups—is set to return to parliamentary government in 1992. Four military governments failed to quell the popular demand for democracy. Instead, they fueled the unpopularity of nonelective governments. Especially encouraging about developments in Nigeria is that it is the only African country that has taken steps to devolve central power by expanding its federal system.

Sudan's experience closely resembles that of Nigeria. Successive attempts to institutionalize military-political regimes have ended in failure; each failure has resulted in a return to civilian government. The country is once again under military rule, but after only a relatively short period signs have emerged that it will fare no better than its predecessors. The bitter armed struggle waged by the Sudan People's Liberation Movement (and the Sudan People's Liberation Army [SPLA]) led by Ohio University trained Dr. John Garang, has as its goal the creation of a democratic, secular Sudan. The earlier civil war between the predominantly Muslim north and the non-Muslim south has given way to a national struggle to establish a single united nation under a democratic parliamentary government.

This trend away from the single-party state is infectious, inspiring the growth of democratic opposition in other African countries. The earlier taboos that inhibited challenges to the notion that Africans are better governed under single-party rule are being eroded. It is no longer fashionable to accuse those favoring democratic parliamentary systems of wishing to imitate Western political systems. In the current political debate, emphasis is placed on the universality of principles that govern democratic parliamentary institutions.

The impression that parliamentary democracy was a foreign-inspired import to the continent undoubtedly was strengthened in the past by Western-based organizations that pressed for African democracy, including Harvard University's Center for African Democracy and the National Endowment for Democracy (NED) funded by the U.S. Congress since 1983. Under their auspices, African politicians and intellectuals were invited to seminars held in the United States. Now, centers for studying and promoting democratic ideas are establishing their own bases on African soil. The Center for the Study of Research of Pluralistic Democracy in the Third World has been established in Dakar, Senegal under the presidency of Jacques Mariel Nzouankeu, a professor of law and economics at Cheikh Anta Diop University. In a recent speech, Nzouankeu spoke of an "atlas of democracies"

beginning to spread across the continent and citing recent elections in a half-a-dozen countries, he commented: "In every case, democratic principles were put to the test . . . and in every case those countries showed that they are moving away from authoritarianism and towards greater democracy."[5] The former Nigerian Head of State General Olusegun Obasanjo has established the Africa Leadership Forum at his successful poultry farm in Ota, Nigeria. At the inauguration of the Forum, the General described its aim as preparing African leaders for the task of undertaking the "profound changes" necessary to halt the backward movement of the continent and to correct "our false political start." The problems now facing Africa, he added, "stem from a human failure to establish institutions that make for a human society . . . In the last resort, only we ourselves know what is really amiss with us and, what is more, only we Africans can tell it as it is to ourselves."[6] A number of other centers for the study and promotion of democracy are emerging in other parts of the continent.

This movement for democracy is fueled by the increasingly outspoken dissent expressed by academics, journalists, and politicians in books, articles, and seminars. Writers like the Nobel prize winner Wole Soyinka of Nigeria are in the forefront of the campaign against misgovernment and abuses of human rights. It is not enough, they say, to inveigh against the misdeeds of the apartheid regime in South Africa while ignoring the offenses of African governments. Among those in the vanguard of the demand for the creation of open societies are politicians who earlier were prominent in boosting the advantages of single-party states but who have themselves become victims of their system. Edem

Kodjo, the former secretary general of the Organization of African Unity (OAU), who is now in exile in France, has severely attacked African leadership in a recent book.[7] Another former African minister, Abdulrahman Mohamed Babu, who first came to prominence as a leader of the Zanzibar revolution, was later detained for seven years in Tanzania. His political writings in the London-based *African Events* and in other publications argue passionately for the need for political democracy. A dozen African academics, who organized a workshop in Kenya to review the past and future of democracy, recently produced the book *Democratic Theory and Practice in Africa*.[8] Peter Wanyande, a lecturer in government at the University of Nairobi, summed up their conclusions:

> Partly as a result of their failure to meet the popular and legitimate demands of the people, the one-party states have not only become sensitive and insecure, but also very oppressive and unresponsive to the demands of the mass of people whom they rule. They have tended to control and limit the rights and freedoms of the people who would want to participate voluntarily in the political life of the nation. Institutions such as parliaments have been rendered largely ineffective as sources of legitimacy for government decisions. The people, therefore, no longer control and limit governmental authority in the one-party states of Africa.[9]

The fact that these intellectuals, who were mainly from Kenya, had the courage to launch a methodical attack on the idea of a single ruling party in a country whose leadership is particularly "sensitive and insecure" is representative of the resolution and concern of the great majority of the continent's intellectuals who, today, fill the void created in most single-party states that deprive ordinary people of effective participation. The situation is better in a country like Tanzania where the *wananji* (the ordinary people) do enjoy the right to select and deselect their parliamentary representatives, but where other essential aspects of democratic government, including a free press and the right to organize opposition parties, are absent.

President Jimmy Carter was correct in making human rights an essential feature of U.S. foreign policy. Despite the inability of his and subsequent administrations to apply the principle consistently, the focus has given a fillip to the human rights movement in the Third World and has provided a cutting edge to the campaign for wider democratic rights. Speaking up for human rights has become respectable and hard to oppose, except by such uncaring despots as Zaïre's President Mobutu Sese Seko who, especially in the post-Carter administrations, has been allowed to get away with murder, figuratively speaking. It is no longer possible to campaign for human rights without linking them to the abuse of undemocratic governments. The growth of the human rights movement in Africa is an intrinsic element in the growth of the democratic movement.

That human rights is an idea whose time has come is evidenced by the OAU's adoption of the *Charter of Human and People's Rights* that has been ratified by over two-thirds of its 51 member states. Notable among those who have so far refused to ratify the Charter are the governments of Colonel Mu'ammar Qadhafi of Libya and President Mengistu Haile Mariam of Ethiopia. The African Commission for Human and People's Rights (ACHPR) has been established with headquarters in Banjul, The Gambia, in recognition of President Dawda Jawara's initiation of the Charter. The purpose of the ACHPR as outlined at the 1989 OAU summit is to make Africans aware of and to promote their rights and obligations, and to ensure that these are properly protected. Just how these rights are to be protected properly in those countries that imprison and subsequently often torture dissenters remains to be tested. Two years after its establishment, the Commission so far has received 30 complaints that are still under investigation. The 11-member Commission has been selected by the OAU heads of state for "their integrity and morality." It appears that the first 11 measure up to those standards. Ten years ago, the idea of such a Charter and Commission was inconceivable; that these pan-African institutions exist today is a measure of the changing climate of political opinion in the continent.

The African Lawyers Association, whose membership includes lawyers and judges, has played a major role in the campaign for human rights. Its meetings are noteworthy for the freedom and outspokenness of lawyers to expose the injustice and political interference in the judicial processes of many countries.

If one takes account of the five trends described above, it is hard to escape the conclusion that the protest movement against undemocratic government is gathering in strength and importance. The possibility of new tyrants emerging in Africa—equal to the likes of Amin, Nguema, and Bokassa—cannot be ruled out. What seems more certain, however, is that the African silence that shrouded their misdeeds is much less likely to occur in the future. Still, one cannot be too confident so long as criticisms of Qadhafi, Mengistu, and Mobutu remain muted. What is important, nevertheless, is that their misdeeds should be trumpeted by Africans—rather than by Americans or Europeans.

Impacts on African Democracy

Many, if not all, of the nastier regimes were able to survive in Africa because of their client relationship with some of the major powers. The Americans have supported and continue to support Mobutu's regime in Zaïre and, formerly, President Jaafar al-Nimeiri's in Sudan. The Soviets supplied arms to Amin and give strong support to the Mengistu regime in Ethiopia. The British provide substantial aid to Moi in Kenya. The French encouraged and supported Bokassa until nearly the end. Without such foreign support, usually accompanied by an uncomfortable silence about the behavior of the client regime, such dictators would not have survived for as long as they did. Now that the major powers' struggle in Africa seemingly is coming to an end, it could be easier for the major powers either to withhold support from crass offenders or, at least, to speak out against them, which would be a major contribution to the evolving democratic challengers.

African democrats perceive the new thrust of Western policy as exporting the idea that capitalism is the answer to the continent's problems; that privatization, à la the government of Margaret Thatcher, should be the keynote of development, and that the writ of the International Monetary Fund should extend continent-wide. Governments that are willing to toe this line are more likely to figure prominently with regard to the allocation of Western resources. Whereas Moscow sought to export Marxism, the major Western countries now seek to export their versions of capitalism.

This development is likely to produce new tensions among Africans, including between those favoring democracy and the West. What African democrats are seeking is both freedom from their own unrepresentative governments and freedom from foreign economic dictates. Not all African democrats embrace capitalism as the answer to the continent's problems. Many, possibly the majority, favor a mixed economy along the lines of European social democracies. Out-and-out democratic socialism, as in Tanzania, has its adherents; while others favor a diluted form of socialism, as in Sweden, France, and Spain, or as advocated by the British Labour Party and the West German Social Democrats. The future of African democracy is likely to be as diverse as it is in Western Europe. Undiluted capitalism has little support—not even among those who nail their flag to the mast of free enterprise, as in the Côte d'Ivoire.

On the other hand, communism is no longer a lodestar—even for African radicals. Some still aspire to their invention of African Marxism, but the recent developments in Eastern Europe already have had a visible impact on African political thinking and practice. The formerly small, but tenacious, Marxist people's democracies in Benin and the Congo already have abandoned even their slender pretensions of being Marxist states. The Frente de Libertação de Moçambique (FRELIMO) government of Mozambique recently erased Marxism from its program. Angola can be expected soon to follow suit. Only the Mengistu government in Ethiopia still clings to the bloody, tattered flag of its Communist revolution, but its survival is doubtful, to say the least. The African National Congress (ANC) of South Africa never has been a Marxist movement, despite its convenient alliance with the South African Communist Party and Moscow; but the bitterness of the anti-apartheid struggle in South Africa—where apartheid understandably is linked to capitalism—has bred a new generation of younger black leaders who see a Marxist state as the only way of transforming the country's inequitable political and economic system. Nevertheless, the *rigor mortis* of West European communism and Gorbachev's *perestroika* cannot fail to affect the continent's future political climate, even in South Africa.

China, once seen as the alternative lodestar to the Soviet Union, lost its attraction with the demise of Mao Zedong and the rise of the revisionist government in Beijing. The last lingering doubts about the "Chinese model" seem to have been dissipated finally by the revolt in Tiananmen Square. In a summing up of the uprising of Chinese students and workers, Ghanaian journalist Baffour Ankomah has written:

> The ignorance of the Chinese people about politics made it possible for the dictators to hold power so tightly for so long. It used to be so in Africa, today it is all changing. Like Chinese students, Africans are now a widely travelled people and can compare the differences between countries. They know we have chains to break at home, and are angry . . . The fact that so few African leaders have condemned the killings in China shows how guilty they feel about repression at home . . . But, thank God, Africa has precedents and time on its side. We can begin, today, to reform our political systems, to do away with the 'culture of silence,' to restore basic personal freedoms to our people—before the bubble finally bursts.[10]

What of Cuba—that island of communism? Fidel Castro undoubtedly still has his admirers in Africa. Many Africans feel a sense of gratitude for the Cuban support of the Angolan government's resistance to South Africa's military pressure. Nevertheless, this kind of appreciation does not translate easily into influence. Africans seem to understand that Castro's Cuba was made possible only by the solid support of pre-Gorbachev Moscow. Because Gorbachev is perceived widely in Africa as having abandoned the earlier policy of solidarity with the international working class, Africans no longer put their faith in the possibility of "new Cubas" in their continent. Anthony Lewis recently wrote that "Marxism is *passé*" in Africa.[11] He would have been more accurate if he had said that the Soviet Union is *passé*. Although Marxism still has its supporters, there seems little chance that it will offer the new wave for a continent in transition from one generation of politicians to the next.

Finally, one possible development that could affect progress toward the achievement of democracy in Africa is the Islamic factor, in countries with large Muslim populations. Sub-Saharan countries have been relatively untouched by the rise of Islamic fundamentalism in Africa's northern littoral. This type of Islam undoubtedly constitutes a challenge in the countries of the Maghrib—notably Tunisia, Algeria, Libya, and (arguably) Morocco—as well as in Egypt, Sudan, and, more marginally, Somalia. Whereas frustration and disillusionment in sub-Saharan Africa have led to an awakening of interest in the alternative of multiparty parliamentary government, in countries with strong Islamic ties, such frustrations and disillusionment have produced a reaction favoring religious fundamentalism.

The Muslim Brothers have strong pockets of support in North Africa. One case is Sudan, where the promise of a return to parliamentary democracy has been checked, at least temporarily, by a military coup with links to the local Islamic fundamentalist organization. Unless democracy can be implemented in Algeria, Tunisia, and Egypt, those countries risk a strong challenge from religious fundamentalism.

Conclusion

Africa stands poised for its second period of liberation. The current dominant trend strongly favors the seeding of democratic ideas. Historic change, however, is seldom swift, never easy or harmonious, and always unpredictable.

Notes

1. Kwame Nkrumah, prime minister of Ghana from 1952 to 1960, led that country to independence in 1957. Serving as Ghana's first president from 1960 to 1966, Nkrumah pursued policies of African socialism and pan-Africanism and helped establish the Organization of African Unity. While there is no agreed definition of African socialism, African leaders widely subscribed to the philosophy, especially during the 1960s and 1970s. Generally, African socialism emphasizes equitable development and a major role for the state in its pursuit.

2. For a convincing exposure of this myth, refer to Vincent Simiyu's writing in *Democratic Theory and Practice in Africa* (London: James Curry, 1986).

3. *Guardian* (London), June 11, 1986.

4. Refer to Carol Lancaster, "Economic Reform in Africa: Is It Working?" in this volume.

5. Cited in the United States Information Agency, *Africa Wireless File* (Paris), May 3, 1989.

6. Quoted by Flora Lewis, *International Herald Tribune* (Paris), October 31, 1988.

7. Edem Kodjo, *Et Demain l'Afrique* (Paris: Stock, 1985).

8. *Democratic Theory and Practice in Africa.*

9. *Ibid.*

10. *New African* (London), August 1989.

11. *International Herald Tribune* (Paris), January 31, 1989.

III. Democracy, Prosperity, and Governance

The Informals Pose an Answer to Marx

Hernando de Soto

WHY ARE WE poor? Why after a century of industrialization, massive capital transfers, the postwar development decade, revolutions of one sort or another, and the hard labors of working people does much of the developing world remain in a state of economic backwardness if not abject poverty? Clearly, something is seriously amiss with the conventional wisdoms of both development specialists and their critics on the left or right.

In Peru, we have set out to find some answers to these questions and to begin to formulate a strategy for development grounded in a realistic understanding of the ingredients of prosperity. Our method is one based on strict empirical observation. We have set out to understand how and why things really work, not to find and fit facts to predispositions of ideology or dogma. Our results have been surprising. They have also been inspiring. The work of the Institute for Liberty and Democracy (ILD) has drawn attention throughout Latin America and in many other parts of the world.

The very essence of our conclusion

is that developing economies do not work for two reasons. First, the structure of governance and economic activity in most Third World countries effectively squeezes out the entrepreneurial element of economic activity, an element that is key to employment, capital formation, and growth. Second, we have failed to grasp fully the fundamental link between economic participation and political participation and to understand that prosperity without democracy is impossible in a modern economy.

How Developing Economies Work—Or Don't

Even the most untrained of observers cannot but be impressed by how much economic activity in the developing world occurs outside the formal economy. Visit any Third World city and see an abundance of purveyors of goods (street vendors and small markets) and of services (transportation or housing construction) who fall outside of the parameters of economic activity measured by the state and subject to its laws. This impression was the point of departure for our work in Peru.

We set out to study these economic actors outside the formal economy—which we deemed the informals. Existing techniques of economic analysis did not make this study easy. The informal sector is hardly a new discovery

Hernando de Soto is president of the Institute for Liberty and Democracy in Lima, Peru. His major work, *El otro sendero: la revolución informal* (The Other Path: The Informal Revolution), has become a bestseller in Latin America, with over 100,000 copies sold. This essay is based on a summary of this work which Dr. Hernando de Soto presented at CSIS.

in the development business, but the role it plays in development cannot be fully understood if it is equated to the microenterprise sector. To start off with, most measurements of the informal sector as the sum of the small enterprises are based on an arbitrary measure of the number of employees in an enterprise. Such a criterion defines informal as microenterprises employing fewer than a set number.

This is a quite different task from counting those activities that fall outside of the legal framework. In Peru, we discovered that at least 60 percent of the population works illegally all of the time. Based on subsequent inquiries, we have found that the 50–60 percent level is fairly consistent throughout Latin America. This is a staggering sum with profound implications for governance. For example, how can the government expect social and political stability when its authority extends to less than 40 percent of the population? It is no wonder that the Third World has such an embarrassing history of coup d'état.

It is inconceivable that 60 percent of the population could be in the informal sector without the consent of the government. Obviously, it is not so simple a matter to think that a president sits down with a representative of the informal sector to allocate parcels of property and sectors of the economy. Our research also shows that it is not so simple a matter as corruption—that informals have bought their way into the legal domain.

We spent three years honing our empirical methods and identifying, seeking out, and learning from the informals in Peru. Here is what we found out.

In housing, of every 10 buildings under construction in Lima today, 7 are built illegally. Overall, 37 percent of Lima's housing is informal and illegal. We know because we counted them one by one. That is $9 billion worth of housing in Lima. In Peru as a whole the total is $18 billion, which is more than the whole of our foreign public and private debt. Regarding just housing for the very poor, the government has built 1 out of every 50 homes; the informals have built the other 49. The informals build at about two-thirds of the cost and about 6 square meters more per inhabitant.

In transportation, we found that 87 percent of Lima's buses are operated illegally. If we add taxis, 95 percent of public transportation in Peru is informal. The value of the informal Lima bus fleet and infrastructure is about a $1 billion. It is run without deficits. The other 5 percent of public transport run by the government runs a deficit of $12 million per year.

In addition, we counted 90,000 street vendors in Lima. They are essential to the distribution of food stuffs in the city. In an effort to leave the streets for a place with electricity and running water, many have banded together to build producers' markets. Within Lima, 331 such markets have been built since the colonial days, of which 57 were built by the state and 274 by former street vendors. Today of every 12 markets under construction in the country, 11 are being built by former street vendors and 1 is being built by government.

In sum, therefore, the informal sector is a very economically powerful sector. Though it consists of relatively poor entrepreneurs, it is significant. These poor entrepreneurs produce, according to our calculations, 38 percent of the gross national product (GNP). This means that Peru's GNP is 27 percent higher than official statistics report.

Why Are Informals Informal?

Why is so much economic activity going on illegally? Many outsiders look at the economies of Latin America and assume that social or cultural attitudes unique to the region account for the fact that so many people do not participate in the formal economy. Empirical analysis challenges these conventional wisdoms and stereotypes.

Why have the millions of people who have flocked from the countryside to the city in recent years (Peruvian cities have quintupled in size in the last 30 years) found the path to prosperity in the informal sector instead of the formal economy? We set out to understand what it actually takes to get into business—not for a large, established corporation but for an entrepreneur.

We began with a simulation. We set out to establish a small workshop in the outskirts of Lima. We engaged one lawyer and four assistants who, with a stop watch, went to each office in the state bureaucracy in order to register a small clothing workshop with two machines. Working 8 hours a day it took a total of 289 days to be able to start operations legally. We did the same exercise in Tampa where most of the legalities could be done by the mail, and it took us 3 and 1/2 hours to start the business. In New York, it took us 4 hours. In short, it takes a Peruvian entrepreneur 700 times more time than his or her U.S. counterpart to start a small business.

We repeated the exercise in the housing industry. Anyone familiar with Latin American cities knows the surrounding belts of inferior housing which often house half or more of a city's population. Why do so many people end up in hovels when, in most Latin countries, there is a process of legal adjudication whereby a group of families can band together and lay claim to a certain sand dune or plot of land for the construction of a new village? Our institute examined the red tape involved in this process. One individual representing 100 families working 8 hours a day requires 6 years and 11 months to get the necessary permit, requiring the completion of 207 different official statements and visits to 52 government offices. Is it surprising that in Peru in 1985 there were 282 invasions of land and only 3 legal adjudications?

This kind of bureaucratic bottleneck is not limited to the clothing and housing sectors. The small markets cited above built to serve the needs of street vendors provide another case in point. Those built within the framework of the law require about 12 years of preliminary bureaucratic work before the first step can be taken.

Some observers try to explain away the existence and size of the informal sector as simple reflections of crafty tax avoidance. Therefore, we studied the role of taxation in the economy and who pays what kind of taxes. Only 120,000 people in Peru pay income tax, generating less than 1 percent of government revenue. Tax on gasoline provides the largest increment of government revenue—45 percent. Clearly, the 95 percent of the transport industry that operates informally pays a very substantial gasoline tax. Of course, they also pay a consumption tax of 60 percent.

Informals are also subject to other kinds of taxes not usually borne by the formal economy. They must pay a very substantial inflation tax because informal enterprises require large cash balances in lieu of banking credit, balances that erode at the rate of inflation (quite substantial in most developing economies). Informals also pay a daily fee to the local police to ensure their presence and support. The annual total collected this way in the Lima streets is twice as much as the property tax collected legally in the whole country. This sectoral analysis produced the unexpected fact that the informal sector pays more tax than the formal sector.

Law and the Economy

It is too simple to conclude, as many do, that, by sweeping away all of the bad legislation, everything will improve. In point of fact, the law serves useful purposes. Our focus should be on improving the law. In trying to move from analysis to prescription, we found it useful once again to study the informals for signs of what works and what does not. Not unsurprisingly, the informal sector has generated its own body of laws.

The laws that govern the informal sector in Peru are not all that different from the kinds of law that we have seen at other times and in other places in the world. Their law looks very much like law in the Western world of the nineteenth century. Many rules parallel the rules that came to govern the California gold rush and the settlement of competing claims.

A case in point is property law. In Peru it is not uncommon to see side-by-side neighborhoods of sharply contrasting standards even if they have been settled by people of similar socioeconomic backgrounds. We studied an area near San Travino for 9 months: the fundamental difference seemed to be that one neighborhood secures the right of property and the other does not. In the more prosperous community, property titles were maintained and defended in a court of law. After 10 years the value of property in the

neighborhood that protected those titles was 41 times that of the property across the street.

Another example of the importance of effective law to the development of an economy is liability law. The absence of liability law renders nearly impossible creating contracts or making long-term arrangements. The formal sector takes liability law for granted. However, without such protection, the risks that fall on an entrepreneur are exorbitant. One wonders why so many entrepreneurs are willing to run this risk and how much more would be possible within the framework of effective law.

Informals do not have access to this kind of law because it takes them 289 days to get it, making entrepreneurship nearly impossible. Many business ventures are not begun because the risks are too high. Businesses that do evolve are not the best that the economy and society might generate. Family connections become an important basis of business organization because they are the most durable kind of pressure to sustain business commitments in the absence of recourse to law. The Latin work ethic is shaped more by the absence of good institutions and tort law than by culture.

These factors suggest a novel explanation of the popularity of enterprise nationalization in the developing world. Private business creates numerous negative externalities that the courts cannot control—the normal subjects of legal wrangling over liability in a developed economy. State ownership creates at least the appearance of public control absent a system that provides real control. This also suggests that the formal sector lacks adequate legal protections.

As a consequence, we examined the burden of legal affairs on enterprise in Peru. Our analysis of the formal sector revealed that entrepreneurs spend about 40 percent of their time on politics. It also revealed that legal demands require that managers of firms located outside of Lima spend a great deal of time in the capital. For example, 85 percent of the general managers of enterprises with fewer than 100 workers and outside Lima actually live in Lima because they need to be close to where the rules are being made.

Toward More Effective Governance

The key question is how did these things come to pass? How could there be so much law that is so stifling to our national well-being? Cynics argue that it is a cultural matter, that Latin Americans aspire to the atmospherics of legality and imbue the legal profession with high prestige. Others argue that it is a matter of bureaucratic inertia that can be changed by sweeping away the bureaucracy. In fact, research reveals that the bureaucracy is one of the least significant culprits. The answer is, of course, much simpler.

The generation of law is a matter that is easy to measure. The central government of Peru produces 27,400 rules per year, which is 111 rules per day. Of these 111 rules, the executive branch of the central government produces 99 percent while the legislative branch produces just 1 percent. This arrangement does not provide for much public accountability in the generation of law.

The generation of law in a developed society and economy proceeds quite differently and provides for a systematic check to creating 289-day obstacles to economic activity. An example is the system in the United States. In the judicial branch, thousands of courts are involved in producing jurisprudence based on the evolution of common law. In the legislative branch, representatives who are elected on the basis of their popularity with the voter, not with the political machine, generate public law. In the executive branch, the regulatory agencies are subject to public accountability and must defend their cost-benefit analyses publicly. There is freedom of access to public information. The entire system ensures effective feedback and the evolution of the legal framework of economic activity.

How does the system work in Lima? In the courts, winning a case against the state is nearly impossible. In the legislature, politicians are beholden to their political mentors, not the public. In the executive branch, there is no public accountability. There is no access to public information—in fact, it is forbidden by law. The government owns about 90 percent of the paper produced in the country. It controls 40 percent of advertising. The result, of course, is a system that forces entrepreneurship from the normal economy.

All of this suggests the central importance of effective democratic governance to the prosperous functioning of an economy. If our concept of democracy is limited simply to periodic electoral exercises, then our concept is too narrow to meet the demands of economic well-being.

Shifting the Pendulum

History provides a reassuring degree of perspective, however. There is nothing fundamentally different from the way Latin Americans govern themselves today and the way Europeans governed themselves 200 years ago. In England 200 years ago, for example, an entrepreneur obtained a charter from the king in a step-by-step negotiation for political permission. This kind of capitalism without competition is just like the Peru of today. So Latin Americans can be reassured that they are not culturally inferior— we are simply legally backward.

The Lima of 1988 is not the London of 1800—nor is it even the Lima of the mid-twentieth century. In 1940 Lima had 300,000 inhabitants; today it has 7 million. A King George could run a Lima of 300,000 and allocate economic prizes to politically preferred clients. However, when the population migrations began, the old system was doomed. The market economy began to work and the need emerged for general rules and mechanisms.

The informal sector may yet emerge as the new middle class as its predecessors did in Europe and North America. At the moment, it is fair to say that the informals share common interests and objectives. The research of the ILD addresses these people in terms of their entrepreneurial interests: their desires for private property and contracts. We have also learned to understand their frame of reference and their language, setting aside the largely useless conceptual references common to the developed economies and the Peruvian upper class. We have gained respect for the way the informals have confronted an environment rich in obstacles and made it work.

History shows that the structure of law and governance is something that can be reformed. In fact, a constituency exists to change that structure. They are the informals—economic actors who rebel against the system and build their own system. These actors are unfamiliar to policymakers in the developed world. To return to an earlier analogy, the developed world is used to dealing with the King Georges of the developing world, ignorant of

the Boston Tea Party that is happening in any country with a large informal sector.

The ILD has begun to articulate a pragmatic policy agenda for Peru that builds on the insights enumerated above. We have drafted legislation on property titles. We organized an ombudsman system to oversee adjudication. We pushed through an initiative that greatly expanded access to banking credit by broadening the definition of collateral. We make policy statements available to the general public and gather signatures to endorse new laws. Our goal is to start a process for more open rule-making and more reasonable application of the law. Through this more activist profile for the ILD, we have learned that pragmatism is politically viable. If politicians are shown that they can be popular by doing the right thing, they will.

Clearly, the problems of Peru or the developing world can have no long-term resolution if governments have to turn to organizations such as the ILD to tell them what to do. All organizations have limits. The only real solution is for governments to do what people best require. People are much wiser and smarter than they are generally given credit for being. If all of the wisdom that exists in Peru about its economic and governmental structure could be incorporated into some kind of an institutionalized feedback mechanism, the economy would improve—quickly. Generally speaking, decisions in the developed world are smarter than ours because the collective wisdom of the society is brought to bear in an open process of learning and accountability. However, the developed world is very unskilled at explaining how the system evolved and how decisions are made—reflecting, I suspect, a certain enviable complacency.

The Role of Outside Actors

This raises the important question of what external actors can do to assist this process. Two ways of providing assistance are helping development and doing charity work. Charity work has many virtues. Financial assistance to microenterprises, for example, may not generate much capital on a national scale but it makes an important contribution by delegitimizing the myth that the poor are incompetent economic actors.

Our research suggests that assistance can actually be useful if it is directed toward changing the structures of economic activity—principally, the legal system. Registry systems, adjudication measures, customs regimes, and other regulations are critical components of the overall business environment. Multilateral agencies could have an enormous impact in a country such as Peru if they would stop pouring money into projects that compete with what the informal sector does quite well (e.g., providing housing) and focus instead on the much less expensive matter of improving the legal infrastructure.

An Answer to Marx

Our conviction that democracy and market economies are the only path to development grows out of a pragmatic test of what works and a historical perspective that offers substantial supportive evidence. The kind of analysis undertaken at the ILD can lead to only one conviction—a clear commitment to broadened economic and political participation.

Advocates of stable long-term growth in the developing world based on the foregoing principles must confront two challenges. First, many of the conventional wisdoms about the way modern economies emerge are simply irrelevant to the circumstances in the developing world—and we have much homework to do to put our intellectual house in order. Nobody in the West has drawn a blueprint of how to traverse from the mercantilist system to one based on a market economy and an open political framework. The traverse happened from adjustments here and there. Or, it did not happen at all, and such states as the Soviet Union came along. We must do the ideological work of putting together a body of ideas and policies that hang together convincingly and embody human aspirations and our moral preferences.

Second, the advent of Marxism-Leninism means that we cannot trust in the leisurely drift of history, as the West could, to stumble on a modern political economy. The simple answers posed by this philosophy have a certain powerful appeal, especially among politically active elites. It is ironic indeed that a system that has produced such oppressively dismal economic results throughout the world has nevertheless taken over half of the world's governments. The importance of change in basic sociopolitical affairs is a subject that should not be left to the Marxists—historically, it has been their province, but we must lay claim to it.

The first two clashes in Latin America between the informal sector and the old regime were in Cuba and Nicaragua, and we can see who won. There is no reason why the only people who have to be deliberate are Marxist-Leninists. We can also be deliberate by studying the history of the developed world to understand how deregulation, administrative simplification, and good macroeconomic policy can be translated into the reality of the developing countries so as to produce a language that the majority—a group the developed world knows little about—will support. Economically prosperous and politically liberal systems are not beyond the reach of the developing world. People who want real answers instead of dogma must understand the forces at work and address their recommendations to those powerful and emerging actors in the developing world whose efforts are the cornerstone of a better future.

Adam Smith Was An Optimist

Ralf Dahrendorf

AT THE BEGINNING of Book Three in *Wealth of Nations*, Adam Smith has a chapter entitled "Of the Natural Progress of Opulence." In it he argues that once prosperity exists anywhere, it will inevitably spread from the towns to the country, from one country to another, and from those who enjoy it through all ranks of society. There would be a natural progress in economic provisions from "subsistence" to "conveniency" and on to "luxury," from the indispensable to the agreeable and even the superfluous. But Adam Smith was not blind. He knew that such progress was not happening. Therefore he introduced a small, but crucial proviso. This natural process of progressive economic change would have taken place, he adds, "if human institutions had never thwarted those natural inclinations," or "had human institutions never disturbed the natural course of things." In other words, the invisible hand of the market would see to it that all get a share of the goods and services produced, but, alas, the visible hand of human institutions interferes with this natural process.

The following essay offers a somewhat more benevolent view of human institutions and a more skeptical view of the market. Markets are wonderful inventions, but without institutions, we probably would forever remain in a Hobbesian war of all against all in which crude power prevails. The purpose of this analysis is to illuminate a facet of the old problem of the relations between economics and politics, and more particularly, the political conditions of economic participation.

An example may help to define the issue. In recent years, many businessmen have looked to the People's Republic of China as a potential gold mine, where vast undeveloped spaces and a potential market of one billion people offered the prospects of unlimited business. They were quickly disappointed. After the first two trips to China, one could hear mutterings about the waste of management time and the expense of setting up anything in Beijing or Shanghai. The unlikelihood of one billion or even 250 million washing machines, color television sets, or motor cars being sold on the Chinese market in the foreseeable future slowly dawned on these would-be profiteers. In fact, the relevant market is much smaller; it does not even include all those living in the special economic zones. If a market of 50 million people could be created, the success would be remarkable. What is it that defines whether people are a part of the market or not? What "human institutions" stand in the way? And what can be done to extend them?

The Marshall Plan Is Out

At least once every year, some former politician demands a modern-day equivalent of the Marshall Plan for a

Ralf Dahrendorf is warden of St. Antony's College, Oxford University.

region of the world which he or she has just visited. The belief that a massive injection of capital is necessary to extend the frontier of economic activity is widespread. The example is, moreover, topical: this year celebrates the fortieth anniversary of George Marshall's Harvard speech in which the project of a recovery program for Europe was publicly launched. The occasion warrants a brief reflection. Why was the original Marshall Plan so successful? Why, on the other hand, do many feel more doubtful about its replication elsewhere? One reason, undoubtedly, is that there is no sign of a generous donor at this stage (unless one wants to interpret the recycling of funds in the 1970s which gave rise to the debts of the 1980s as a recent equivalent). But the main reason runs deeper: there existed in postwar Europe certain structures which are not at all a given in those parts of the world to which the notion of a Marshall Plan would be applied today. These included an infrastructure which, while in tatters, was laid out and ready to be revived. It consisted not only of roads and railways and canals, of industrial facilities and concentrations, but also of flows of raw materials and finished products—indeed, an entire economy.

One might argue that all this can be rebuilt. It can also be built, and in so doing one might even avoid the mistakes of the past. This is true, although it is not as easy as it sounds. But it points to an even more significant given in postwar Europe. Let me call it people's attitudes. The Europeans were ready to make use of the economic opportunities offered to them. To say that people were ready means at least two things: they were in a position to take part in economic life, and they were motivated to do so. The motivation was evident, not just

in retrospect. Once people had recovered from the shocks of the war, they sought for themselves and their children at least the lifestyle they remembered from happier days, if not a better one. And they were in a position to achieve this. They had the skills, the habit of work (and, not to forget, of saving), the framework of laws, the patterns of social relationships which are prerequisites of modern economic activity. None of this had to be created when the European Recovery Program was started. No one could know at the time how much further the process would be advanced; the economic miracle that followed could not be foreseen, and it had other ingredients than Marshall Plan funds. But the first steps all began with the prefix "re": rebuilding, recreating, reconstructing, recovering.

A Marshall Plan in which people are neither capable of taking part in economic life nor motivated to do so would have a very different effect. The funds might end up in the pockets of the few who are already doing well. They might lead to the construction of large projects of infrastructure which then remain unused or underused. They might lead to a short consumption boom based on imports which soon ends in a rude awakening. The Mexican drama of import desubstitution during the oil boom—that is, the weakening of domestic industries by the misuse of available funds—is an example. China's special economic zones have made similar mistakes. Actually, so have some European countries after the war. The Marshall Plan is not a story of unequivocal success. But it is ill-suited as a model of economic development in which there are obstacles to economic participation, obstacles which were absent in postwar Europe.

These obstacles take us back to the

"human institutions" Adam Smith mentioned. I would like to single out two.

Motivation Is Key

People want to live, and in order to do so they have to engage at all times in certain activities. These activities could be called economic, in the widest sense of the word. We are talking about modern economic activity—that is, economies on a path of steadily improving human welfare and thus of growth. We are talking about participation in expanding economies. This presupposes a break with the secular cycle of poverty or at best self-sufficiency. It involves the motivation not to leave things as they are, but to make progress.

This is not the place to pursue either the moral or the philosophical implications of modern economic life, important though they are. It is not *a priori* clear that the modern growth path is a good thing. Growth undoubtedly means the destruction of traditional ways of life; it does not promise quick results but often leads through a trough of uprooting and destitution; it is guided by an image of life which may be alien to the majority of mankind even today. But no one has the right to deny people opportunities which exist in the world. Furthermore, there are as many paths to economic progress as there are cultures. The American experience is emphatically not the model for all; it has neither been the model for Germany or Japan, nor for the newly industrializing countries today. For the purposes of this argument I am going to assume that modern economic development is a good thing and that it need not homogenize the world into one huge supermarket.

By philosophical implications I

mean the old debate about religion and the rise of capitalism. What values are peculiarly suited or unsuited to get modern economies going? Is there a built-in conflict between the values of some religions and modern economies? Does fundamentalism have to be antimodern in economic terms? One would wish to know much more about the Iran of the shah and that of the ayatollahs than we learn in the heat of battle, about Confucianism and economic progress in China, about Catholicism and modernity in Latin America.

The more immediate issue of motivation has to do with a subject John Kenneth Galbraith treated with characteristic flourish some time ago in his lectures on *The Nature of Mass Poverty*. He argues (largely, no doubt, in the light of his Indian experience) that a cycle of bare subsistence is in many ways the normal way of life in most parts of the world. People accommodate to a life of stable, modest needs and wants under uncertain conditions. In order to make modern economic participation possible, such accommodation has to be broken. This can be done in many ways. Communities can be pulled into a new economic environment brutally, as by the appearance of a large transnational enterprise on the scene. They can also be drawn in slowly, as by the introduction of means of transport which turn subsistence farming into limited marketing of produce. One hopes that there are also modes of gradual change which do not leave a trail of destruction. The stimulation of cooperative efforts by some of the more thoughtful catalysts of development—churches, foundations, small organizations—is perhaps an example.

But it would be wrong to romanticize a process which is a shock even at the best of times. The most dramatic chapter of Galbraith's book deals with migration. Galbraith points out that once people have broken out of their accommodation to the age-old cycle of poverty, they have little hope of seeing their newfound aspirations realized in their environment. The market is not where their motivation has been awakened. At any rate, it will take a long time before it arrives there. As a result, the temptation is great to go where the market is: to Bombay and Rio de Janeiro, or even to Los Angeles and Miami. Motivation for economic participation invariably means mobilization; it does not by itself create markets, but people for markets. Over time, it may lead to the extension of existing domestic markets. But those who want results are most likely to seek them where markets are known to exist. More often than not, they end up in favellas and huts in the outskirts of glittering cities, between a past which is lost and a future which is not yet gained. Even this is not an argument against modernization, although it is a challenge to our social and political imagination. Mobilization is thus one precondition of economic participation. Obstacles to the mobility of people, of needs and wants, and also of goods have to be removed.

The other obstacle to participation takes us back to the ability of people to take part in the economic process. This is a matter of what I call entitlements. People have to have a certain status in order to be able to participate in the economy. This status has several ingredients. One is civil rights. When Adam Smith published *Wealth of Nations*, almost a century had passed since England's "glorious revolution" of 1688. For England and later for Scotland, this had established certain fundamental rights of citizenship for all (or at any rate for all men of certain

categories). It had created, for example, the preconditions of the modern labor contract—equality before the law. It is true that some modern economies are based on varieties of forced labor, but not one of them has been successful. Unless people are in a position to take part in the economic process as free and equal partners, the process is not likely to lead to great improvements in welfare. In that sense, civil rights and the rule of law—a civil society—are preconditions of economic participation.

Civil Society

Marx was perhaps the first to point out the limitations of civil rights in view of inequalities of economic power. To speak of a free and equal contract between a laborer who needs to survive and an employer who runs a large company and makes a handsome profit seems cynical. In some ways it is. Yet such criticism should not lead one to underestimate the importance of equality before the law and civil rights of participation. They are not only the first step toward modern economic growth, they are also the biggest step. The reason for placing the creation of civil societies everywhere at the top of the agenda of development is partly moral. But it is also economic, for there will not be a reliable trajectory of growth before all citizens have basic equal rights.

It is difficult and painful to remove this particular obstacle to participation. Even in England, it took a revolution to achieve it, however glorious the events of 1688 may appear in retrospect. The French Revolution a century later was fought over the same objective. As long as the revolution of citizenship has not happened, economic development remains confined to a limited section of the population.

The experience of recent decades shows that it was wrong to believe that the wealth of the few will in due course trickle down or filter through. The filter is impenetrable or can be made so by a privileged class bent on defending its position rather than allowing the basis of its privilege to be shifted.

Perhaps the greatest political question of development is whether it is possible to break privilege without revolution, or rather, how it is possible to do so, for one of the side effects of revolution is almost invariably economic decline. Once the problems of a country are perceived to be wholly political, the economy is bound to suffer. There is no shortage of examples in the postwar period, including, in recent years, Nicaragua as well as Poland. One of the reasons why so many of us were watching events in the Philippines with such intense interest last year is that for a while it appeared as if "people power" might be mobilized to bring about those structural changes that are necessary to enable the deprived and underprivileged to take part in the economic process. At times one wonders whether that moment has already passed.

One of the great achievements of John Maynard Keynes was that he identified the point at which a change in entitlements actually helped set the economic growth process back on course. Stimulating demand meant enabling people to participate, thereby pulling up supply. It is not my intention to recommend the specific Keynesian remedy today as an instrument of economic development, although I suspect that the opposite— the stimulation of the supply side—is almost bound to leave some behind and create the entitlement problems of the long-term unemployed or the hard-core poor. But we do need, in the process of economic development, someone with Keynes' flair for combining progressive policies with conservative predilections. We need a true radical who seeks and finds the levers of change in entitlements which do not destroy economic prospects. While I confess to being unable at this time to recommend the necessary policies, perhaps defining the need will help find the response.

Entitlements and Participation

Civil rights are a key part of the entitlements needed to enable people to take part in the modern economic process, but they do not constitute the whole story. Some entitlements are themselves economic, including a certain level of income. Let me leave to one side the complicated and controversial issue of a guaranteed minimum income and other methods for turning real wages into entitlements, and instead pick up an aspect of the problem which is topical in many countries. Modern economies are money economies; growth is impossible without money as a medium of exchange. However, not just any money will do the trick. A stable and convertible currency clearly cannot guarantee that everyone will possess a fair share of it, but without a stable and convertible currency, reliable real incomes are impossible to sustain. In that sense, good money is a condition of economic development.

The key event in Germany's postwar economic recovery was probably the currency reform of 1948. For those who had lived to see it, it was a most remarkable event. On the day before the reform, the shops were empty, and the only way to get many products was to pay with cigarettes on the black market. This meant that the few who owned cigarettes and other substitute currencies had all they needed, whereas the many who did not had to rely on the meager rations promised, though not always supplied, by the government. On the day after the currency reform, the shops were full, and for one famous week everyone had 40 marks per person, which were handed out initially. From that day onwards, the intrinsically privilege-free currency of money provided access to the market. One generalized entry ticket determined exchanges, and the question was no longer whether one had carpets to exchange for pigs, or cigarettes for potatoes.

In an article about the fortieth anniversary of the announcement of the Marshall Plan, the *Neue Zuericher Zeitung* remarked recently, "It rarely happens that economic events and decisions make history and are remembered." The point is that economic developments are incremental and can be plotted on smooth curves. Political developments, on the other hand, are not. At any rate, major entitlement changes are usually associated with memorable dates. People remember the day of the West German currency reform, June 20, 1948, as they remember George Marshall's speech on June 5, 1947. These are in fact not economic events, but political events with a bearing on economic developments. Probably the extension of economic participation needs such dates everywhere; in any case, it requires decisions which are not themselves economic.

In most developing countries there has been too much fiddling with exchange rates. Moreover, not all currency reforms have had the desired effect. Positive effects of the Plan Austral can still be felt in Argentina, while the Cruzado Plan in Brazil, which looked more effective at first, has already been followed by a Cru-

zado Plan 2. One lesson here is that currency reforms have to come at the right moment, have to be gauged right in their dimension, and have to be accompanied by the right measure of economic policy. Such reforms should not be seen merely as a part of International Monetary Fund-style economic adjustments. To be successful, they have to provide a new basis for individual expectations as well as for exchanges within and without. They have to stabilize entitlements.

Needless to say, the international monetary system plays an important part in the process. The breakdown of the Bretton Woods system after 1971 was a most serious setback for international attempts to create a framework of stable expectations. Perhaps there was no other choice; certainly the United States had tried to bring about a negotiated settlement before the unilateral decisions of August 15, 1971 (another memorable economic data which is in fact political). Not surprisingly, it has since proved difficult to find a way to a new regime of stability in the world. The European Monetary System is a second-rate substitute for a limited region. It would be wrong to raise false hopes; but in the light of these reflections there can be little doubt that monetary stability is a necessary condition of political decisions which extend economic participation.

The list of obstacles to economic participation is far from complete. Above all, it leaves undiscussed the economic equivalent of the political difference between active and passive suffrage. There are those who vote and those who are elected; there are those who earn money and buy goods and services, and those who produce and sell these goods and services. A modern economy cannot rely on passive participation alone. In one form or another, Joseph Schumpeter's entrepreneurs have to be added to Keynes' measures to stimulate demand. Their emergence too is anything but a matter of course; in fact, many modern political and economic regimes seem to conspire against innovation and initiative.

Entitlements and Politics

People have to be mobilized to be motivated, and they have to be entitled to take part in the economic process. Neither of these two changes is easy or painless. As current events in the Soviet Union and other developing countries demonstrate, the entitlements required for economic development have a political price, and mobility runs counter to a system of total control. In the final analysis, economic, political, and general social participation are part and parcel of the same process. There are certainly examples of countries which have gone further in some respects than in others. The imagination of reality is always greater than that of textbooks. But countries which systematically curb political participation and try to control social participation more generally are not likely to get very far with their economic development. Institutions for participation are a necessary framework of successful human endeavor. There is not just one blueprint for them, but the principle is clear.

Conclusions

It is thoughtless and misleading to go around the world calling for Marshall Plans. The Marshall Plan had its time, its place, and its method, none of which can be replicated in the world today. (One hopes that there will never be another time and a place where the method will have to be repeated.) This is not to say that the only issue of development is participation. We may well need an initiative that relaunches the process of world development. It will have to combine measures of mobilization and entitlement with transfer of resources. To some extent there will even have to be a division of labor between internal, domestic reforms and international assistance. I would hope that the former are not purely political and the latter is not purely economic. Economic efforts have to be made within countries, and the international community has a place in the extension of civil rights. The result is a very different mix of measures from that proposed by most international plans. It is more like a Keynes-Schumpeter Plan because of its combination of participation and initiative. Let us hope that at least the ideas are there when the time is ripe.

Turkey's Path to Freedom and Prosperity

Turgut Ozal

ASPIRATIONS FOR GREATER democracy and prosperity are nearly universal. Yet the obstacles to these goals are numerous. Differences in sociopolitical and economic structures, and diversity in behavior determined by historical and cultural background make each country's situation unique. Yet broad similarities exist even between two widely different countries. Thus there is some value in sharing individual experiences to reach mutually beneficial conclusions. The purpose of this analysis is to examine the Turkish experience—a venture to foster democracy and prosperity through a new liberal economic policy.

Homo Economicus and Freedom

Economic liberalism and political democracy are heterozygote twins. Who is first delivered is beside the point. Their distinctions, however, have given an impression that they were the products of two separate historical processes. I do not share this view. The concept of participation in economic and political life can only be understood within the framework of this twin and inseparable reality. Being a politician, idealism is not my creed— I try to work out what is possible and feasible within the constraints of a given system.

Our special emphasis on liberal eco-

nomic policies is a radical departure from the previous experience. We believe that homo economicus is the basis of individualism. An economic actor free from the strings of state is better placed to defend his individual political rights as well. On the other hand, since he is bound only by impersonal market forces, he operates more efficiently. He makes his decisions himself and faces their consequences. This makes him more responsible, more motivated, and individually stronger. The day-to-day decisions of businessmen are a direct form of participation in the economic life of the nation.

The value of economic freedoms is underestimated. Traditionally, anything measurable in monetary terms is considered unworthy of this qualification. The conceptual scope of freedom is reduced to mere intellectual activity and the protest movements which this activity breeds. We cannot deny the importance of this form of freedom, nor can we accept its confinement solely to the intellectual sphere.

Economy affects our daily life. In order to earn our livelihood, we have to invent, innovate, and create. In economic activity deeds count. But this difference does not make economic freedoms less important to society. On the contrary, without these freedoms society cannot develop, and intellectual activity takes a pessimistic, even destructive turn.

Turgut Ozal is the prime minister of Turkey.

Economic freedoms encourage constructive activities and provide rewards to the participants in accordance with their ability and contribution. In this way, those who are most capable move up the ladder of prestige and power in the society. This process is not, of course, free of problems. Nevertheless, there is no better alternative to serve both individual development and social efficiency. Thus, the state has the prime duty to remove constraints on economic freedoms and create conditions of free competition.

Turkey Embraces Liberalism

The developed world may look upon these views as commonplace. But in the developing world, they are quite radical. In a developing country, the general tendency is to protect businessmen from competition, either internally or externally. This survival instinct is felt acutely by a comparatively weak economy. In addition, Turkey used to have certain historical misgivings against the liberal economy. This has created a strong and stubborn bias in favor of statism and excessive state intervention in the economy. This makes our introduction of free market policies in Turkey all the more significant.

Our policies should not be reduced to the exclusive desire of an elite against popular opposition. On the contrary, my party, which was not supported by the regime at that time, ran its election campaign on the ostensibly unpopular austerity program and free market economy. We explained frankly and openly to the people that without difficulties we could not achieve the desired ends. This was a new phenomenon in Turkey. Political analysts did not give us any chance, but we enjoyed a landslide victory.

This victory is of supreme impor-

tance. First, the people proved that they were mature enough to stand up to difficulties. Second, by doing so, they have overcome the historical constraints of the system. Third, their response constituted an extraordinary example of collective participation in a fateful decision. As a result, Turkey at one stroke left behind the Third World evolutionary phase and entered a new one full of the promises and challenges of modern industrial society.

The Policy Agenda

As soon as we came to power, we further liberalized foreign trade and continued the realistic exchange rate and positive interest rate policies. These policies helped to integrate the Turkish economy into the global economy. Realistic exchange rates facilitate our exports, enhance Turkish competitiveness, and improve the quality of products. On the other hand, these rates restore a rough balance to the trade account without much need for quantitative restrictions. Positive interest rates channel the savings into the official system and together with realistic exchange rates prevent capital flight. Although these policies were well-known in industrial countries they were quite new in Turkey at that time.

Our real innovations are in the mechanisms we introduced to increase savings. Previously, certain items labeled as luxuries, such as American cigarettes, were smuggled into the country. Nor was the importation of foreign cars allowed. We legitimized their imports and charged a fairly high levy on them. Revenues collected in this way created the housing fund. We now build 150,000 units annually. Credits have already been provided for more than 500,000 units. Recently we

modified the system further and introduced small compulsory contributions
to the fund by the state and the employer. This will enable us to provide
housing to everybody. Within this
framework, we envisage solving the
housing problem within 10 years. This
will be achieved through a transfer of
wealth from high- to low- and me-
dium-income groups, a transfer which
is realized without much fuss.

Another instrument we have invented is the Public Participation
Fund. We publicly sold revenue sharing bonds for some of our large public
works such as the Istanbul Bridge, the
Keban Dam, and, lately, the Karakaya
Dam. With this money, we accelerated some of the already initiated projects and embarked upon new ones.
We are now building the Ataturk
Dam, the fourth largest in the world,
in addition to an advanced communication network, toll highways,
bridges, etc. As new projects are completed and put into operation, we will
sell their revenue sharing bonds. The
system is effective and self-propelling.
A similar fund was established in the
field of defense industries, supporting
joint ventures which are calculated to
contribute to the economy.

All these funds are outside the budget. Their advantages are many. Budgetary bureaucracy has been eliminated. Since funds are allocated to
specific projects, financial shortages
and delays are also eliminated and
planning is simplified. Thanks to this
system, projects of great importance
to the economy are completed earlier
than scheduled. Savings also have increased from 16 percent in 1983 to 24
percent in 1987.

As a result of policies geared to
opening up the economy, Turkish exports have increased almost fourfold in
six years and the share of industrial
goods has risen from 35 percent to 75

percent. This development is a clear
sign of integration with the world
economy.

In addition, one can mention increasing foreign direct investment
flows. Here again, we have elaborated
a new mode of investment which we
call "build, own, operate and if you
like, hand over." This approach is accepted by investors and their countries. As a first step, some large ther-
mal power plants are on the way to
realization. The advantage of this system over credits is that the contractor-
investor is encouraged to invest only
in economically sound and viable projects.

As part of our drive to open up our
economy, Turkish contractors have
won international tenders in the Middle East worth almost 20 billion dollars. Their efforts also contribute to
increasing our exports to neighboring
countries, thus balancing our commercial relations between regions.

Economic relations with the Socialist bloc have not been neglected. We
proposed a gas pipeline from the Soviet Union which has recently arrived
at its first destination and which will
bring our total trade with this country
to 6 billion dollars in 1992. A similar
pipeline for the northeastern part of
Turkey is under review.

Turkish growth rates have increased. For the last three years, the
Turkish economy has registered the
highest rate among the OECD countries, with a record of more than 8
percent in 1986. Turkish GDP per
capita, calculated on the purchasing
power parity basis by the OECD and
the Eurostat of the European Community, reached $3,600 in 1985 and is
now more than $4,000. This has been
achieved at a time of slow growth and
mounting protectionism in the world
economy. At the same time we reduced the triple digit inflation to 34

percent in 1986 and service regularly heavy old debts rescheduled in the early 1980s.

Prosperity and Social Justice

Our understanding of prosperity is based on sound and high economic growth, which goes hand in hand with social justice. Without growth we can redistribute only poverty. In 1986, thanks to an exceptionally high growth rate, for the first time we reduced unemployment by creating real jobs. Another aspect of our social development strategy is to extend services to the remotest rural areas. Electricity has now reached all villages. The number of automatic telephones in villages has increased in three years from 11 to 11,000. Rural roads are being upgraded at a rapid pace, and much more.

Agricultural development is of the utmost importance. Turkey is proud of having one of the most liberal agricultural sectors. According to the OECD figures, this sector is protected only by 10 percent of the value-added as against 45 percent in the United States and 90 percent in the EC. Yet agricultural development is impressive due mainly to new seeds and increased irrigation. In education we have given priority to enhancing quality by the increased use of new technologies and a switch to technical education and apprenticeship. Recently, we have launched an ambitious program of computerization in education. Turkey enjoys one of the highest computer-pupil ratios in the world. In a decade Turkey will have a new generation of graduates who will be abreast of the information requirements of a technological society.

Special attention is being given to regional imbalances. We have introduced new incentives to private sector investments in eastern and southeastern Turkey. What is more, we launched a scheme of projects called GAP in southeastern Turkey. This comprises 13 dams that will irrigate almost 2 million hectares and produce 20 billion kilowatts-hour annually. Once it is completed, Turkish agricultural production and hydroelectric power will be doubled. We are confident that this development will eradicate externally instigated ideological activities in this part of the country.

In the light of the results achieved and the perspectives unfolding, we had the courage to apply for full membership in the EC. We are convinced that the Turkish economy will be an asset, a very valuable one, rather than a liability to the EC. It is the only market in Europe with a real growth potential. We hope the Europeans will duly appreciate it and overcome their narrow and archaic sociocultural objections.

Another reform toward democracy is decentralization. Turkey has had a centralized system of government since the founding of the Republic. The municipal and local authorities have atrophied financially and administratively. People had to go to the capital in order to get things done in the localities. Because of this, central authorities have been overburdened, even paralyzed, at times. This situation has prevented people from making decisions for themselves. It goes without saying that this was not only incompatible with democracy, but also with socioeconomic development.

We immediately increased the authority of municipalities and provided them with corresponding autonomous resources. Thus their share in the public expenditures has risen from 2–3 percent to almost 15 percent. In a short time, cities and towns have turned into vast construction areas.

Municipalities have embarked upon the laying down of the urban infrastructure, which has been long neglected despite a very high rate of urbanization. The municipalities began to pay immediate attention to rehabilitating the environment, upgrading urban areas, etc. Their councils, dormant for quite a long time, became the active focal points of participation in decision-making. The press, both national and local, began to give more prominence to municipal activities. In short, municipalities have taken a very important burden from the rigid central government, releasing it to concentrate on nationwide projects.

Recently, we completed the process by promulgating another law on local authorities. We have increased the scope of their prerogatives and financial resources through budgetary appropriations. In the near future we expect a parallel activity to start up in the localities by extending services to rural districts.

These reforms have taken shape in line with the general progress of democracy. After the 1983 general elections, we had one general municipal election, then by-elections and recently partial municipal elections. The frequency of these elections allows the population to reflect its political choices and tendencies at various levels.

Freedom and Prosperity

Today, a democratic regime with all its institutions is in force in Turkey. The parliament comprises all political parties and is very active. The press is entirely free, although, in my opinion, overly critical and hyperactive. Public opinion is sensitive and responsive to events. Turkey has chosen democracy and a liberal economy as mutually supportive ways of life. It seeks its freedom and prosperity in the same vein. The process is in full swing, and there is no other alternative.

Parliaments, Congresses, and the Nurturing of Democracy

Malcolm Churchill

IT IS PERHAPS unfortunate that the ballot box has come to stand as the symbol of democracy for people around the world. Americans are among those who accept this symbolism and who have encouraged its spread. Regrettably, preoccupation with the act of voting has diverted attention from the institutional dynamics of the divergent governing processes encompassed in the term "democracy."

In most developing countries democracy has been introduced, has sickened, and, in many cases, has died. Democracy's withering is generally attributed to the failings of people, the people who seek to retain or to gain power. Thoughtful examination suggests, however, that there are institutional forces at work that lead power seekers in certain directions and that what Americans see as failures of the concept of democracy are in fact the failures of a particular structure of democracy.

In seeking to nurture democracy in countries where it is an unfamiliar form of government, Americans have relied largely on exhortations to encourage democracy and free elections. In reality, Americans' task as practitioners of democracy ought to be to

Malcolm Churchill is a former Foreign Service officer. An economist and Southeast Asian specialist, he now publishes a stock market newsletter, "The Insiders' Way."

promote particular democratic forms, consciously tailored to the country and structured to endure despite the frailties of people. This was precisely the task that faced the Founding Fathers.

To understand the role of the institutional framework, one must look at the origin and evolution of democracy, particularly at the fundamental distinctions between British parlimentary democracy and U.S. congressional democracy. The features of the U.S. system resulted from conscious decisions by men who were grappling with real-life problems. These problems seem distant—irrelevant—to U.S. democracy today. Accordingly, Americans tend to look at the problems of democracy in newly emerging countries from the perspective of the United States in the twentieth century instead of the more relevant perspective of the United States in the eighteenth century.

The Evolution of Parliamentary Democracy

The democracy that evolved in Great Britain had its origins in the struggle by the privileged for a share of the power of the monarch. However, the legitimacy of the monarchy was not under challenge, and the notion of sharing power with the people never entered into consideration. By the 1700s the British Parliament that evolved from this struggle was an established institution but one where only the nobility and upper classes shared with their king the power to rule the country.

Like the king, the governing class in England was born, in effect, to rule. As an elite, the governing class shared attributes of wealth, education, and a common outlook. These shared attributes provided cohesion to the body politic, as well as differentiating the rulers from the ruled.

That the ordinary people of Britain should share in governing was unthinkable in eighteenth-century Britain. As a consequence, parliament in the 1700s used in its practices and procedures few if any notions of participatory democracy. This absence of participatory democracy was particularly evident, of course, in the upper house, the nonelected House of Lords. But it was also true in the House of Commons. There was long even a ban on publicly reporting speeches heard in the House of Commons.

British parliamentary democracy thus embodied the concept that there were those who were suited to govern and those who were suited to be governed. The rules and procedures of parliamentary democracy, incorporating this worldview, have remained intact for the most part. This is so even though their philosophical underpinning cannot be voiced credibly as a serious philosophy in the twentieth century.

The American revolutionaries challenged the legitimacy of the monarchy and Parliament. They did so by enunciating a radical, new philosophy, which denied to king and Parliament the right to rule. The power to govern, they asserted, belongs to the people, not to kings and noblemen. Just as monarchs earlier had turned heavenward to justify their rule—the divine right of kings—so, too, did the Founding Fathers turn to the Divine to justify their rejection of kingly rule. "All men are created equal . . . they are endowed by their Creator with certain inalienable rights . . . that to secure these rights, Governments are instituted among men, deriving their just powers from the consent of the governed. . . . "

The Role of the Masses in Twentieth-Century Parliamentary Government

Of course, the masses have gained a say in the parliamentary system in Britain and elsewhere. Their role remains limited by the structure of parliamentary government, however. Their primary function is the selection of those who will govern them. After the elections, the people participate relatively little in the political process. In contrast, in the U.S. congressional system obtaining the "consent of the governed" is a continuing and integral part of governing. As an astute American, long resident in a Commonwealth country, observed, "Americans are citizens; (residents of country concerned) are subjects."

The exclusion of the electorate from governing begins in a parliamentary country with the nominating process. Not for parliamentary systems is the simple declaration of party preference by which millions of Americans make themselves eligible, as Republicans or Democrats, to select nominees. In a British parliamentary country, nominees are chosen in what are essentially district caucuses, known as pre-selection. To participate in pre-selection one must have enrolled formally as a party member. The term "card-carrying member" of a political party thus has a literal meaning in a parlimentary democracy. Formal enrollment has such limited appeal that few bother with it. Accordingly, candidates for parliament are nominated by about the same number of voters as would be found in a U.S. caucus at the precinct level. The selectors, those who attend pre-selection meetings, are party loyalists, largely those an American would think of as precinct workers.

The relatively closed nominating process is an important element in enforcing party discipline. If a member of parliament flouts the party leadership, he ordinarily can expect to lose pre-selection. Loyal party members are not sympathetic to those who break ranks.

The limited popular participation in pre-selection is attributable to another feature of parliamentary democracy. Because the majority party in parliament chooses the prime minister, if one wants to select a particular prime minister, one must vote for the candidate of the same party in one's district. Thus, for most voters it matters little who the individual candidates are in a parliamentary district. Although an outstanding parliamentary candidate may win some votes on his own merits, most votes are cast for the party label.

Voting for the party label rather than the person creates no dilemma for the voter in a parliamentary system because members of parliament, once elected, cannot be responsive to the views of their electorates. A member of parliament must vote with his party, regardless of his personal views or the wishes of his district. Were he to do otherwise, he would jeopardize his prospects for future pre-selection. Furthermore, for him to vote with the opposition would be futile, unless thereby he would create a majority. Creating a majority for the opposition brings down the government, however, precipitating the election process

with its party-dominated pre-selection. Given these constraints, representing the district in an American sense is of so little consequence that it is not even necessary that a member of parliament reside in the district in which he stands for election.

In such a system, once elections are finished the ordinary citizen is left without an effective voice on most matters. It is futile for him to write to his representative on any but petty matters or to lobby on all but the most earthshaking of issues.

Parliamentary Government and the Magnifying of Differences

Because party discipline is absolute, the minority party in parliament is virtually without power to modify legislation. Americans sometimes unthinkingly envy a prime minister his resultant ability to enact programs quickly and without modification. This overlooks the reality that bad or unpopular legislation as well as good legislation can be enacted quickly and without modification. In fact, bad legislation is actually more likely when one is accustomed to ignoring the opposition.

Backbenchers, of course, may influence the prime minister in private party meetings. On truly major issues, public opinion may have an impact. The cabinet in some parliaments may exert considerable collective influence. But in the last analysis, the prime minister's view generally dominates in deciding what legislation will be passed.

Because the opposition party is destined to lose on 999 bills out of 1,000, the only power left to it is the power to speechify. Accordingly, speechifying has become a high art in the British parliamentary system. However, the level of vitriol is shocking to American ears, and differences are magnified rather than bridged.

This magnifying of differences resonates through society at large because of the absence of checks and balances in the government. With few formal checks and balances, in a free society extraparliamentary institutions arise to provide a countervailing power. Mainly, it is the labor movement that fills this function. Labor union membership percentages in British countries are high, and labor solidarity is taken seriously. The power of unions to thwart government policy on particular issues is unquestionable, and labor's extraparliamentary power is exercised sometimes on issues, such as the environment, which in the United States would be considered nonlabor issues and left to citizens' lobbying groups.

The emergence of an extraparliamentary power source to check the excesses of parlimentary power introduces a major source of divisiveness to society. This divisiveness must be experienced firsthand to be comprehended fully. The methods of labor in British parliamentary countries—strikes, bans, and slowdowns—are ill-suited to the complexities of twentieth-century social issues.

In the eighteenth century the divisiveness of the parliamentary system was not apparent to those creating the new U.S. system. The ideological differences of the twentieth century largely hinge on economics, and Marx was not yet on the scene, while Adam Smith and his *Wealth of Nations* were only then arriving.

The Challenge for the Founding Fathers

The young U.S. nation faced divisions of another sort, however—those arising from regional loyalties. The Founding Fathers thus faced two challenges: establishing a governmental structure that would bridge regional differences, and ensuring that power would not be usurped by a self-appointed monarch. In solving these two problems, the framers of the U.S. Constitution unknowingly created a system that muted the divisiveness of the parliamentary system. It is a system that not only is the product of compromise but that requires compromise to function.

This contrast with parliamentary democracy has been little commented upon. This undoubtedly is because in Britain strong unifying traditions developed over the centuries when members of Parliament shared a common class outlook. These norms or traditions hold the system together despite class and ideological differences, while they provide a strong and effective check against dictatorship.

However, a system that combines executive and legislative power places its trust entirely in such societal norms and traditions to avoid dictatorship. There are no institutional checks to say to an ambitious individual, long before he reaches the point of seizing power, "This far you can legitimately go, and no farther." Moreover, each ideological faction in a strongly British society knows that its opponents also play by the rules of the game. Policy may swing wildly with a change of power, and the redressing of ill-conceived initiatives must depend on the slow rhythm of the election cycle, but each faction is content to wait and play the game.

Not so in many other countries, where British norms and common bonds are lacking. Where such norms and bonds are absent, unless there is some other strong unifying element (frequently a dominant political party supported both by the electorate and by society's instruments of power), parliamentary democracy does not endure.

Safeguarding Democracy in the U.S. System

The safeguard against authoritarian rule in the U.S. system was the separation of executive from legislative power. However, the introduction of checks and balances changed the dynamics of the system in ways other than the obvious.

The framers of the Constitution, in addition to assigning specified powers to Congress, withheld from the head of state the power to dissolve Congress. It is Congress' immunity from dissolution—not its specified powers—which assures its independence. For the power to dissolve a legislature is, ultimately, the power to control it. The independence of Congress from the chief executive, as well as its responsiveness to the electorate, is what most distinguishes U.S. from British democracy.

The obverse of congressional independence is presidential independence. It was achieved by denying Congress the power to select or dismiss the president. To have allowed Congress this power would have given it influence and perhaps dominance over the president. Instead, the electoral college was created as an alternate mechanism to select the president. The electoral college was to function exactly as did Parliament in selecting the head of government.

Foreign observers, deceived by the president's position at the pinnacle of government as well as by his independence from Congress, frequently characterize the U.S. system as that of a strong presidency. In fact, a much more accurate appellation than presidential democracy for the U.S. system is congressional democracy, the direct counterpoint to parliamentary democracy.

The Flow of Power to the People

The U.S. president's power in fact is limited. When he was denied the power to dissolve Congress, his power to penalize directly members of Congress for crossing party lines also was limited. Moreover, voters can turn out a legislator without affecting the selection of a president.

Legislators thus have more to fear from displeasing their electorate than from displeasing their president. The legislator who ignores the strongly expressed views of his constituents on a sufficient number of issues is likely to be a legislator no longer.

Those taking part in the nominating process want winners. Whatever enthusiasm there might be for nominating ideologically pure party loyalists is difficult to sustain if it means abandoning the seat in question to the opposition. Thus, the structure of the system also encourages those controlling the nominating process to place a higher value on popularity with the voters than on party loyalty.

Moreover, a member of the U.S. Congress, by design, has genuine ties to his district. The Constitution requires that a senator be a resident of the state he represents, and members of the House generally are also required by state law to reside in the district they represent.

The greater dependence of the U.S. legislator on his electorate, rather than on his party machinery, gives individual citizens an effective voice between elections. U.S. legislators can be swayed by lobbying. An extragovernmental check on congressional power is both unnecesary and unwelcomed.

Congressional Government and the Diminution of Differences

The ability of the legislator in a congressional democracy to vote his conscience minimizes ideological differences. Knowledge that an opponent on a particular piece of legislation may be the ally one needs to pass another piece of legislation goes far to eliminate the "us" and "them" mentality that permeates a system where the political gulf between "ins" and "outs" is not only vast but often accentuates class and economic differences. Knowledge that a member of Congress will vote the "right" way some of the time even though from the "wrong" party leads to an emphasis on the attributes of the man and the positions he takes rather than the label he wears. Whether or not the Founding Fathers foresaw this, it is a very American type of outcome.

Federalism further encourages this outcome. Although federalism is neither necessitated nor precluded by either a parliamentary or a congressional system (Australia has a federalist system under parliamentary democracy; the Philippines had a unitary system under congressional democracy), federalism is ideally suited to a society that is not homogenous.

In the U.S. system, authority and responsibility are conveyed to the regions, but with important and clearly defined limits. The result appears to accommodate diversity while diminishing separatism. This can be seen in the indirect election of the president. Each state's electoral votes are equal in number to its senators and representatives, and all are won by one candidate. This feature drives candidates to appeal to voters throughout the country. An overwhelming vote in a candidate's home region (or in a few large states) counts for less than small margins in a broad assortment of states. A successful presidential candidate must be more than a regional candidate, as no single region can hope to provide a majority of electoral votes.

Some might challenge the conclusion that the U.S. system accommodates diversity while diminishing separatism, citing the U.S. Civil War. However, the lesson of the Civil War is not that the system failed. Rather, it is that the system succeeded in holding the country together for a considerable period, despite differences so fundamental as eventually to divide families, sometimes literally turning brother against brother.

Federalism has a further important advantage. It provides a check against the seizure of power by an individual at the center, by avoiding the complete centralization of political decision making and power.

The Sine Qua Non of Congressional Democracy

Attractive as the structure that is congressional democracy appears to be, there remains one sine qua non if it is to work. In a system where representatives are responsible to the people, the people themselves must be responsible. Education is the key. In other words, in a system of congressional democracy the people must be educated sufficiently well to comprehend the issues and to identify demagoguery. Simple, easy solutions are often wrong, and the electorate must have the education to distinguish between the appealing and the true.

In this respect, there is a fundamental difference between congressional democracy and parliamentary democracy. A parliamentary government basically receives from the voters a mandate to govern until the next election. While the government is accountable at election time for its overall record, legislators cannot be held individually accountable for votes on specific issues. With legislative majorities predetermined by virtue of party discipline, there is, in fact, no need for an electorate sufficiently well educated to understand and accept their legislator's vote on individual issues.

The Founding Fathers were, of course, Englishmen before they became Americans. They shared with their parliamentary brethren the perception that property ownership was a necessary attribute of a responsible citizen. While this elitist view now appears undemocratic, in colonial days there was a greater congruence between property and education. As it became apparent in the United States that good citizenship was not dependent on property ownership, the emphasis on education was increased.

Under the U.S. Constitution, qualifications for voting were left expressly to the states. The early property requirements were largely abandoned by 1850. But literacy requirements were introduced in the nineteenth century, in northern as well as southern states, in response to concern about the influx of large numbers of unlettered blacks and immigrants into the body politic after the Civil War.

One might be tempted to dismiss the literacy requirements as attributable only to antiforeign sentiment and racism were it not for the rather astonishing fact that aliens were able to vote in many states in the 1800s. It was not until well into the twentieth century that aliens became ineligible to vote in all states. Thus, while the motives

for literacy tests were not always pure, they reflected what by then had become an element of American political belief, that education was a requisite of good citizenship.

The Concern for a Qualified Electorate

The concern of the drafters of the Constitution that electors be informed and responsible also was made manifest in the decision that neither the senators nor the president be elected by direct vote. It was believed that these positions were so important that an additional measure of wisdom and responsibility was required of the voters. Senators were to be elected by the legislatures of each state. The president, of course, was to be selected by the electoral college, which was expected to consist of the most prominent citizens. These prominent citizens would select a president from among men whose qualifications they were personally familiar with.

The electoral college was to have functioned very much as an eighteenth-century British parliament would have in selecting a prime minister from among its worthy members. As it turned out, the actions of the electoral college in selecting a president are as predetermined as those of a parliament selecting a prime minister. The reasons are similar. A political party will select as candidates for the electoral college only those whom they are reasonably certain will support the party's choice for president. Voters, choosing between a distinguished but uncommitted citizen or a candidate committed to a particular presidential candidate, almost invariably will prefer the candidate who supports their presidential choice. The institutional framework again determines the manner in which the system functions, notwithstanding the contrary intentions of the system's founders.

Indeed, one could abolish electors while retaining precisely the same indirect selection method, i.e., electoral votes for each state equal to the number of its senators and representatives, presidential candidate with the most popular votes to receive all of the state's votes, and a majority of electoral votes required to win the presidency. Proceeding without electors clearly would be preferable for any country starting anew with a federal congressional system. Omitting electors would ensure that coercion, fraud, or personal idiosyncracies could not alter the expressed intention of a state's voters.

The great concern that the drafters of the Constitution displayed for limiting the selection of the nation's leaders, particularly the president and senators, to a subset of uniquely well qualified persons was in time rendered irrelevant by the evolution of the U.S. educational system. With the expansion of good public education in the 1800s, the enlarged electorate was an increasingly well educated electorate. Whatever one's criteria for considering persons to be uniquely well qualified, such persons represented an ever growing proportion of the electorate.

Though the process by which the president is elected continues to be indirect, for a long time it has been the citizens of each state who, by direct vote, have made the choice for their state. By the twentieth century there was little reason for these same voters not to select their senators also. No longer were state legislators as a group significantly better qualified by virtue of education, wisdom, or experience than the broad electorate. Hence, the Seventeenth Amendment, providing for direct election of sena-

tors, was put forward in 1912 and quickly ratified in 1913.

The Transferability of the U.S. Approach to Education

Although Americans valued education from the earliest days of settlement, what probably made U.S. education unique was the system of land grant colleges. Not only has universal, free public education through twelve years of secondary school become a norm, but virtually unrestricted access to college education has become generally available through the state universities. Most Americans take the U.S. educational system so much for granted that they are unaware of just how unusual it really is.

In most countries there are different schools and different types of education for those who will go to universities and those who will not. In most countries this separation of university-bound from others denies the opportunity for a university education to those not identified early as university-bound. Moreover, in most countries education is considered to be a tool rather than a value. People view education as preparation for a specific occupation rather than as preparation for life. Reflecting the foregoing, in most countries it is considered appropriate, or even desirable, for those not headed for university to drop out of secondary school in order to work.

Though a unique approach to education evolved in the United States, the system as it has developed is transferable to other countries. Moreover, developing country status is not an insuperable obstacle to its transfer.

When the United States acquired the Philippines in 1898, one of the first priorities was universal education. U.S. volunteer teachers, beginning with the Thomasites (named for the ship that transported them), introduced U.S.-style education. Today, in the Philippines as in the United States, it is considered desirable for those from all levels of society to acquire as much education as possible, certainly through high school and preferably through college, regardless of the particular occupation that eventually will be pursued. College attendance in both countries is unparalleled, constituting approximately one-quarter of the college-age population.

What is particulary noteworthy in the case of the Philippines, a developing country, is that tertiary education is primarily a private matter. The University of the Philippines, a government-funded institution, though selective and relatively limited in enrollment, is the counterpart of state universities in the United States. Its graduates are generally viewed as the best and the brightest, and it provides an important avenue for upward mobility for graduates of public schools. But the majority of students attend private institutions: older, church-related universities for those of greater means or higher religious orientation and relatively new, often for-profit, secular institutions for most of the rest. The students or their families fund their studies, often at great sacrifice.

Though the U.S. educational system, like the U.S. congressional system, is unique, it is no longer fashionable to proclaim the superiority of either. After World War II Americans discarded the isolationist ideas of the prewar period and adopted a more universalist approach. Desirable as this was in many respects, the attempt to understand other cultures led to a drawing back from value judgments. It became unsophisticated and even jingoistic to enunciate the view that the American way of doing things was superior to other countries' ways of doing things.

The Emergence of a New Principle for Enfranchisement

At the same time that people began to perceive the U.S. system of government as just another form of democracy, as a variant on parliamentary democracy but not significantly different, another series of struggles for independence commenced. In these struggles of colonial peoples for independence, the right to self-government came to be symbolized by the right to vote. "One man, one vote" was born of necessity, a crucial weapon in independence struggles, just as "government by the people" had been 200 years earlier.

Because the colonizing countries were democracies, at least after World War II, and because government by the people had become a widely accepted ideal, logic required the colonizers to enunciate a basis for denying to colonial peoples a right considered undeniable in the home country. The basis for denial was the colonial peoples' alleged unpreparedness or inability to govern.

The colonial powers controlled the educational systems and limited access to advanced education to native elites somewhat acculturated to the colonial culture and somewhat co-opted by the colonial rulers. The colonizers thereby assured perpetual unpreparedness for self-government by the majority of the population, which favored independence. One man, one vote thus became a necessary counterprinciple.

The demand for a vote for everyone was not just a powerful rallying point in the struggles of the twentieth century for national independence. One man, one vote became equally necessary in the U.S. civil rights movement.

However, in the United States the populace was largely literate and generally well educated by the time of the civil rights movement. Thus, elimination of an explicit literacy requirement restored voting rights to those undeservedly deprived of equal rights without introducing significant percentages of uneducated citizens into the electorate. U.S. democracy, accordingly, was affected positively by one man, one vote.

The Vulnerability of Parliamentary Democracy

In the developing world, where large percentages of the population lack an adequate education, one man, one vote creates an electorate that mirrors the low educational levels of the general population. Parliamentary government, which requires less of the electorate, seemingly is suited better to such situations. However, inasmuch as parliamentary government lacks the checks against despotism found in the congressional system, it is also more vulnerable to takeover by despots.

If one examines successful parliamentary democracies around the world, one finds that most are in countries whose populations are relatively homogenous (e.g., Japan, Singapore, and Western Europe). If political power is transferred in a parliamentary democracy to the opposition party, the break with the policies of the previous government is often dramatic. The society must be relatively stable to be able to endure with equanimity the drastic wrench which is entailed.

Moreover, successful parliamentary democracies in non-Western countries are often those which have avoided the shock of a change of power because they have been governed for extended periods by a single party (e.g., India, Japan, Malaysia, and Singapore). Often they have been led for extended periods by a single prime minister (India and Singapore).

Many of those parliamentary democracies that have failed have been in countries with a relatively high degree of ethnic or regional friction or considerable socioeconomic differences. In such societies, where a long tradition of democratic government is absent, democracy comes under threat not only from leaders with a thirst for personal power. It also is in danger from those who feel threatened by the uncompromising position either of the party in power or the party waiting in the wings.

Parliamentary democracy is not likely to be a viable alternative in most countries where it has not already been implanted successfully. Where efforts to implant parliamentary democracy have foundered on ethnic or socioeconomic divisions and the absence of checks and balances, recreating the same institution is hardly a promising approach.

The Vulnerability of Congressional Democracy

U.S. congressional democracy appears to have answers to the problems posed by regional and social divisiveness, as well as by the temptation to seek absolute power. But to achieve its promise, it requires a relatively well educated electorate.

In a congressional system, a legislature responsive to a poorly educated electorate is likely to generate legislation that either is unwise, thus not in the national interest, or that appears inimical to the haves of society. Such a system will be inherently unstable, either because the nation will suffer or because those with the instruments of power will reject it.

The dilemma is clear: one form of democracy cannot survive without an educated electorate and the other form cannot survive without preexisting unity and democratic traditions. This brings the reader to the central question for U.S. democrats surveying the world scene: how does one best promote democracy where it does not now exist?

Late twentieth-century Americans are reluctant to proclaim U.S. democracy as either more virtuous or more efficacious than parliamentary democracy. Even without this constraint, Americans are an impatient people, and this impatience discourages acknowledgement of education as a sine qua non for congressional democracy with universal suffrage. The idea of less than universal suffrage causes extreme discomfort because of its inconsistency with American egalitarianism. Disenfranchisement of otherwise worthy people who lack an education appears to many to imply a value judgment on the personal worth of the disenfranchised.

From the Thomasites of the U.S. colonial period in the Philippines to the Peace Corps volunteers of John F. Kennedy, Americans have a tradition of dedicated sacrifice abroad for the principles of education. This earlier dedication was not misplaced. Where societies are too unstable for parliamentary democracy, education can provide the foundations for successful congressional democracy.

It appears Americans should reach back to an earlier tradition and once more preach the gospel of free, universal, quality education, in tandem with congressional democracy. But ed-

ucation is a long-term process. For the short term, the challenge is to promote democracy in societies that are not highly literate.

Creating a Democratic System That Will Survive

Universal suffrage is today too well embedded in the structure of democracy to be abandoned. The need, then, is for a mechanism that will be politically acceptable yet will substitute for an educated electorate. The solution appears to lie in the original structure of U.S. democracy.

The Founding Fathers desired that the Senate be a more august body than the House, that it change slowly rather than be responsive to popular whim, and that it represent broader interests than the House. They accomplished this in part through six-year staggered terms and at-large elections by state (rather than election by district). They also sought to achieve this through election by a more highly qualified electorate. Senators were to be elected by legislatures, as state legislators were thought likely to be highly qualified.

With this precedent, it would appear eminently reasonable to suggest that a higher educational level would be appropriate for those electing senators. The lower House, of course, would be elected by universal suffrage, giving voice to the entire population of each district. But the Senate, intended from the outset of U.S. democracy to provide a counterweight to the presumably more impetuous House, could well be elected only by those with a specified level of education.

Voting qualifications for the Senate might appropriately include a post-elementary standard, such as a seventh-grade education, or a high-school education, or something in between. Introduction of such a qualification, easily understood by the electorate, would retain the essential elements of direct, popular election. Yet it would largely accomplish the results sought by the United States' Founding Fathers, in a fashion more compatible with twentieth-century concepts.

Some may object that a more limited electorate for the Senate could produce a Senate so vastly different from the House as to produce deadlocks, perhaps rendering the system unworkable. But if so, these differences would reflect societal differences of such vastness as to lead to dictatorship if not contained within a system with formal checks and balances. Holding back from the reform will not resolve the conflicts.

While deadlock certainly would be preferable to dictatorship, what is more likely is that the congressional system's institutional structure will bring about compromise. The U.S. structure was intended to balance a House elected on the basis of population with a Senate where the smaller states enjoyed disproportionate weight. The interests of large and small states were not completely antithetical, however, just as the interests of rich and poor or educated and noneducated are not totally antithetical. Thus, there are likely to be ample bases for successful legislative compromise, whatever the difference in outlook between Senate and House.

Furthermore, if the masses already share political power, through domi-

nance in one House, then universal education is far less threatening to an elite seeking to preserve its power and status. Indeed, the elite may come to see education as positive, encouraging a responsible electorate that will elect responsible representatives.

Turning Promise into Reality

Americans should continue their support for free elections in nondemocratic societies. But they should accompany this support with unabashed advocacy of congressional democracy, structured as described above. While advocating congressional democracy may appear an illiberal rejection of the democratic contributions of Americans' British brethren, it is clear that the parliamentary model has not met the needs of much of the Third World.

The Third World is no less suited to democratic government than was the newly independent United States—initially a confederation of thirteen disunited states that nearly succumbed to anarchy. However, exhortations to democracy can be meaningful only if the institutional framework allows for success.

Most countries of the world subscribe to democracy as an ideal, but few attain it. Without the proper institutional framework there can be no government "of the people, by the people, and for the people." To convert the universal longing for responsive, representative government into reality is feasible, but it requires first of all the creation of the institutions that can make it happen.

Tocqueville Revisited: Are Good Democracies Bad Players in the Game of Nations?

Josef Joffe

"IT IS ESPECIALLY in the conduct of their foreign relations," Tocqueville wrote, "that democracies appear to me decidedly inferior to other governments."[1] This classic statement has become part of our conventional wisdom, and the twentieth century has not done much to dispel Tocqueville's somber dictum. To be sure, the democracies have won the great wars—but only after they had lost the peace. They were good at fighting to the limits of human endurance but bad at playing the game of diplomacy that requires not cataclysmic exertion but patient, measured, and, above all, steady effort.

Before World War I France and Britain failed either to contain or conciliate the rising power of Prussia-Germany—hence the great test of strength and the unprecedented bloodletting that was the war of 1914–1918. Nor did the Treaty of Versailles, the product par excellence of the new democratic spirit in world affairs, bequeath a stable, let alone legitimate, order to Europe. First, there was the darker side of the democratic ethos: having bled in the war, the masses now demanded

a voice in the peace—and that translated into a settlement suffused with retribution, which in turn planted the seed for the war to come.[2] Second, liberal-democratic ideology made short shrift of the requirements of a stable postwar balance. Instead of drawing viable borders in the East, Versailles decreed borders that were to follow the distribution of nationalities—with scant regard to the conflicts these new entities, such as Poland and Czechoslovakia, henceforth would create by dint of their mere shape or existence.

Finally, having established a complicated peace, the democracies were not very good at securing it, recalling Tocqueville's warning that "a democracy can only with great difficulty regulate the details of an important undertaking, persevere in a fixed design, and work out its execution in spite of serious obstacles."[3] Their energies spent in the Great War, the democratic powers (with the exception of France) did what comes naturally to a democracy. Britain and the United States turned inward, repudiating those (like Woodrow Wilson) who had drawn them into the European balance and refusing to shoulder the diplomatic and military costs the main-

Josef Joffe is foreign editor and columnist of the *Süddeutsche Zeitung* in Munich.

Josef Joffe

tenance of peace required. The disastrous results are familiar enough. With Britain and the United States out of the system, the power of the revisionists Germany and the Soviet Union began to seep into the vacuum. While there was still time to resist a resurgent Nazi Germany, "Britain slept" (as the famous little treatise by John F. Kennedy termed it) and the United States withdrew from Europe. And none of the democracies, France included, paid attention to the military dimension of diplomacy until it was too late.

Whence this pattern that Tocqueville dimly foresaw and that the record of the interwar period so tragically exemplified? Tocqueville's own answer, which echoes the claims of such other nineteenth-century thinkers as Auguste Comte and Herbert Spencer and before them the *philosophes* of the Enlightenment, is that "democratic nations naturally desire peace."[4] Hence, the neglect of military power in times of tranquility.[5] "The warlike passions," he wrote, "will become more rare and less intense in proportion as social conditions are more equal." He listed numerous factors which "concur to quench the military spirit" in a democracy simply because such a system inherently favors the "equality of conditions."

The ever increasing numbers of men of property who are lovers of peace, the growth of personal wealth which war so rapidly consumes, the mildness of manners, the gentleness of heart, those tendencies to pity [which are produced by equality], that coolness of understanding which renders men comparatively insensible to the violent and poetical excitement of arms. . . . [6]

Unlike Condorcet and Turgot, Comte and Spenser, Tocqueville

understood, however, that democracies are neither inherently nor permanently pacific. (This insight is all the more remarkable, given that he wrote before the Civil War and the two world wars that would amply demonstrate the democracies' capacity for violence.) Though "it is extremely difficult in democratic times to draw nations into hostilities," Tocqueville argued, democracies are as bloody-minded as any other system once war has broken out. "When a war has at length. . .roused the whole community from their peaceful occupations and ruined their minor undertakings, the same passions that made them attach so much importance to the maintenance of peace will be turned to arms."[7]

In modern parlance, Tocqueville rendered a "binary theory" of democratic behavior: it is either yes or no, war or peace, passion or passivity. Yet what about foreign policy proper—the actions of nations between those extremes? Here Tocqueville is unambiguously pessimistic. At home, democracies are good at increasing and spreading wealth; they promote the "public spirit" and fortify the "respect for the law." But these advantages are at best incidental to the pursuit of foreign affairs. Here the premium is on endurance, perseverance, and attention to detail. Nor can a democracy "combine its measures with secrecy or await their consequences with patience. These are qualities that more especially belong to an individual or an aristocracy"—and "by which a nation, like an individual, attains a dominant position."[8]

If democracies are at best capable of stark choices—between war or peace, between the *levée en masse* or the life of the *bourgeois gentilhomme*—then it follows that they are equipped badly to deal with the rich spectrum

124

of choices in between, also known as "foreign policy" or "diplomacy." Such a gloomy conclusion should come as no surprise if we lengthen the lines of Tocqueville's analysis and contrast the ways of diplomacy with those of democracy.

Diplomacy is a game of ambiguous rules and stark dilemmas that are not so much resolved as they must be muted or suspended. It is a game of balance and appeasement where force is only the last resort—and even then it must be carefully constrained by the overarching purposes of policy. Diplomacy is the art of ruse and reinsurance, and as such, it does not divide the world into permanent friends and foes. Democratic politics thrives on publicity and public discourse; in fact, democracy cannot endure without the clamor of contending ideas and interests. Diplomacy, on the other hand, must act with circumspection and even secrecy; it frequently pretends to aspire to one objective (which it portrays as lofty and universal) even as it pursues another (which happens to be base and self-serving).

In the end the game of nations obeys no other law than that of reciprocity, yet a democracy is nothing if it does not obey the rule of law. Totalitarian-revolutionary regimes have never confused the Hobbesian realm of international politics with the predictable, legitimate, and hierarchical structures of domestic governance; a Stalin or a Hitler held on to contracts or promises only as long as these constraints did not interfere with the supreme interest of party and state. Democracies, on the other hand, are prone almost constitutionally to view the world as an extension of their domestic polities. They confuse the realm of law with the realm of power; they believe that international law has somehow the same hold on nations as domestic law has on citizens; indeed, they even hope (cf. Messrs. Kellog and Briand) that legal norms can undo international politics and then reconstitute it as a subspecies of domestic politics, with peaceful negotiation or compulsory adjudication unseating violence as the supreme arbiter among nations.

If diplomacy must be subtle, democracy lives the rough and tumble of domestic politics that ranges from the din of demonstrations to the demagoguery of the politico on the stump. Democracies decide their fates by choosing between crudely packaged alternatives in the shape of persons or ideologies; diplomacy seeks to enlarge options even as it purports to make a choice. Finally, notwithstanding perennial pleas, such as "politics stops at the water's edge," democracy does not really bow before the concept of raison d'état as a disembodied, almost Platonic idea of the national interest; in a democratic society, any issue is fair game as long as it promises electoral profit. In short, the art of diplomacy does not seem to lend itself to the democratic ethos, let alone to the democratic temper.

II.

Given these contrasts between the two realms and the "two cultures," Tocqueville surely must be right in claiming that, "in the conduct of their foreign relations, democracies appear decidedly inferior to other governments." Still, how do we test this theorem? What shall we put into the sample, and which slice of history shall we apply to the Master's yardstick? While it is true that the democracies failed in the pursuit of peace before and after World War I, what about the record after World War II?

It can be argued fairly that the

United States, as the democratic power par excellence, quite nicely disproved Tocqueville's skeptical predictions in the decades after 1947. Indeed, during these years the United States displayed all the qualities thought to be wanting in a democratic great power. Moving in the ambiguous realm of "neither war nor peace," the United States surely would have flummoxed the French sage who insisted, "Almost all the nations that have exercised a powerful influence upon the destinies of the world, by conceiving, following out, and executing vast designs, from the Romans to the English, have been governed by aristocratic institutions."[9]

In the decades of the postwar era the United States not only executed a "vast design" by singlehandedly erecting a new order on the ashes of the old; it also "persevered" in spite of "serious obstacles," to use Tocqueville's terminology. Within the confines of the democratic-industrial world, the United States built a global trading system (the Marshall Plan and GATT), a global monetary system (the IMF), an interlocking security system (NATO, SEATO, ANZUS, and, as a silent partner, CENTO), and a would-be global government (the UN) at least initially dominated by the United States. Nor did the United States lack the "patience" Tocqueville found absent in a democracy. In fact, the record of the 1950s and 1960s exemplified rather nicely the counsel George F. Kennan laid out in his oft-quoted "X" article of 1947: the "main element of any United States policy toward the Soviet Union must be that of a long-term, patient, but firm and vigilant containment of Russian expansive tendencies."[10]

Indeed, the history of U.S. containment policy during the first quarter-century of its career as a truly global power defies both Tocqueville and Kennan, who would soon go beyond the Master's melancholy critique of democracy and serve up the following acerbic indictment:

> I sometimes wonder whether . . . a democracy is not uncomfortably similar to one of those prehistoric monsters with a body as long as this room and a brain the size of a pin; he lies in his comfortable primeval mud and pays little attention to his environment; he is slow to wrath—in fact, you practically have to whack his tail off to make him aware that his interests are being disturbed; but, once he grasps this, he lays about him with such blind determination that he not only destroys his adversary but largely wrecks his native habitat. You wonder whether it would not have been wiser for him to have taken a little more interest in what was going on at an earlier date and to have seen whether he could not have prevented some of these situations from arising.[11]

In spite of its "roll-back" rhetoric and its quasi-nuclear monopoly until the mid-1960s, the United States did not "lay about with blind determination"; nor did the United States need to have its "tail whacked off" to make it respond to its "interests being disturbed." Indeed, the bulk of U.S. policy was dedicated precisely to prevention and stabilization, which are a central purpose of diplomacy. In contrast to the interwar period, the United States did not withdraw from Europe but mounted a permanent military presence there. Far from ignoring the social and economic roots of military conflict, the United States infused capital, opened its own markets, and goaded the West Europeans into trade-expanding integration. The

United States, in short, did not "obey impulse rather than prudence"; nor did it "abandon a mature design for the gratification of a momentary passion."[12] Had Tocqueville lived, he surely would have added another chapter to *Democracy in America*, modifying his earlier pessimistic conclusions in praise of Republican foreign policy.

It is not clear, however, whether he would have held up the Soviet Union as a model—the totalitarian version of an oligarchy (one bridles at calling it an "aristocracy," which the Tocquevillian vocabulary always contrasts with "democracy"). The Soviet Union has all the presumptive advantages lacking in a democracy: secrecy, a "vast (doctrinal) design," and the ability to "combine, upon a single point and at a given time, so much power as an aristocracy or an absolute monarchy."[13] Yet how well has the Soviet Union fared in the world?

Like the democracies, it failed to deal with the menace of Nazi Germany until it was too late. After World War II the Soviet Union certainly failed to achieve its stated goal, the maintenance of the anti-Hitler coalition, reaping the enmity of its erstwhile friend instead. It did not win hegemony over Europe but rather the nasty fruits of the cold war—with countervailing alliances and constant counterpressure around its borders. In spite of assiduous diplomatic effort, Moscow did not manage to break the encircling ring of bases and allies the United States had thrown up. Where it leapfrogged those barriers, as in Egypt in the 1950s, the Soviet Union was expelled again in the early 1970s. Since then the Soviets have been excluded effectively from a peacemaking role in the Middle East. In Cuba, the greatest test of strength of the postwar era, Moscow was humiliated. After the

defection of Yugoslavia, the Soviet Union "lost" China in the 1960s—as had the United States in the late 1940s. Even within its pontifical and political empire in Eastern Europe, the USSR could hold on to its allies only by regular recourse to force. And where the Soviets did breach the ring, it finished with politically costly or economically wasteful engagements without apparent end—in Afghanistan, Angola, Cuba, and Ethiopia.

The purpose of this list is to make a point so obvious that it often is ignored in woeful comparisons between "us" and "them": by the yardstick of success and failure, it is by no means evident that the totalitarian regimes play a more nimble and intelligent game than the democracies. The postwar tally does not favor the Soviet Union, and, while it is possible to argue endlessly about what is and is not a gain or loss, the United States has done much better than Tocqueville predicted. There is, presumably, a good reason why the Master's record as a soothsayer is less than perfect.

It is never quite clear whether Tocqueville wrote about the failings of democracy as such or the peculiar state of America in the nineteenth century. Though he located the root cause of foreign-policy insufficiency in the constitution of a democracy, his eye was too sharp to ignore the obvious: that democratic America was sui generis by dint of geography. His commentary is filled with references to America's blessed condition, yet he did not engage in "multivariate analysis" by explicitly distinguishing between geography and democracy as they affect foreign policy. With the benefits of hindsight, we can and must draw that distinction today, and the result is arguably that the foreign policy effects Tocqueville attributed to democracy can be linked just as easily—if not better—to America's benign insular state in the nineteenth century. As that condition waned, America's behavior in the world changed—regardless of its abiding democratic constitution.

The "United States is a nation without neighbors," Tocqueville mused more than once. "Separated from the rest of the world by the ocean . . . it has no enemies, and its interests rarely come into contact with those of any other nation on the globe."[14] Elsewhere he asked, "How does it happen . . . that the American Union . . . is not dissolved by the occurrence of a great war? It is because it has no great wars to fear. Placed in the center of an immense continent . . . the Union is almost as much insulated from the world as if all its frontiers were girt by the ocean." He continued, "The great advantage of the United States . . . consists in a geographical position which renders . . . wars extremely improbable."[15] Whence it followed,

As the Union takes no part in the affairs of Europe, it has, properly speaking, no foreign interests to discuss, since it has, as yet, no powerful neighbor on the American continent. The country is as much removed from the passions of the Old World by its position as by its wishes, and it is called upon neither to repudiate nor to espouse them; while the dissensions of the New World are still concealed within the bosom of the future.

The Union is free from all pre-existing obligations; it can profit by the experience of the old nations of Europe, without being obliged, as they are, to make the best of the past and to adapt it to their present circumstances. It is not, like them, compelled to accept an immense inheritance bequeathed by their forefathers, an inheritance of glory mingled with

calamities and of alliances conflicting with national antipathies. The foreign policy of the United States is eminently expectant: it consists more in abstaining than in acting. It is therefore very difficult to ascertain, at present, what degree of sagacity the American democracy will display in the conduct of the foreign policy of the country; upon that point its adversaries as well as its friends must suspend their judgment.[16]

In short, the United States did not have a foreign policy because it did not need one. The jury was still out while Tocqueville was writing; therefore, he was right in tempering his policy-is-destiny theory with the insights from history and geography. He evidently sensed that there was (or more accurately, would be) more to American foreign policy than the peculiarities of a democratic constitution, and that eventually the "international system" would claim its due—overshadowing or reversing what democracy-cum-insularity allowed.

Once the United States was forced into the system for good (after the final collapse of the European balance during World War II) it had to play by the rules of that system and shelve both "abstinence" and "expectancy." Though a democracy, the United States had to adapt to a game as old as the nation-state itself, and to rules determined not by Montesquieu and Locke but at least in part by Hitler and Stalin. To eschew balance, raison d'état, and realpolitik in favor of the Founding Fathers' ethos was one thing while the British navy ruled the Atlantic; it was another once the power of the totalitarians reached out across the sea. No wonder, then, that the predictions of Tocqueville held good only as long as the conditions that had spawned them endured. Once the United States was plunged into the existential condition of the classic great powers, America-the-Democracy was forced to behave like them, regardless of its constitution. Yet even Tocqueville, though drawn to "domestic determinism," clearly anticipated what his own theory apparently excluded—that the "system" would eventually impose itself on the "sub-system," changing a great many questions and answers in the process.

III.

How many questions and answers have changed today? Though events have blunted Tocqueville's glum conclusions, their abiding relevance cannot be gainsaid. Indeed, in many respects his pessimism actually falls short of reality because this relevance unfolded after that quarter-century during which the United States brilliantly and patiently had erected a global order whose benefits still are enjoyed today. Four shibboleths suggest where the problems lurk at the close of the twentieth century: Vietnam, Irangate, the "Post-Imperial Presidency," and nuclear weapons, none of which really demolishes the framework of Tocqueville's analysis.

The Vietnam War clearly showed that a democracy cannot "combine, upon a single point at a given time, so much power as an aristocracy or an absolute monarchy." Nor is this an American failing alone. Israel, the most "Sparta-like" nation in the annals of democracy, ran afoul the limits of democratic power during its "first imperial war" in Lebanon in 1982. France lived through the same experience in Algeria, and Britain presumably would have, too, if the Suez War had not been terminated swiftly by U.S. pressure. By contrast, the Soviet Union has been fighting in Afghanistan for eight years; if and when that war ends, it will not be because of popular revulsion.

The lesson seems clear: democracy cannot "persevere in a fixed design and work out its execution in spite of serious obstacles" if that design is (a) open-ended and (b) dependent on force while only remotely related to "core security," i.e., the protection of the national space. In contrast to Vietnam, Grenada and the Falklands were "worked out" because success came swiftly and relatively cost-free. Yet the U.S. intervention in Lebanon was cut short abruptly once the prospect of no victory combined with the dramatic loss of American lives. Democracies, as Tocqueville would agree readily, are not fond of Clausewitz. While they are wedded to peace and, in the end, willing to plunge into unlimited war, democracies do not move smoothly along the "Clausewitzian continuum" where diplomacy and violence are but shades of one and the same spectrum of options. Hence Tocqueville's dictum, "There are two things that a democratic people always will find very difficult, to begin a war and to end it."[17] Unless they can be mobilized by great threats or great ideologies, democracies will hearken the call of peace and shy away from force as adjunct of policy.

Irangate symbolizes a second constitutional weakness. On the most obvious level, the episode buttresses Tocqueville's point that a democracy "cannot combine its measures with secrecy." (Even that exemplar of a "republican monarchy," France, could not get away with the bombing of a Greenpeace ship in New Zealand.) Yet there is a more profound moral to the story. To act in the name of raison d'état, which sometimes requires saying one thing as one does another, does not sit well with the democratic ethos that demands that the government submit to the same rules abroad that are sanctified at home, even with the Khomeinis of this world. When Lieutenant Colonel Oliver North, in 1987, testified to the Congress (in so many words) that "I lied for the good of the nation, and I would do it again," he expressed the classic tenet of realpolitik, echoing Churchill's famous remark, "Sometimes the truth is so precious that it must be surrounded by a bodyguard of lies." To which the predictable reply was, "If you lied to them, how do we know that you will not lie to the Congress?"

If Col. North invoked the distinction between the two realms, which lies at the heart of raison d'état, the Congress insisted on their congruence. From the vantage point of realism, North was right—as was Hobbes before him. Morality, though cast in universal precepts, does not flourish in independence from political community. To triumph, morality requires law, and law requires a sovereign with the indispensable accoutrements of enforcement, hence the ultimate powers of the state. Lying to the Congress has consequences—all the way to prison. Lying to the Khomeinis, i.e., between political communities not beholden to a common law, is an entirely different game. To begin with, we cannot rely on their veracity, let alone have their duplicity punished by a third, "objective" party. Second, the name of the game of nations is not truth but advantage, and, while it might help to have a reputation for reliability, such a posture might just as well invite the less scrupulous to exploit our credulity. Finally, in dealing with enemies, the measure of an act is not goodness but success: Does it minimize harm and maximize security?

Yet a democracy beholden to moral principles and the rule of law always will be uncomfortable with the eternal clash between ideal and interest, hence with the separation of the two realms. How can a good end justify bad means? If we play the game of the totalitarians, will we not become like them? Can the state still be good at home if it acts immorally abroad? This is why democracies are superb at fighting wars against the "children of darkness": their supreme evil easily justifies the lesser evils forced upon the "children of light." Yet short of Armageddon, the advantage is bound to lie with those who play by their own rules.

The "Post-Imperial Presidency" outlines a third problem area. In terms of his legal rights, the "President of the United States possesses almost royal prerogatives,"[18] Tocqueville noted. The Founding Fathers intended the president to embody the interests of the nation as a whole, giving him powers unequaled among the chief executives of the Western world. Presumably, his brief was to run widest where the "national interest" came into play vis-à-vis other nations. This idea was hardly different from the classic European concept of raison d'état or the *Primat der Aussenpolitik*; indeed, there is even a perfectly American phrase for it: "Politics stops at the water's edge."

Though many tend to idealize the era cut short in the aftermath of the Gulf of Tonkin Resolution as the golden age of the presidency, American politics—perhaps with the exception of the two world wars—has never stopped at the water's edge. The very idea of reason of state is, in itself, inimical to the idea of democracy. If the people are the sovereign, why should certain issues be excluded from public debate? The very idea of the primacy of foreign policy is antidemocratic (and was so conceived by its German inventors under the guise of lofty precept in the nineteenth century) because it presumes a "national" interest defined and guarded by an elite beyond the sway of the domestic political contest. In the democratic arena, any issue is fair game—whether it is federal taxes or Iranian terrorists. While the welfare of the state ought to be a limiting factor, it is not so in practice as long as the foreign issue at hand holds out electoral gain.

The cycles may come and go, and perhaps there soon will be another time when party discipline is restored along with the power of congressional committee chairmen, when there will be one rather than 436 secretaries of state, when a presidential aspirant like Jesse Jackson will not usurp the role of the U.S. ambassador in Syria. Yet the basic problem is endemic to democracy, and it is as manifest in Bonn, one of the youngest democracies, as it is in Washington, the oldest. The totalitarians always will be able to deliberate *in camera*, the democracies always will have to debate in the public square, and then untrammeled by any disembodied notion of raison d'état. This imposes a double handicap on the democracies: the nondemocratic players will know much of their opponents' hand before it is played. And in part, they even can determine how the deck is stacked. In a society dedicated to the freedom of information and speech, even non-nationals can enter into the debate, make their case heard and manipulate the domestic line-up while insulating their own society against the intrusion of their democratic rivals. It is a handicap, however, that knows no other remedy than the loss of liberty—a price too high to pay for "equality of opportunity" in the contest of nations.

Fourth and last, there is the problem of nuclear weapons. Until 1945

U.S. history surely conformed to Tocqueville's "binary theory" of democratic foreign policy, with peace and war being rigorously separated states of the American condition. While the Europeans experienced both in endless alternation, with nary a decisive outcome, the United States did manage to achieve "final solutions" that obliterated the threat once and for all. If enemies could not be reformed, they were crushed. At home, the British were expelled, the Indians reduced to a harmless minority, and the South beaten into submission. Abroad, the Spaniards similarly were extruded from the hemisphere, and in the twentieth century Wilhelm II, Hitler, and Hirohito were forced to surrender unconditionally (whence political conversion at last, could take its course).

Yet the nuclear age definitely has eliminated defeat as an objective of U.S. policy, and, as a result, the enemy's domestication, too, remains only a distant hope. Sheltered by vast deterrent strength, the United States and the Soviet Union cannot hope to prevail over each other. Yet precisely because they possess overwhelming destructive power, they cannot trust each other. Hence they are doomed to unending rivalry that resembles the condition of Europe's great powers in the eighteenth and nineteenth centuries—and for reasons Tocqueville would have understood easily.

On the one hand, because there is nobody else to shoulder the global burden, the United States now has to play the classic game of nations—of balance, containment, and partial accommodation (also known as arms control and détente). On the other hand, that crown does not sit easily on America's head, given an older American tradition characterized by the familiar oscillation between radical intervention and radical isolation. Such a tradition does not make for stable behavior. Thus, by Tocqueville's standards, U.S. foreign policy was at its best in the early postwar decades—when the Cold War functioned as the long-term moral equivalent of a real war against the "children of darkness," when the electorate was in a steady state of ideological mobilization, when presidents from Truman to Johnson were handed a "blank check" denominated in the currency of popular support for each and for any task assumed by the "Imperial Republic," as Raymond Aron called it.

Yet democracies, and most of all a true child of the Enlightenment like the United States, do not cherish the idea of permanent conflict. The historical optimism of the Enlightenment revolves around the core idea of transcendence, and in that teleology evil and strife appear as mere stepping stones on the path to ultimate salvation. With salvation foreclosed by nuclear bipolarity, there are the familiar cycles of postwar American policy. Set in motion by grand hopes for a "real" settlement and by ideological demobilization, they are completed by inevitable disappointment and moral as well as real rearmament. If Roosevelt brought us "Uncle Joe," Truman unleashed his containment doctrine (and war in Korea), followed by Dulles's "pactomania." Johnson's globalist vision foundered in Vietnam, spawning the antiwar movement and McGovern's cry, "Come home, America." In reaction to Nixon's realpolitik, Jimmy Carter offered "world order" and the call to "shed our inordinate fear of Communism." In turn, that brought about militant neo-containment à la Reagan, massive rearmament, and the doxology of the "evil empire." Hardly into his second term, Reagan II turned against Reagan I,

taking the road to Reykjavik and descending with the message of wholesale nuclear disarmament. Such cycles do not make for a foreign policy where a "mature design" overwhelms the "gratification of a momentary passion."[19]

Another implication of nuclear bipolarity, though more in the nature of a possibility, returns us once more to the conclusions Tocqueville drew from America's unique insular situation. By an ironic twist of history and for the first time since the British navy ruled the Atlantic, nuclear weapons and intercontinental missiles have brought the will o' the wisp of isolationism at least within theoretical reach. Robert W. Tucker suggested the following logic of a nuclear Fortress America:

> Having withdrawn once again from the world beyond this hemisphere, though now possessed of a surfeit of deterrent power in form of nuclear missile weapons, we would have little reason to fear attack, for an attacker would know with virtual certainty that he had far more to lose than to gain from so acting. To this extent, nuclear missile weapons give substance to the long-discredited isolationist dream. So long as it is clear that they will be employed only in the direct defense of the homeland, they confer a physical security that is virtually complete, and that the loss of allies cannot alter.[20]

Though the case can be refuted plausibly,[21] it should not be dismissed because the isolationist instinct has by no means disappeared. The Strategic Defense Initiative is surely one manifestation; the neoconservative (and liberal) critiques of America's presence in Europe is another. Insofar as nuclear weapons "give substance to the isolationist dream," they also dramatize Tocqueville's fundamental point about America's "great advantage"—and its enduring temptation: a "geographical position which renders . . . wars extremely improbable."[22] Physical insulation has been pierced by technology. But ironically, nuclear weapons have replicated that American *Ur*-condition, which evokes security without dependence and entanglement, hence the blessings of a setting where sagacity, patience, and attention to detail might no longer need to contend with the democratic temper.

IV.

Tocqueville wrote about the tension between democracy-in-America and America-in-the-world and kept in suspense by the country's blessed geographical condition. Nuclear bipolarity embodies a similar tension. Bipolarity bids the United States to play the game of balance and containment on a global scale, to compensate for each and every shift, to harness allies, and to deny them to its great adversary. Nuclear weapons, contrarily, transmit a countervailing message. They spell not nervous vigilance and steady exertion but safety and indifference. When it comes to "core security," the United States can deter by itself any and each challenger, singly or in combination. Though nuclear weapons invoke supreme terror, they also confer a margin of security no great power ever has enjoyed.

Such an asset translates into great leeway for error, but unlike the physical distance that once separated the United States from the rest of the world, lesser nations risk deadly punishment for smallish errors. Even for great powers (e.g., France in the 1930s), existential consequences can grow from faults Tocqueville saw rooted in the ethos and temper of democracy. Yet there is also solace in Tocqueville's diagnosis, for America in particular and the democracies in general.

"Though a democracy is more liable to error than a monarchy or a body of nobles," he postulated, "the chances of its regaining the right path when once it has acknowledged its mistake are greater also; because it is rarely embarrassed by interests that conflict with those of the majority and resist the authority of reason." Nonetheless, there is a nasty twist to this soothing message: "But a democracy can obtain truth only as result of experience; and many nations may perish while they are awaiting the consequences of their errors."

Yet the United States is different: "The great privilege of the Americans does not consist in being more enlightened than other nations, but in being able to repair the faults they may commit."[23] Historically, this verdict is surely correct—with Pearl Harbor and the victorious aftermath serving as the most dramatic piece of evidence. Yet it is not clear whether the solace stems from democracy or rather from geography and sheer power (which is just another word for a wide margin for error). And so the fundamental question persists: Is the United States wise or just lucky? Does America's "great privilege" grow from its marvelous political system—or in fact from past physical insulation and its latter day nuclear equivalent?

Notes

1. Alexis de Tocqueville, *Democracy in America*, vol. I (New York: Random House, Vintage Books, 1945), p. 243.

2. It is instructive to compare Versailles with the outcome of the Prussian war against Austria in 1866 and the Franco-Prussian

War of 1870–1871. In 1866 Bismarck still could resist the popular cry for a march on Vienna, exacting no more than the cession of Holstein while countering the *grossdeutsch* nationalists with the classic counsel of diplomatic prudence, "We shall need Austrian strength for ourselves later." A mere five years later the handwriting of mass participation was already on the wall, and the clamor of the populace could not longer be stilled. Though Bismarck was loath to take Alsace and Lorraine from defeated France for fear of provoking a future war, nationalist sentiment forced his hand, thus paving the road to World War I.

3. *Tocqueville*, p. 243.

4. Thus the title of chapter 23, *Democracy in America*, vol. II.

5. "Among democratic nations in time of peace the military profession is held in little honor and practiced with little spirit." Vol. II, p. 292.

6. Vol. I, p. 279.

7. Vol. II, p. 292.

8. Vol. I, p. 243–244.

9. *Ibid.*, p. 245.

10. "The Sources of Soviet Conduct," *Foreign Affairs*, July 1947, p. 575.

11. George F. Kennan, *American Diplomacy, 1900–1950* (Chicago: University of Chicago Press, 1951), p. 66.

12. Vol. I, p. 244.

13. *Ibid.*, p. 238.

14. *Ibid.*, p. 131.

15. *Ibid.*, p. 178.

16. *Ibid.*, p. 242–243 (emphasis added).

17. Vol. II, p. 283.

18. Vol. I, p. 131.

19. *Ibid.*, p. 244.

20. "Containment and the Search for Alternatives: A Critique," in Aaron Wildavsky, ed., *Beyond Containment* (San Francisco, Calif.: Institute for Contemporary Studies Press, 1983), p. 81. Tucker states the case only in order to reject it.

21. I have tried to do so in *The Limited Partnership: Europe, the United States, and the Burdens of Alliance* (Cambridge, Mass.: Ballinger Publishing Company, 1987), ch. 5.

22. Vol. I, p. 178.

23. *Ibid.*, p. 239.

IV. The United States and the Democratic Revolution

Developing Democracy at Home and Abroad

Charles S. Robb

THE SEARCH FOR social justice and economic prosperity in the decades ahead must learn from both the successes and failures of past efforts to achieve these twin aspirations. We are fortunate to enjoy a rich variety of national experiences in overcoming obstacles to political and economic participation. This analysis draws from one particular experiment—that of the United States—for lessons of broader implication.

I am mindful of the danger in offering the United States as a model for democratic and socioeconomic development. If I were to emphasize the United States' achievements in developing democracy, I would risk the arrogance of implying the universal applicability of our institutions and ethics. Yet, there is little to be gained in a one-sided critique of the failings of U.S. social policy.

I will try to resolve that dilemma by assessing first the ways to make U.S. democracy more worthy of emulation by others. Then I will suggest how the same principles can be applied to foster democratic development abroad.

The Continuing U.S. Experiment

If the U.S. experience is to have any bearing on the problems other nations

Charles S. Robb, a former governor of Virginia, is currently U.S. Senator from Virginia (Democrat).

face, we must remember that neither our achievements nor our failures in developing democracy were just the natural fruits of the constitutional tree planted long ago by our Founding Fathers. Today's United States is the outcome of intense struggles between individuals, minority and interest groups, and parties to build better laws and policies upon the foundation of our political institutions and democratic ethic.

Early in our history there occurred a pivotal struggle between the ideal of limited government and popular sovereignty, attributed to Thomas Jefferson, and the more statist reliance on strong central authority to serve national objectives, attributed to Alexander Hamilton. Efforts to reconcile these two tendencies have propelled the development of democracy in the United States. In the heat of the Civil War, Abraham Lincoln expanded government authority in pursuit of Jeffersonian liberties for the emancipated slaves. From the turn of the century, progressives aligned with Woodrow Wilson tried to harness government power to legislate tax, regulatory, and electoral reforms in order to increase equal opportunity for the individual. In the depth of the Depression, Franklin Roosevelt's New Deal used massive government investment to tip the balance of economic power back from entrenched interests to the individual.

In our own generation, Lyndon Johnson's Great Society legislated an end to open racial discrimination in education, employment, housing, and voting. Although the Great Society's use of coercive federal authority probably would have repelled Jefferson, its objectives conformed to the Jeffersonian ideal of assuring each citizen an equal opportunity and the freedom to rise to his or her full potential.

But the Great Society's application of Hamiltonian means to Jeffersonian ends also resulted in failures. While barriers to black participation in life in the United States were rapidly dismantled, vast pockets of poverty and social inequity remain.

Thus, through the use of the central government as an agent of social change, we have overcome many obstacles to political and economic participation by its citizens. But other, more intractable problems have arisen.

The Underclass

None is more dramatic than the failure of the United States to stem the rise of a dependent, demoralized, and self-perpetuating underclass in our cities. This disturbing development mocks our Jeffersonian ideal of equal opportunity for all and provides propaganda fodder to the critics of democracy around the world.

For the first time in our history, the bottom segment of our society has become immobile. In our city centers, millions of people, mostly black, are trapped in a tragic cycle of deprivation, family disintegration, disorder, and dependency. They are headed toward permanent status as wards of the state, without jobs, hope, or a meaningful sense of membership in our society.

We need to draw careful distinctions between the underclass and the poor generally. The vast majority of the poor in the United States, both white and black, move in and out of jobs and the welfare system, always hoping to work their way out of poverty. The underclass represents only a fraction of the poor, but it generates social turmoil and absorbs public resources far out of proportion to its size.

The underclass represents the reverse side of the coin of black progress. The black middle class has grown rapidly and moved out of the ghettoes, leaving behind blighted inner city communities bereft of commerce, cohesive civic and fraternal organizations, positive role models and, finally, hope.

Those who remain are the least equipped to live independent, self-sufficient lives. Too many fall prey to the self-destructive patterns of behavior that tend to perpetuate the underclass: the failure to finish school, teenage pregnancy, welfare dependency, idleness, drug abuse, and crime.

The entrenchment of these social pathologies, after a period of unprecedented government activism aimed at lifting people out of poverty, has been a disturbing and confusing phenomenon to many Americans. Social policy has retreated to providing a safety net of transfer payments to the underclass, which has only seemed to subsidize the spread of nonparticipatory and self-destructive behavior in our poorest communities.

As the social dilemma facing the United States has changed, so has the debate on what government ought to do about it. There is a new emphasis on mutual obligation—not only on society's obligation to the poor but also on the obligations of those who receive society's aid. There is also a new emphasis on decentralization, on targeted, community-based initiatives designed and administered locally to address local problems.

In our democratic ethic in the United States, all citizens have a right to expect an equal change to get ahead, not an assured outcome. The U.S. quest for democratic equality is not to level or raise people's income and status toward some common mean, but to ensure their equal political rights and equal social and economic opportunity to compete for income and status.

Our citizens also view equality as entailing certain obligations to participate both socially and economically in society. As noted U.S. political scientist Lawrence Mead recently expressed it in his book, *Beyond Entitlement*:

> Equality is not so much an entitlement, a status, as an activity. To be equal an American must do things, not just claim them . . . duties such as obeying the law or paying taxes become, not just burdens, but badges of belonging.

Thus most U.S. citizens feel obligated to educate themselves, work, provide family support, and obey laws.

To expand our promise of equal opportunity to the underclass will require moving beyond a safety-net policy of transferring entitlements. It will require enlisting the alienated members of the underclass into the reciprocal rewards and obligations of meaningful work. At present the United States has established no new political consensus about what national strategy could bring this about. Public opinion polls only reveal an overwhelming desire to attack the problem, coupled with strong disillusionment over the effectiveness of past welfare policies.

This majority sentiment does not come solely from compassion, however, but from an ethical demand for a just social order, without which the individual cannot feel his own accomplishments to be legitimized. Americans realize that the enduring presence and spread of the underclass, even if it does not vote or revolt, undermines the very legitimacy of a democratic society.

The United States will soon have to undertake a fundamental restructuring of its public welfare system, based on a whole new approach to social policy. We need a social policy that fosters upward mobility, rewards self-discipline and hard work, encourages families to stay together, and instills basic values of citizenship. Above all, our new social policy must be designed to restore our poor and dispossessed to full citizenship—to both the benefits and the obligations that citizenship entails.

Yet it is not the objectives, but the effective means to attain them, that present the biggest problem. The big hands of government bureaucracy failed in their initial attempts. The burden of solving the problem of the underclass will now have to be shifted from the national government to a combination of local government and the myriads of mediating institutions and private volunteer organizations at the local level. At the same time, Washington's limited resources can be put to more effective use by letting the national government concentrate on the two most important prerequisites for breaking the poverty cycle: promoting economic growth and strategic public investments.

Our democratic development would have been impossible without a steady economic growth. At this point in its history, however, U.S. prospects for growth have been mortgaged by a domestic deficit of unprecedented scale. Thus there is little chance that we will be able to both substantially increase social welfare spending and decrease the deficit to the extent needed to promote overall economic growth.

To grow, we will need to make strategic public investments in public education and the rapid redeployment of labor from shrinking industries to the emerging knowledge-intensive sector. We will need to lift the quality of general education to the level now enjoyed by only our best students. And we need to focus special attention on skills training for those who are not college bound.

National Service

But there is a more direct way to involve members of the underclass in a concerted effort to increase their own participation in the democratic experience. That way is national service.

Each year, between three and four million youths in the United States turn 18 years old. Many studies have identified about the same number of jobs to fulfill unmet social needs in such civilian sectors as education, health, housing, child care, and conservation. Yet, full-time service programs at all levels of government now employ less than 7,000 18-24 year olds.

So why are we not matching such resources to needs? The reasons have been twofold. First, there is the concern that national service might spawn yet another large, costly, and inefficient bureaucracy. Second, there is the continuing Jeffersonian concern that the central government should wield its authority as little as possible over the free associations of its citizens.

But the key innovation that could make national service effective is decentralization. Defining and administering the service of the volunteers would be done by local private voluntary organizations in conjunction with local government. Not only could such services expand opportunities but they could provide the "servers" from poor and disadvantaged families both the incentives and the manpower to develop widespread volunteer groups within their own communities.

Thus, many are beginning to come around to the idea that Jefferson was right, that the greatest strength of our democratic society is the incredible mosaic of our free associations, not the central governmental authority. If, as I hope, it is our national purpose to deepen democracy by rooting out the tragic inequality of opportunity that still plagues our underclass, then citizens should be rallied to serve, while localities must be empowered to do the job.

Autonomy and Political Culture

How relevant is the United States' struggle to match democratic principles and practice to other nations? For instance, compared to the immense problems of economic and social development in India, the world's largest democracy, what lessons can be offered by U.S. attempts to overcome such barriers to participation as poverty, crime, illiteracy, teenage pregnancy, and joblessness?

The principle lesson I would draw from our historical experience is that the two most valuable assets for developing democracy in the United States have been the political culture and competence of its citizenry, and the degree to which it has fostered such a dense network of free institutions and local associations, autonomous from state control. Nevertheless, even under our relatively favorable cultural and institutional circumstances, it has taken us over two centuries and many stages to bring our laws into line with our fundamental ideals.

My own experience as a former state governor has underscored a second lesson—that a society that empowers local representative governments with policy-making autonomy can establish a more equitable balance of benefits for its citizens.

Thus the autonomy of private pursuits and the decentralization of public power have provided the key conditions under which democracy in the United States has tried to overcome barriers to political and economic participation.

Building Democratic Competence Abroad

What can the United States do to help such conditions take root and flourish outside of the industrialized democracies? We certainly cannot offer our political institutions or principles as models to people abroad if we have stopped trying to perfect them at home.

Complacency about the spread of a destitute and demoralized underclass in our cities leads all too easily to indifference toward the brutalizing effect, on both whites and blacks, of apartheid in South Africa, toward Ethiopia's murderous resettlement policy, or toward the dirty wars of Latin America.

Thus, just as we must find new ways to help the poor in the United States free themselves from poverty and dependence, we must also help others around the world create the right conditions for democratic development.

We must, in a word, help build something I would call "democratic competence," which I would define simply as the ability of self-rule. The same basic idea is also expressed by the word "citizenship," which entails the individual exercise of both rights and obligations. In essence, the success of a democracy depends on the quality of its citizenship.

A society blessed with democratic competence is one that can contain and constructively channel the clash of competing interests. In such a society, citizens may press their personal interests and may create free associations to magnify their influence and may build even broader coalitions that give them great political clout.

In such a society, where conflicting ideas and interests are allowed to compete freely and openly, citizens become skilled in the arts of give-and-take, compromise, and consensus building. Political change becomes evolutionary rather than revolutionary.

Building democratic competence abroad should the central aim of U.S. foreign policy, for in the long run, the best way to promote our national interests is to promote basic democratic values. Our policy should consist of measured but persistent efforts to fortify the democratic center where it exists and to encourage its emergence where it does not exist.

What do I mean by the democratic center? I do not mean the central authority of government, but the brave men and women in society who are struggling for individual and economic freedom, for equal opportunity and human rights, and perhaps most fundamentally, for the inalienable right to choose their own destiny. I mean those men and women who have the courage to tolerate diversity and dissent, who believe that basic rights are inherent in the individual and not in the state, and who prefer the occasional indignities of democratic self-

141

rule to the constant degradation of despotism. And I mean those who reject the rigid and inhuman demands of ideology in favor of a more flexible—and forgiving—view of human nature and human potentiality, a view that sees the possibility of orderly progress and peaceful resolution of conflict within a democratic framework.

The democratic center may consist of elected public officials, union members, peasants, church, civic, or business leaders, students, teachers, human rights activists, or of ordinary men and women who understand, if only instinctively, that individual rights and liberty are the best bulwark against oppression by the state.

We have seen the democratic center grow in Latin America, where nine nations—including such giants as Brazil and Argentina—have replaced military rulers with popularly elected civilians within the last decade.

We have seen it grow in Poland, despite the suppression of the Solidarity union, in the Philippines, and in South Korea, where it is still growing daily.

And we have seen it grow stronger in Turkey, where the people have decisively rejected attempts by armed extremists to impose their will through terrorist violence.

The Uses and Limits of Aid

What can the United States do to fortify the democratic center in these and other nations? Clearly, in some countries, especially Communist countries, we can offer little more than moral support. But elsewhere, we can and must do more.

For example, in El Salvador, President Napoleon Duarte presides over a shaky civilian government besieged by violent extremists on the Right and

the Left. His freely and fairly elected government deserves our help. At first glance, El Salvador might seem to illustrate how, if we are serious about bolstering fledgling democracies, we cannot ignore the grave security threats they face. The capacity for self-defense is basic to democratic competence. To pour large amounts of economic aid into countries whose stability is threatened by insurgencies is a futile gesture. Improving the lives of people must begin with the basic security that we too often take for granted.

Yet El Salvador also illustrates how economic and security aid, as critical as they are for struggling democracies, are not enough. The sizable amount of U.S. economic aid we have transferred directly to the El Salvadoran ministries has had the indirect and unintended effects of both increasing central governmental authority over the masses of people and intensifying political struggles between bureaucratic elites to obtain bigger portions of the budgetary pie. It has done comparatively little to empower Salvadoran communities to organize the kind of self-reliant, participatory efforts necessary for truly successful socioeconomic development.

U.S. foreign aid programs need to draw from the lessons of our own recent experience at home: that government bureaucracy, no matter how well intentioned, can itself become an obstacle to participatory self-development by marginalized groups of the population.

Not only the United States but the whole network of international development agencies as well should reexamine how we provide direct monetary aid and begin channeling it, to the extent possible, to local governmental or private voluntary development organizations, rather than through government bureaucracies. Our priorities should be shifted toward catalyzing and investing in participatory development projects such as the Grameen Bank in Bangladesh, the Solidarista movements in Central America, and the Mondragon worker-managed enterprises in Spain.

We should also use our aid to encourage economic and social reforms that can both broaden and bolster the democratic center. For example, we should press developing nations to widen the scope for private participation in the economy by scaling back public bureaucracy and subsidies, easing government economic and trade controls, and dismantling inefficient state enterprises. On the other hand, we could do far more to encourage such countries to foster participatory economic development by such indirect means of aid as reducing U.S. trade barriers and arranging various forms of credit and debt relief through private sector banking.

Economic growth alone will not do. Equally important are efforts to spread its benefits more widely—for example, land reform, public investments in education and health, and other steps that foster upward mobility and a more equitable distribution of wealth.

U.S. citizens in both public and private capacities can also help build democratic competence by providing expertise in the strengthening of free institutions and processes, such as honest elections, police and security forces subject to strict civilian control, and fair and impartial judicial systems. And we ought to reach out to the next generation of political leaders by offering more scholarships to our colleges.

Private efforts to build the infrastructure of democracy are also essential. In Central America, for example, U.S. labor unions are supporting land reform efforts and the growth of free trade unions. The National Endowment for Democracy also promotes democratic pluralism abroad through its support for greater voter participation and a free press.

In countries ruled by Communist or authoritarian governments, the United States should do what it can to nurture the notion of popular sovereignty and the growth of democratic sentiment. Though we cannot remake the world in our own image, neither can we afford to give the appearance of uncritical support for corrupt or despotic regimes that profess to be our friends. That undermines the moral authority of our foreign policy, just as tolerating social inequity and injustice in our own society corrodes the democratic ethic at home.

Conclusions

Democracy in the United States does indeed offer a model to others—not a set of institutions and laws that can be successfully replicated everywhere, but a continuing experiment by its citizens to enlarge the scope of individual freedom and opportunity. The revolutionary principles on which this country was founded were narrow in their application, but universal in their implications. Our democratic development over the last two centuries is the record of a determined struggle by those excluded from full citizenship to achieve equal participation in a free society. In the United States and around the world, that struggle must continue.

Human Rights and U.S. Foreign Policy

Paula J. Dobriansky

PUBLIC DEBATES ABOUT the role of human rights in U.S. foreign policy have been a regular fixture of American political life at least since the early 1970s, spanning the presidencies of Richard Nixon, Gerald Ford, Jimmy Carter, and Ronald Reagan. All too frequently, however, these debates have featured a tendency to caricature opposing views and even have served as surrogates for broader disagreements about the proper course of U.S. foreign policy. The oft-propounded myths have been that the pursuit of an assertive U.S. foreign policy, imbued with a strong dose of anticommunism and realpolitik, is necessarily inimical to human rights and that Nixon, Ford, and Reagan failed to pay adequate attention to the promotion of human rights abroad.

Regrettably, the excessive zeal and the conceptual oversimplification that permeate these debates, to a considerable degree, have precluded public scrutiny of the real dilemmas of U.S. human rights policy. They have also obfuscated the key underlying problem of how to integrate the pursuit of human rights into the overall national security agenda. Equally unfortunate has been the tendency either to ignore

outright complex American heritage and historical experiences relating to human rights issues or to misconstrue them to support a given view or bias pertaining to current human rights policy.

The American Tradition

Although human rights have been a much discussed component of U.S. foreign policy since the early 1970s, American interest in human rights developments in other countries is not a new phenomenon. Indeed, American history and political tradition clearly evidence a long-standing concern with protecting the rights of individuals and national groups, whether at home or abroad. At the same time, American political culture manifests an ever-present tendency to flirt with isolationism, direct national attention inward, and foster ambivalence about the maintenance of strong national institutions, which would be required to implement an assertive foreign policy. This somewhat contradictory combination of American moralism, the tendency to universalize the peculiarly American experience, and the deeply entrenched abhorrence of power politics accounts for a certain tension and inconsistency in the U.S. human rights tradition.

Upon reflection, this tension is not surprising. The United States was

Paula J. Dobriansky is deputy assistant secretary of state for human rights and humanitarian affairs. Previously, she served at the National Security Council as director for East European and Soviet affairs.

born from a crucible of revolutionary struggle, animated to a large extent by a desire of the colonists to restore and protect their rights against arbitrary state power. Early American leaders believed all individuals possess certain inalienable natural rights. Such natural rights are neither conferred on people nor can they be taken away by governments; rather, they are integral attributes of all human beings. American leaders always viewed protection of such rights as a key task of a civilized society. As philosopher John Locke explained, the end of government is the preservation of liberty.[1] In fact, having witnessed firsthand the ravages of tyranny, the Founding Fathers were determined to create a society in which systematic violations of natural rights of individuals by the state could not occur.

Influenced by their study of such philosophers as Locke, Montesquieu, and Hume, the Founding Fathers also believed that relying solely on the goodness of man's nature, or on enlightened policies espoused by individual rulers, was foolhardy. Accordingly, in their view, the only reliable way to ensure that tyranny and abuses of state power could not arise was to create a full-fledged democracy with a system of checks and balances. Eventually, a panoply of structural and procedural safeguards was established to protect the civil and political rights of citizens.

Additionally, one important and abiding conviction felt by the Founding Fathers and their successors was that the lofty ideals of freedom, democracy, and human rights were not just for Americans. The United States had something unique to share with the world. This belief in the universal nature of the U.S. experience arose neither from cultural arrogance nor

from a desire to impose U.S. views on the rest of the world. Rather, it reflected a conviction that, as a young society with a uniquely democratic political system and one far removed from acute power struggles then raging in Europe, the United States was in John Winthrop's formulation, a "city upon the hill."[2] It was in a superb position to offer moral and spiritual leadership to the world.

The belief in the universal nature of the American experience was reflected in key documents associated with early U.S. history. For example, the Declaration of Independence proclaims it is self-evident "that all men are created equal, that they are endowed by their Creator with certain inalienable rights, that among these are life, liberty and the pursuit of happiness." The concept of the protection of natural rights of individuals also permeates numerous state constitutions and the Bill of Rights of the U.S. Constitution. These documents offer perhaps the most vigorous and spirited defense of the concepts of human dignity, democracy, and freedom. The universality of these documents was viewed as a nearly self-evident proposition, leading Thomas Jefferson to state in a 1787 letter to James Madison that "a Bill of Rights is what people are entitled to against every government on earth."[3]

Given its political, cultural, and constitutional traditions, the oft-manifested U.S. concern about alleviating human suffering and promoting democracy abroad is not surprising. In fact, throughout the years, the United States spoke forcefully against oppression in other countries, ranging from pogroms in Tsarist Russia to Ottoman atrocities against the Slavs and Armenians. The multiethnic composition of U.S. politics and the keen interest of many U.S. ethnic groups in conditions in their former homelands contributed to the U.S. government speaking against human rights abuses. In time, as public involvement in U.S. foreign policy grew, the impact of domestic considerations on U.S. human rights policy also increased.

Many early American leaders advocated an even more assertive policy. In Thomas Jefferson's words, the U.S. "empire of liberty" was destined to serve the cause of freedom throughout the world and assist those who were fighting to promote it. Combined with this assertion was an innate American optimism about the human condition and a view that even complex international problems would eventually prove amenable to rational solutions. At the same time, other Americans took a more minimalist view of the proper U.S. policy. In the words of John Quincy Adams, "We are the friends of liberty everywhere, but the custodians only of our own." Thus, the debate over the limits and proper uses of U.S. power began. Questions of implementation aside, rich American cultural, constitutional, and political traditions provide a hospitable milieu for a foreign policy concerned with human rights situations in other countries.

However, it would be far too simplistic to claim that U.S. political traditions automatically translate into an assertive and coherent human rights policy. For example, alongside an understanding of the need to combine morality and power in public policy, U.S. traditions also feature a moralistic streak and confusion about the realm of international relations, largely dominated by power politics, and the realm of domestic relations, organized by the rule of law. To a certain degree, a sense of geopolitical invulnerability

and a long separation from the rough and tumble of world politics reinforced the proclivity for adoption of moralistic foreign-policy stances.

Another unfortunate trait in U.S. political culture has been the tendency toward geopolitical withdrawal and isolationism, periodically espoused by a considerable proportion of the American elite and body politic. Interestingly enough, the American preoccupation with human rights was seemingly compatible with the isolationist component of the American tradition. Thus, human rights problems and deviations from democracy found in many foreign countries were eagerly seized on by isolationists. They argued that the United States ought not to involve itself in inherently immoral foreign-policy ventures and should limit its international pursuits to maintaining ties with those few genuine democracies.

Yet, despite this seeming congruence of isolationism and focus on moral and human rights issues, proponents of an assertive U.S. foreign policy correctly noted that isolationism was boosted precisely when normative and ethical components of U.S. foreign policy were ignored. Thus, as noted by Charles Krauthammer, the promotion of freedom has been an indispensable foundation of any assertive U.S. international stance. Without it, U.S. foreign policy lacked strong domestic support and was prone to devolve into isolationism. Henry Kissinger affirmed an identical view:

Our nation cannot rest its policy on power alone. Our tradition and the values of our people ensure that a policy that seeks only to manipulate force would lack all conviction, consistency and public support. This is why America has been most successful in our relations with the world when we combined our idealism and our pragmatism.[4]

Overall, the public concern about human rights abroad is a truly unique element of American cultural and political traditions. It is compatible with all the other components of the U.S. experience and capable of, but not always successful in, providing an impetus for a sustainable and assertive foreign policy.

Continuity and Change in U.S. Policy

Historically, human rights considerations have played a major role in shaping U.S. foreign-policy initiatives. Examples include the Kellogg-Briand Pact, Woodrow Wilson's Fourteen Points, and the establishment of the United Nations' system. In the early 1970s human rights factors began to play a much more visible role in day-to-day U.S. foreign-policy operations. The original impetus for this development came from Congress, where in 1973, the House Foreign Affairs Subcommittee on International Organizations conducted lengthy hearings on human rights issues. Substantial legislative initiatives ensued.

Congress amended a number of foreign policy-related statutes—the Foreign Assistance Act, the Mutual Assistance Act, the Trade Reform Act of 1974, and the International Financial Institutions Act of 1977—to specify that human rights considerations should play an integral role in dispensing U.S. military, economic, and financial assistance. These statutes were also amended to indicate that governments, guilty of "a consistent pattern of gross human rights violations," should not be granted U.S. as-

sistance, unless the president requests a waiver on national security grounds.

In addition to amending these generic statutes, Congress also passed thematic human rights clauses. One of the earliest examples of such thematic provision was the 1974 Jackson-Vanik amendment (section 402 of the Trade Reform Act of 1974), which provided that "nonmarket economy" countries that impose restrictions on free emigration are not eligible to receive most-favored-nation status. Congress also enacted numerous country-specific statutes.[5]

The executive branch also played a major role in the development of this new human rights atmosphere. Thus, for example, president Ford devoted considerable attention to publicizing the U.S. commitment to the cause of human rights during the 1975 meeting to sign the Final Act of the Conference on Security and Cooperation in Europe (CSCE). Senator Patrick Moynihan, during his tenure as the U.S. ambassador to the United Nations, also delivered a series of key speeches advocating genuine international commitment to eradicate human rights abuses. Human rights issues played a visible role in the 1976 and 1980 presidential campaigns and during the Carter and Reagan administrations.

This ebb and flow of U.S. human rights policy has been institutionalized and supported by an active human rights community in Congress and the private sector. The pursuit of human rights causes has become a major element of U.S. foreign policy. It is solidly rooted in U.S. political culture and constitutional tradition and generally enjoys strong and bipartisan support of Congress and the American people. Thus, debates about whether the United States should pay any attention to human rights considerations in devising its foreign policy or should pursue some version of pure realpolitik are intellectually sterile and practically irrelevant.

The real dilemmas facing the United States have been how to resolve specific human rights problems, how to reconcile human rights considerations with other foreign-policy factors, and last but not least, how to generate a sustainable public consensus behind its human rights policy. These efforts are unlikely ever to succeed fully. Human rights policy seems to enjoy bipartisan support only at a rather abstract level. At the operational level, it is often controversial, cannot be reduced to rigid formulae, and necessarily has to be flexible.

For example, although the pursuit of human rights has been generally a popular undertaking, considerable confusion still permeates American discussions of the concept of human rights itself. Recent years have seen efforts to obfuscate and even replace the recognized civil and political rights with the so-called "economic and social rights." During the Carter administration, for example, a concerted effort was made to equate civil-political rights with economic-social rights. Specifically, secretary of state Cyrus Vance said that U.S. policy was to promote human rights defined as: "1)the right to be free from government violation of the integrity of the person. . . . 2)the right to fulfillment of such vital needs as food, shelter, health care and education. . . . 3)the right to enjoy political and civil liberties. . . ."[6] Traditionally, however, it has been the U.S. view that political rights, reflecting natural law, provide a vital foundation for any democratic society.

Traditional liberal political philosophy also spoke primarily of individual's rights against the government—what Justice Brandeis once termed the fundamental human right to be let alone—the right to enjoy the fruits of one's labor and to carry on one's own life as one sees fit, so long as this does not unduly infringe on the rights of others. These individual rights have been held so sacred in U.S. constitutional tradition so as to supercede, in some important respects, political rights. Accordingly, even the will of a majority, expressed through the democratic process, cannot abridge certain fundamental individual rights. Yet, undue emphasis on economic and social rights, construed as entitlements, is bound to clash with the very essence of U.S. political tradition, insofar as any attempt to secure these rights necessarily entails the mobilization of all societal resources, leading eventually to an unlimited or even totalitarian government. It is difficult to comprehend why the United States, dedicated to the idea of a limited government of checks and balances at home, should be promoting abroad a version of human rights that leads to an unlimited government.

Moreover, under present conditions, economic and social rights are really more in the nature of aspirations and goals than rights. This seemingly semantic distinction is important. It does not make much sense to claim that particular levels of economic and social benefits constitute rights if most governments are not able to provide them. In contrast, any government can and ought to guarantee natural rights to its citizens (for example, freedom from torture and arbitrary detention). Furthermore, equating all types of rights and aspirations trivializes the concept of human rights and may ultimately lead to the denial of fundamental rights. As Michael Novak aptly observed:

Rights do not come free. Each right has a corresponding cost.

When a great many things are asserted as a matter of right, then there comes into existence a kind of hierarchy of rights. Asserted of too many things, the word 'right' becomes empty of meaning. This, in turn, leads to a situation where human rights violations are viewed as almost inevitable transgressions, committed by all countries.[7]

Not surprisingly, blurring the distinction between a goal of economic and social development and fundamental human rights breeds not only conceptual confusion but also is a tactic often invoked as an excuse by human rights violators. The United States has usually found that repressive governments often deliberately denigrate political rights. Those governments falsely claim that, in order to promote economic and social rights, they must deny their citizens political and civil rights. Such governments usually seek to justify their own egregious violations of political and civil rights by disingenuously asserting that, after all, even the United States has not fully conquered poverty, and a number of Americans have been unable to secure shelter or stable income. This, of course, is a flawed argument. The fact that economic privation has not yet been fully eradicated provides absolutely no justification for denying people their political rights or torturing one's political opponents. Sadly, the whole subject has become so heavily laden with hypocrisy that dictators, who often torture and maim their subjects, see fit to lecture the United States on human rights.

Yet, a symbiotic relationship clearly exists between the observance of high standards for human rights and economic development. Experience demonstrates that individual freedom unleashes creative forces in any society and best fosters economic and social development; repression stifles it. Thus, those who justify denigrating political and civil rights on the grounds that they are concentrating on satisfying economic aspirations of their subjects invariably deliver on neither. Resolving, to the extent possible, this conceptual human rights muddle is a necessary prerequisite for a successful U.S. human rights policy.

In addition to serving as the repository of rich political and historical human rights tradition, the United States also has made a major contribution to the development of international human rights law. Human rights have become a legitimate subject of international discourse only recently. Traditionally, maintenance of human rights standards was considered a matter of domestic jurisdiction of individual states. Although concerned with the right of national minorities, the League of Nations did not even attempt to champion individual human rights cases. Now, however, repressive governments no longer cloak their human rights violations behind national sovereignty. Even the Soviet Union is prepared to discuss human rights matters in bilateral and multilateral fora.

The United States played a key role in this development of substantive international human rights norms through the establishment of the UN system and the drafting of the UN Charter. In fact, one of the earliest and most important international documents dealing with human rights matters—the Universal Declaration of Human Rights, adopted by the General Assembly on December 10, 1948—was prepared under the guidance of Eleanor Roosevelt, then the U.S. representative to the United Nations Human Rights Commission (UNHRC). The United States adheres to the principles of the UN

Charter and the Universal Declaration of Human Rights and continues to play a constructive role in the development of new international human rights documents and norms. Through the Security Council, the UNHRC, the Third Committee of the UN General Assembly, specialized UN agencies, and other international forums, the United States has consistently sought to bring to the attention of the international community, and to eradicate, violations of human rights and fundamental freedoms. In addition to focusing on human rights violations within specific countries, the United States has also urged the international community to consider thematic human rights issues (for example, religious freedom). Having helped develop new international human rights obligations, the United States then has played a pivotal role in monitoring compliance and holding violators accountable for their actions.

The United States was also instrumental in placing human rights issues on the agenda of regional organizations. For example, prompted by U.S. appeals, the Charter of the Organization of American States and the 1948 American Declaration of Rights and Duties of Man incorporated strong human rights language. The United States has advanced the cause of human rights in another multilateral forum, the CSCE. The United States ensured the inclusion of Basket III in the 1975 Helsinki Accords which spelled out a range of human rights obligations assumed by the signatories.

U.S. efforts notwithstanding, it would be premature to claim that multilateral forums and international organizations invariably display an objective and serious attitude toward human rights issues. In 1976, then–U.S. ambassador to the United Na-

tions, William Scranton, criticized the considerable hypocrisy of many UN human rights deliberations. He noted, "the only universality one can honestly associate with the Universal Declaration on Human Rights is universal lip service." The situation has not improved much since 1976. International institutions are still beset with numerous political and ideological rivalries and have been unable to foster major improvement in human rights situations in many countries.

Although in many respects U.S. human rights policy manifests considerable continuity, it has also undergone a major transformation over the first decade. Yet, the actual changes in U.S. human rights policy have been quite different from those attributed to the United States by numerous critics. An oft-voiced misconception is that the Carter administration pursued a vigorous human rights policy and the Reagan administration allegedly came into office intending to abandon active pursuit of human rights causes. It is further claimed that only belatedly and begrudgingly did the Reagan administration embrace the human rights banner, repudiating its alleged earlier doctrinal hostility to human rights supposedly set forth in Jeanne Kirkpatrick's famous article, "Dictatorships and Double Standards."[8]

This view, however, features both an erroneous assessment of Reagan's human rights policy and of how it differed from Carter's. Without doubt, the Carter administration deserves credit for bolstering the role of human rights in U.S. foreign policy and for educating the American public about human rights issues. Despite the sincerity of its commitment to the cause of human rights, however, critics challenged the manner in which Carter's administration executed its human rights policies. Arguably, the major conceptual deficiency of Carter's policy was his attempt to separate the pursuit of human rights from the broader struggle between democracy and totalitarianism. Carter's assistant secretary for human rights and humanitarian affairs, Patricia Derian, succinctly summarized this notion, opining that "human rights violations do not really have much to do with the form of government or the political ideology or philosophy."[9] In fact, president Carter went to great lengths not only to separate his human rights stance from the erstwhile anticommunist trends in U.S. foreign policy but also to contrast it with the alleged anti-Soviet realpolitik of his predecessors. Thus, in his May 22, 1977, speech at Notre Dame University, Carter dismissed the "inordinate fear of Communism," which allegedly formerly animated U.S. policy. He stated, "It is a new world—but America should not fear it. It is a new world—and we should help to shape it. It is a new world that calls for a new American foreign policy—a policy based on constant decency in its values and an optimism in its historic vision."

The claim that a new world was emerging was not inherently wrong, albeit perhaps somewhat overstated. Nor can one take issue with the claim that an "inordinate fear of Communism" is a poor policy guide. Yet, claiming that the reverse is necessarily true is a fallacy. As Senator Moynihan aptly noted, "It is as if—with no further consideration—we should divert our attention from the central political struggle of our time—that between liberal democracy and totalitarian Communism—and focus instead on something else."

Another problem with the pre-Reagan human rights policy was its evident inability to establish any rational connection between power and morality. All historical analogues are inherently suspect, but this trait bore a rather strong resemblance to Wilson's moralism. Thus, critics have maintained that Carter's efforts to promote human rights were excessively rigid, elevated to the status of absolute imperatives, and failed to take into account historical and social traditions in countries whose human rights policies the United States was determined to change.

All of these issues represent a very real difference between the approaches of the Carter and Reagan administrations. They did not, however, in any way substantiate the allegation that the Reagan administration, as a whole, did not care about human rights.

Another popular myth holds that Reagan's human rights policy, under Jeane Kirkpatrick's influence, originally cozied up to authoritarian regimes. Yet, this claim both is factually incorrect and significantly distorts the essence of Kirkpatrick's arguments. Even a casual reader of "Dictatorships and Double Standards" would notice that Kirkpatrick was not advocating coddling authoritarian regimes. Instead, she merely pointed out that authoritarian regimes may evolve into democracies, although the prospects of the similar transformation for totalitarian regimes are virtually nil. In fact, Kirkpatrick was not alone in articulating this distinction. Henry Kissinger also pointed out that "in recent decades, no totalitarian regime has ever evolved into a democracy."[10] Indeed, the developments of the last decade support his premise.

Democratic governments have replaced a large number of authoritarian regimes. The closest a totalitarian regime even came to this transformation was Czechoslovakia in 1968, but Soviet tanks crushed the development. In that regard, as Irving Kristol correctly noted, authoritarian regimes are preliberal entities, which may evolve into liberal or totalitarian societies. "Totalitarian societies, on the other hand, are post liberal realities—they emerge out of an explicit rejection of the Western liberal tradition, are declared enemies of this tradition, and aim to supercede it."[11]

Based on this conceptual premise, Kirkpatrick criticized the Carter administration's handling of crises that beset authoritarian regimes in Iran and Nicaragua. Clearly, few would argue that the overthrow of the Shah in Iran and of Somoza in Nicaragua either improved the human rights situation in these countries or benefited U.S. strategic interests. Instead, debate within the U.S. foreign-policy establishment (mainly fought in memoirs of various high-ranking Carter administration officials) still brews over whether specific U.S. decisions on how to handle the turmoil in Nicaragua and Iran contributed to the rise of the Sandinistas and of Khomeini. Kirkpatrick, however, focused on the broad underlying assumption of Carter policies: (1)whenever an authoritarian regime is beset with a domestic crisis, a democratic alternative is always available; (2)any beleaguered autocrat cannot survive for long; and (3)any change in a repressive government is always for the better.

Taking issue with Kirkpatrick's criticisms is difficult. They were valid at the time they were written and they remain true today. It should be noted, however, that Kirkpatrick's article criticized the policy excesses of the Carter administration, rather than laid a comprehensive framework for the Reagan adminstration. Thus, although it would be wrong to claim that the Reagan administration's human rights pol-

icies repudiated Kirkpatrick's theses, it cannot be said that the article contained the entire intellectual credo of Reagan's policy.

The Reagan administration began with the conviction that it wanted to learn both from the mistakes and accomplishments of its predecessor. It realized that even the pursuit of idealistic goals required pragmatism and careful implementation. While desirous of bolstering U.S. power and influence, the Reagan administration realized that U.S. ability to cause democratic change abroad was not unlimited. The Founding Fathers understood this point well. In modern times, Walter Lippman cautioned U.S. decision makers that successful policy requires maintaining a balance between commitments and resources. Human rights pursuits are not immune from this overriding imperative.

To be sure, during the first few months of the Reagan administration, one could find a few statements by administration officials that seemed to de-emphasize human rights concerns. Most of these statements were rhetorical flourishes criticizing Carter's policies—a phenomenon endemic to most new administrations. This adjustment period was over by the end of 1981.

Operational Dilemmas of Reagan's Policy

In developing its human rights policy, the Reagan administration confronted five critical issues.

How far and how fast to pressure an authoritarian regime to reform? There are no standardized prescriptions. Rather, what is required is a differentiated policy that deals with individual countries taking into account all the relevant facts and circumstances. Thus, a country with a strong democratic tradition and a government with a willingness to consider reform ought to be encouraged, through both positive inducements and punitive means, to accelerate the process of change. An authoritarian government, battling procommunist insurgents, should be urged to liberalize but not pressured (through U.S. sanctions) to the point that it collapses. Between these two extremes lies an infinite variety of situations which have to be dealt with pragmatically and based on the sound analysis of local events. The Reagan administration based its encouragement of democratic change in Brazil, El Salvador, Honduras, and South Korea on this differentiated approach.

The United States should be prepared to deal sympathetically with those countries that are genuinely trying to cooperate with it to improve their human rights record, even if the initial progress is slow. To maintain credibility, the United States also should be prepared to assist governments that, having commenced human rights reforms at U.S. urging, have encountered domestic opposition from the Right or Left or simply widespread domestic turmoil. For the United States not to render help in such circumstances would not only be hypocritical, but it would also diminish the prospects that other countries would cooperate with the United States in the future.

Evidence is clear that, contrary to the allegations of its critics, the Reagan administration did not ignore human rights violations committed by anticommunist regimes. Thus, for example, the administration denied military and economic aid to Chile because of the repressive human rights policies of the Augusto Pinochet regime. The administration also went to considerable lengths to curb death-squad activity in El Salvador. Then–vice president George Bush traveled

to El Salvador in December 1983 to meet with key military, police, and political leaders. As a result of this meeting and other U.S. actions, human rights abuses in El Salvador considerably decreased. Significantly, the Reagan administration accomplished this without destabilizing the governments of presidents Magaña and Duarte which have been successfully battling the Marxist insurgency.

How to handle a crisis besetting a repressive regime? In such situations, good intelligence and timely U.S. action are the key to success. The United States must know whether it faces a viable democratic opposition or an antidemocratic force. If both elements are present, the United States needs to know which is likely to emerge victorious. This mode of analysis was extremely important in structuring U.S. policy toward the Philippines. U.S. decision makers also should avoid a false sense of historical determinism and a conclusion that, once a given authoritarian regime has come under attack, it is certain to fall and the United States better jump on the bandwagon of change before it is too late. Yet, these cautionary notes do not suggest that the United States should never encourage the demise of an entrenched repressive government. In fact, the Reagan administration successfully handled crises in Haiti and the Philippines. Its record compares more than favorably with that of the Carter administration.

How to balance the pursuit of individual human rights cases and efforts to stimulate broad reforms? Generally, the United States has to pursue both aspects of human rights policy simultaneously. The exact balance between these policy elements, however, should properly vary from country to country. In very repressive societies, for example, where prospects of general human rights reform are not high, initially the United States can emphasize individual cases or select aspects of human rights—for example, freedom of emigration.

In fact, during the Reagan administration, the United States actively worked to resolve individual human rights cases. Literally thousands of individuals were helped in countries ranging from Eastern Europe and the Soviet Union to Latin America, Africa, and Asia. Yet, even in the case of totalitarian governments or highly repressive authoritarian regimes (for example, South Africa), the United States is committed to fundamental reform of their political systems. Joshua Muravchik noted, "the struggle for human rights, far from being . . . indifferent to political systems, is fundamentally a struggle about political systems. It cannot sensibly be merely an endless chase after an infinite number of individual violations. It must aim instead to erect political systems which have the idea of human rights, and means for their protection, built in."[12]

Relation between human rights and other determinants of U.S. foreign policy. Another often misunderstood matter is the proper relationship between human rights considerations and other factors shaping U.S. foreign policy. Critics of U.S. human rights policy often highlight U.S. decisions to provide military or economic aid to a country with a less than perfect human rights record. In their view, this indicates that the United States is not serious about promoting human rights. This, of course, is a highly simplistic and flawed notion. Human rights are an important, but not the only, consideration in determining the course of U.S. relations with foreign countries. Other factors have to be taken into account. Yet, this is true of any for-

eign-policy consideration, all of which have to be balanced against one another.

This view was not peculiar to the Reagan administration. Indeed, the Carter administration took an identical position. Lincoln Bloomfield, a staff member of Carter's NSC who was responsible for human rights, stated:

> When it came to specifics, whether the aid was military or non-military, complex interests had to be balanced in reaching decisions on individual cases. Inescapably, there were numerous cases in which the Administration was exposed to the charge of inconsistency. Human rights performance became a dominant factor in conventional arms transfers to Latin America; but such considerations were clearly subordinate in weighing military aid to Egypt, Israel, North Yemen and Saudi Arabia.[13]

Vance put forth an identical view. In justifying Carter's decision not to cut aid to such U.S. allies as Iran, South Korea, and Zaire, which had been found to commit human rights violations, Vance indicated that "in each case, we must balance a political concern for human rights against economic and security goals."[14] To put this process in perspective, it should be noted however, that the pursuit of U.S. security and economic goals, in the long run, is fully congruent with the objective of improving human rights. U.S. policy toward Poland during the martial law period offers an excellent example of this fact.

Another frequently heard criticism is that Reagan's human rights policy was too closely intertwined with the overall thrust of U.S. foreign policy, purportedly stimulated by an anticommunist bias. This situation allegedly added a note of hypocrisy to Reagan's human rights stance and damaged the administration's credibility. This claim, however, is absurd. There is nothing inherently wrong with a human rights policy that is congruent with other elements of U.S. foreign policy and serves U.S. national interests. In fact, a human rights policy that combines both morality and a pragmatic pursuit of U.S. national interests is most likely to succeed in the long term. The Reagan administration's success in dealing with human rights problems in the Soviet Union validates this point. To be sure, major differences between Brezhnev and Gorbachev's regimes have contributed to the relative improvement in Soviet human rights. Nevertheless, another significant variable is the thrust and quality of overall U.S. foreign policy, of which human rights concerns are a major component. It is the successful reinvigoration of U.S. foreign and defense policy during Reagan's tenure that has contributed to the administration's success in engaging the Soviets on human rights matters.

Some human rights advocates have clamored for greater consistency in U.S. policy. As opined in a 1979 report of the United Nations Association, "obvious inconsistencies of attitudes or actions on the part of the U.S. will undercut the moral force upon which the persuasiveness of the nation's policy largely depends. This risk is especially great if inconsistencies in its responses fall into political patterns. . . . "[15] Yet, given the range of factors that shape specific U.S. responses toward human rights abuses in individual countries, perfect consistency is impossible to attain. Whether this dissipates the moral force of U.S. human rights is unclear, as well as irrelevant. A repressive government may be induced to follow U.S. guidance for improvements in the human rights area

by various factors; moral force, however, is not one of them.

Moreover, as far as the promotion of human rights is concerned, the United States, to be successful, has to act with a sense of realism and prudence. This means that, while striving to improve human rights situations in various countries, the United States usually ought not to expect immediate results. A pattern of improvement, however modest, deserves encouragement. The United States has to be attentive to the circumstances facing each specific country. Clearly, a country plunged in the turmoil of civil war, or which has been battling right-wing or left-wing terrorists who seek to overthrow a fledgling democracy, cannot be expected to improve human rights as promptly as a country enjoying political and economic tranquility. Yet, some human rights abuses (for example, torture) are so horrendous that no reason of state can ever justify them and ought to be vigorously condemned at all times.

The U.S. sense of realism has resulted in a human rights stance that carefully weighs the consequences of U.S. policies—for example, whether the imposition of sanctions would lead to improvement in human rights. Even less extreme U.S. human rights steps might have negative consequences and ought to be carefully scrutinized. For example, in February 1977 president Carter attacked then-president of Uganda Idi Amin for human rights violations, noting that the latter's "actions have disgusted the entire civilized world."[16] Amin's reaction was entirely predictable for those who bothered to study the habits of this particular dictator. He ordered that several hundred resident Americans, most of them missionaries, not be allowed to leave the country. To secure the safety of these Americans, the

United States had to retreat in humiliation and solicit help from its African friends. A better assessment of the situation should have prevented this policy debacle.

From the moral standpoint as well, it is necessary to move beyond the monodimensional ethics and consider the costs and benefits of U.S. actions. For example, destabilization of a repressive or authoritarian regime may bring to power an even more repressive and durable regime of a totalitarian stripe. Failure to consider both the limits of U.S. influence and the consequences of U.S. actions can result in a human rights policy rich in moral posturing and poor in positive, concrete results. Yet, when the United States witnesses a country commit an egregious pattern of human rights violations, the United States usually must respond by condemning the perpetrator, even if no immediate prospect for success is in sight. Expressing moral outrage contributes to public education and heightens international cognizance of human rights problems.

Policy approaches to attain U.S. human rights goals. In fostering human rights improvements, many claim that public representations by the U.S. government and overt pressure are the only sound approach to attaining human rights objectives. Yet, experience shows that, to attain human rights goals, the United States must use numerous approaches, with specific circumstances, determining the extent to which one or the other is used. To begin with, the United States should not underestimate the impact of the simple functioning of its democratic system on the human rights situations abroad. The United States provides a powerful example to other peoples that both obtaining material prosperity and maintaining a democratic system are possible.

Private groups, such as Amnesty International or Helsinki Watch, offer another avenue to pursue human rights. Such groups have access to numerous media outlets and exert considerable influence on world public opinion. Moreover, private parties and nongovernmental organizations sometimes accomplish more than the U.S. government. This usually occurs in dealing with individual human rights cases because a nationalistic government sometimes finds it easier to give in to the demands of world public opinion than to grant the official request of the U.S. government. Private U.S. corporations can also play a useful role in promoting the U.S. human rights agenda by following, for example, internationally recognized labor standards in their activities.

Quiet diplomacy also plays an important part in implementing the U.S. human rights agenda. Time and again, using regular diplomatic channels, the United States has resolved individual human rights cases. The Reagan administration's efforts to free Kim Dae Jung in South Korea offer the perfect example of the success of this approach. In such instances, the government involved can resolve the case without appearing to cave in to U.S. pressure and without a loss of face.

Occasionally, public protests and demarches against actions of a particular oppressive regime or overt pressure on a recalcitrant dictator are useful. The U.S. shift from quiet diplomacy in dealing with Ferdinand Marcos and Jean Claude Duvalier are good examples of successful overt pressure to attain U.S. human rights objectives. Likewise, when necessary, the United States has been prepared to suspend economic and military aid to the country involved. An even more extreme measure is to impose economic sanctions, which may range in severity from a limited embargo to a total ban on economic activities. The Reagan administration used these punitive measures against such countries as Afghanistan, Chile, Nicaragua, and Poland. (In some of these cases, human rights violations were not the only reason for the imposition of sanctions.)

Another component of U.S. human rights policy has been the granting of asylum to victims of human rights persecution. To be sure, domestic, economic, and political considerations determine asylum policy. The United States lacks an ability to assist all victims of economic or social oppression. Thus, it has to be selective and, based on its conception of human rights, grant asylum primarily to those individuals who are able to establish a well-founded fear of persecution in their home countries.

The government must also broaden its conception of how to promote human rights. The United States has sought to eradicate specific human rights problems. Fundamentally, however, it believes that the best way to promote human rights in the long term is to spread and bolster democracy throughout the world. As noted in the State Department's Country Reports on Human Rights:

> It is in our national interest to promote democratic processes in order to help build a world environment more favorable to respect for human rights and hence, more conducive to stability and peace. We have developed, therefore, a dual policy, reactive in the sense that we continue to oppose specific human rights violations wherever they occur, but at the same time active in working over the long term to strengthen democracy.

In fact, it is at this level that the nexus between moral and pragmatic elements of U.S. human rights policy is most evident. The promotion of democracy and human rights abroad is not only a moral imperative but also a sound strategic approach to bolster U.S. national security. To begin with, a causal link exists between repression and turmoil in other societies and regional tensions and conflicts. Aleksandr Solzhenitsyn noted, "one cannot have peace only for oneself and calmly accept that for most of mankind, or most of the globe, repression reigns and suffocates people."[17] In addition to purely military benefits, a world of democracies engenders an international environment most conducive to U.S. political, economic and cultural interests. This view is also not unique to the Reagan administration. Indeed, it was the foundation of the world vision of many activist U.S. presidents, including Woodrow Wilson and Harry S. Truman.

The Reagan administration sought to promote democracy and human rights abroad by providing assistance to democratic and nationalistic movements, which were battling foreign occupation or homegrown oppressive regimes. This aspect of the adminstration's policy was dubbed the Reagan Doctrine and involved the provision of U.S. assistance to freedom fighters in Afghanistan, Angola, Cambodia, and Nicaragua. Although some uses of the Reagan Doctrine enjoyed wide domestic support, such as support of Afghan mujaheddin, U.S. efforts to support the Nicaraguan and Angolan resistance were more controversial.

This perhaps is not surprising. The trauma of Vietnam still endures in the American psyche, and, in general, debating the wisdom of specific overseas ventures is very much a part of the U.S. political tradition. It is far more regrettable, however, that certain individuals and groups, although professing an abiding commitment to the cause of human rights, invariably oppose U.S. efforts to aid anticommunist rebels. It is hypocritical, indeed even outright dishonest, to claim that the United States ought to intervene through a variety of means to bring down an authoritarian or a racist government, yet ought to abstain from assisting those battling an oppressive Marxist-Leninist regime. This is not to suggest that the United States ought to assist any movement raising the banner of anticommunism. The United States should consider many factors before it undertakes such a momentous step, and the assessment of the human rights prospects under a new regime should be a major policy consideration.

Fundamentally, however, the Reagan doctrine, was predicated on an optimistic assessment of international trends. It assumed that the democratic trends were much in evidence in numerous Third World countries and the pro-Soviet regimes clearly manifested their brutality, illegitimacy, and inability to promote political and social developments. Such regimes are being battled by vigorous rebel movements, and it is in the United States' interest to render concrete assistance to these freedom fighters.

Future Human Rights Agenda: Challenges and Opportunities

Although human rights policy has become an institutionalized and accepted component of U.S. foreign policy in the last decade, considerable problems remain, and new challenges lie ahead. As far as the new challenges are concerned, perhaps the single most important dilemma for U.S. decision makers is how to promote human rights improvements in newly created democracies. In the past the

major problem for U.S. foreign policy has been how hard to press authoritarian regimes to mend their human rights ways. The major concomitant concern has been that, if pushed too far, such regimes may be overthrown and replaced by a totalitarian or simply a virulently anti-American government. In contrast, the international scene today includes many new democracies (for example, Brazil, El Salvador, Guatemala, the Philippines, and South Korea), many of which came to power with U.S. assistance. They have faced difficult domestic problems, ranging from economic chaos to right- or left-wing insurgencies. Many of these democracies have human rights problems. The new dilemma for U.S. statecraft is how to promote human rights in these countries without jeopardizing democracy.

Moreover, although the desire to foster freedom and democracy abroad is an appropriate tenet of U.S. statecraft, decision makers ought to manifest a greater awareness of the fact that the peculiarly American conception of human rights may appear alien and even dysfunctional to many foreign cultures and societies. In particular, many Third World traditional cultures emphasize corporate group rights (for example, those of churches, commercial and industrial interests, military, peasants) as distinct from individual rights. As noted by Howard Wiarda, in this cultural context, "generally, a government is considered democratic to the degree it respects the corporate group rights of the societies' constituent units; to the extent it does not respect them, it not only violates basic human rights, but runs the risk of its own overthrow."[18]

Clearly, the United States should not impose its conception of morality and ethics in public policy on anyone. Thus, a government that operates within the context of a traditional political culture, respects the corporate group rights of its subjects, and provides opportunities for democratic elections deserves U.S. support and encouragement, even if it does not subscribe to all of the tenets of U.S. democratic tradition. Yet, while taking into account cultural and historical features of various countries, the United States can properly seek to develop common international human rights norms and secure their acceptance by all members of the international community. Many human rights activists throughout the world support this approach. Andrei Sakharov noted, "the global character of [human rights] is particularly important . . . the defense of human rights is a clear path toward the reunification of our people in the turbulent world."[19]

As far as the perennial challenges to an effective U.S. human rights policy are concerned, the most important one is that its major components generate debate, both among the public and the foreign-policy establishment. To a certain degree, this is inevitable and reflects the fact that human rights policy has graduated from being mere rhetoric to becoming a serious component of U.S. foreign policy, subject to the same controversies and debates as all the other foreign-policy matters. Yet, room for improving human rights policy clearly exists.

In that regard, several guidelines appear to be particularly promising. Most of them involve improving public and congressional support for U.S. human rights policy and enhancing its bureaucratic status. In addition, better executive-legislative cooperation is desirable and feasible in such matters as the development of new human rights legislation and oversight hearings to consider the implementation of existing statutes. The most difficult,

but necessary, task is the eradication of the ideological polarization that has often beset human rights policy. Some of the conservatives must overcome their suspicion of human rights policy as a liberal ruse to bash pro-U.S. regimes abroad. Some liberals need to be convinced that vigorous efforts to promote the cause of human rights by assisting democratic movements abroad are not illegitimate and ought not to be dismissed *a priori*. In other words, building democratic institutions abroad—a goal enunciated by Charles Robb on behalf of the moderate wing of the Democratic party—may require, when appropriate, the dispatch of U.S. arms and advisers.

To maintain broad public and congressional support behind human rights policy, three key points need to be stressed continuously: the pursuit of human rights causes is in the national interest, is compatible with U.S. traditions, and most important, is a realistic undertaking if properly pursued. To be sure, these points have already been stated; yet, any foreign-policy consensus is inherently fragile and requires careful maintenance.

Notes

1. John Locke, *The Second Treatise on Government* (Library of Liberal Arts edition, Indianapolis, Ind.: Bobbs-Merrill Co., Inc., 1952), p. 124.

2. John Winthrop, "A Model of Christian Charity," sermon delivered on board the Arbella, 1630, quoted in *Bartletts' Famous Quotations* (Thomas Brown and Company, 1980), p. 264.

3. *Thomas Jefferson Writings* (The Library of America, 1984), p. 916.

4. Henry Kissinger, "Morality and Power," The *Washington Post*, September 25, 1977.

5. At one time or another, Congress proscribed U.S. assistance, trade, and investment, either partially or in full, with such countries as Angola, Argentina, Brazil, Cambodia, Chile, Cuba, El Salvador, Gua-

temala, Mozambique, Nicaragua, Paraguay, South Africa, South Korea, Uruguay, and Vietnam.

6. Law Day Address by Secretary of State Cyrus Vance, University of Georgia, April 30, 1977, cited in "Toward an Integrated Human Rights Policy," monograph (New York: American Association for the International Commission of Jurists, 1979), p. 1.

7. Michael Novak, "Human Rights and White Sepulchers," in *Human Rights and U.S. Human Rights Policy*, Howard J. Wiarda, ed. (Washington, D.C.: American Enterprise Institute, 1982), p. 79.

8. Jeanne Kirkpatrick, "Dictatorships and Double Standards," *Commentary*, November 19, 1979.

9. Quoted in Roger Pilon, "The Idea of Human Rights," *The National Interest*, Fall 1986, p. 97.

10. Kissinger.

11. Irving Kristol, "Human Rights: The Hidden Agenda," *The National Interest*, Winter 1986–1987, p. 7.

12. Cited in Pilon, p. 98.

13. Lincoln Bloomfield, quoted in "From Ideology to Program to Policy: Tracking the Carter Human Rights Policy," *Journal of Policy Analysis and Management* 2:1 (1982), cited in *Human Rights* in *U.S. Foreign Policies: The First Decade 1973–1983* (New York: American Association for the International Commission of Jurists, 1984), p. 21.

14. Vance, cited in *Human Rights in U.S. Foreign Policies*, p. 21.

15. *United States Foreign Policy and Human Rights: Principles, Priorities, Practice*, December 1979, p. 31.

16. Jimmy Carter, cited in *Human Rights in U.S. Foreign Policies*, p. 20.

17. Aleksandr Solzhenitsyn, *Amerikanskie Rechi* (American Speeches [Paris: YMCA Press, 1975]), p. 77.

18. Howard J. Wiarda, "Democracy and Human Rights in Latin America: Toward a New Conceptualization" in Wiarda, p. 45.

19. Andrei Sakharov, article reprinted in *Trialogue*, Fall 1979, cited in *Human Rights in U.S. Foreign Policies*, pp. 52–53.

England, the United States, and the Export of Democracy

Enrique Krauze

NOT LONG AGO, the Mexican media announced that the U.S. government had developed a program to promote democracy in the hemisphere. The official document recognized that "the American people find it more expeditious to work with democratic governments than with authoritarian regimes," and it announced a continent-wide meeting to be held in mid-1989 to approve and "proclaim the Magna Carta of Pan-American democracy." Not one editorialist took the trouble to criticize the news by asking the obvious question: Since when has the United States been so interested in hemispheric democracy? In fact, the editorials did not miss the point: showing their natural scepticism, those who transcribed the document simply put the word democracy in quotes.

This short anecdote reveals a longstanding mistrust. It illustrates the problem the world's most powerful democracy will have if it persists in exporting its own political system. The problem is not the system itself: democracy is the best system invented by man thus far. Nor is there an alleged cultural resistance or incompatibility that would make adopting Western-style democracy difficult in

Enrique Krauze is a historian and essayist of Mexican development and democracy who also serves as coeditor of a periodic review, *Vuelta*. He has written a number of books and essays on cultural and political history of Mexico.

countries that have lived with other traditions for centuries. The problem lies in the poor track record the United States has in the hemisphere and in the inadequate U.S. understanding of its misbehavior.

Throughout history, not all the powerful democracies—or, for that matter, all democratic empires—have had the same limitations. England provides the clearest example of this. A cursory inspection of a map of the former British empire reveals a constellation of democracies. Let us leave aside the most obvious ones, that is, those that were founded directly by British immigrants: Australia, Canada, New Zealand, and of course the United States. Small Caribbean islands which live, or have lived, under the British flag are democratic: the Bahamas, St. Lucia, St. Vincent. Others, such as Barbados, Jamaica, and Trinidad, have survived the most difficult test of democracy and—with the exception of Grenada—have established and removed quasi-totalitarian regimes in a peaceful manner. On the mainland, Belize is a model democracy. Furthermore, one must ask oneself if the resistance along the Misquita coast of Nicaragua does not owe at least something to the liberal English tradition that dominated the region until the end of the nineteenth century.

One can rightly say that the British were less successful in passing along democracy to the African colonies.

Perhaps counteracting the tribal cultures was difficult; perhaps the imperialists' greed was excessive there. In either case, one can not deny that in many former British colonies concerns over democratic form have been maintained, even if the democratic institutions themselves have disappeared. Nigeria refuses to resign itself to living under a dictatorship. Sudan, devastated by hunger and civil war, has a *Times* that has nothing to fear from its namesake in London. Zimbabwe, formerly Rhodesia, has been one of the greatest political surprises of recent times, proving that democratic methods can prevail over more radical views, reducing them and channeling them into the mainstream. Far from Africa and the American continents, the greatest testimony to England's ability to pass along its democratic traditions is the jewel of the empire—India.

It is disheartening to compare this democratic map with that of the United States' area of influence, particularly regarding Latin America. Of course, historical experiences have differed: the United States has not been a formal empire in the European fashion. In considering the Central American countries, England and the United States perhaps should not be compared; England and Spain are the better comparison. However, the United States has been active in the region for over a century and a half. The United States could have promoted active democratic emulation without the inconveniences and costs involved in a colonial system. The seeds for emulation were already taking root among many nineteenth-century liberals from Sarmiento to Júarez. It is clear that this was not done, but what is not clear is why not.

Many books of genuine national self-criticism have recently appeared in the United States (for example, Alan Bloom's *The Closing of the American Mind* and Paul Kennedy's *The Rise and Fall of Great Powers*). If they are more than just another trend, the time will come when Americans will have to ask themselves why they have failed in their relationships with the world, why the ugly American is more than a stereotype, and just why their democratic convictions lack credibility abroad. To deal with these subjects, they will need to use a humanistic approach—such as comparative history—which is completely alien to their normal evaluative style. It will be difficult for an American academician to ask himself, "What did the British have that we do not?"

One potential methodology would involve comparing English and American attitudes toward the political life of a key country in each of their respective areas of influence, say, India and Mexico. The fundamental differences between these two cases not withstanding, the analogy may help reveal the ways in which democracies may or may not—or should or should not—help to establish or strengthen democracy in countries where it is unknown or is practiced in a limited fashion.

Woodrow Wilson's Exception

Following Mexico's independence, the local strongmen sought to bury their Spanish heritage and develop a new institutional order. Mexico emerged with its eyes set on the natural model, the United States. In 1824 Mexico adopted a constitution inspired by the Founding Fathers of the United States which the contemporary Mexican newspaper El Sol considered "one of the most perfect creations of the spirit . . . the foundation on which the simplest, most liberal and con-

tented government in history rests."
Among some Mexican liberals, this admiration for U.S. institutions and political ideas overshadowed even the most basic feelings of nationalism. The Texan secession of 1836 and the War of 1847, in which Mexico lost over half its territory, helped convince the liberals that the doctrine of manifest destiny was inherently racist and gave little credit to their democratic efforts. So, while Mexican poets were reading *The Federalist Papers*, Walt Whitman justified the expansionistic thirst as a democratic accomplishment: "It is our wish that our country and its laws extend only so far as is necessary to ensure that the shackles that prevent men from enjoying the opportunity of being good and happy are removed."

In the nineteenth century Mexico experienced a civil war with marked ideological connotations. On one hand, conservatives sought the continuation of the Spanish political tradition—with the help of some European governments. On the other, and in spite of the War of 1847, the liberals struggled to implement a democracy like the one to the north. The possibility of the gradual consolidation of a democratic, federalist republic along the southern U.S. border did not particularly impress the American statesmen. If they supported the liberals, it was in exchange for real or promised commercial or territorial concessions.

The complete subordination of U.S. diplomacy to the country's economic interests was also the guideline in 1867, when Mexico repelled the last French soldier from its territory. This event was followed by 10 years of as close to democratic governance as the country had ever seen (under the administrations of presidents Benito Júarez and Miguel Lerdo de Tejada). Yet the attitude of the American diplomats did not change a bit. James

Blaine's bias in favor of a "pacific penetration" that spread "deposits of national vitality across other countries" theoretically left territorial greed behind. However, democracy was not included among the deposits. During the long dictatorship of Porfirio Díaz, Mexico finally turned its sights toward Europe and began to distrust the imperialistic democracy for its policy of "votes on the inside, and the big stick on the outside."

History could have been different if William H. Taft's administration (1909–1913) had been more sensitive to democratic life beyond its borders. Mexico underwent what is probably a unique chapter in the history of Western democracy. A young entrepreneur, Francisco I. Madero, led an innocent and purely democratic revolution against Díaz. Madero had studied at Berkeley, where he learned the progressives' message. He devoutedly applied this message in Mexico upon his return. Democracy was not an ideology for Madero, but a religion.

Beginning in 1903 Madero transferred his personal mysticism to the struggle for democracy and planned the details of a 7-year crusade which would end, to his regret, in revolution. Before the upheaval, Madero encouraged opposition newspapers, founded political clubs, personally bankrolled a broad range of critical initiatives, and finally, in that land without an independent political life, created an opposition party. Staunchly following the U.S. model, he made the first campaign trips through the Mexican states. According to Alan Knight, the path of the "progressive" democratic awakening was clear:

The Mexican reformists emulated the methodology and issues of progressivism: the moralist criticism of politics of the *caciques* (bosses); the civic preoccupation with installing representative and honest governments. On a more profound level, Maderism—as much as progressivism—was a movement of the urban middle class, which was simultaneously the beneficiary of the economic growth and the bearer of the traditional values of constitutional liberalism.

In October 1911, following a mild revolution and the definitive exile of the dictator, Madero won the presidency in the cleanest elections recorded in contemporary Mexican history. During Madero's 15-month administration, Mexico experienced full democracy (a much more profound and broadly based democracy than that of the Júarez period) with electoral cleanliness, a division of powers, a variety of parties, respect for municipal and state autonomy, and effective federalism, all within the context of complete freedom of expression and criticism.

Unfortunately, the Americans who provided Madero with limited support against Díaz (the old dictator flirted too much with Europe and Japan) soon longed for peaceful times and actively sought a return to the status quo. "If you consider Madero's economic and foreign policy," Knight noted, "the extreme and virulent U.S. opposition to his government seems incomprehensible." Madero overturned Díaz's pro-British policy and scrupulously respected the right to private property. Washington, however, paid little attention to these facts, and preferred to be scandalized by the adoption of such minimally democratic measures as the legalization of trade unions. It is true that Madero faced growing political, military and revolutionary opposition, but the political upheaval was merely a result of the years of dictatorship.

The people who voted for him never withdrew their support.

Madero was overthrown not by a revolution but by a *cuartelazo* (barrack's revolt) led by a U.S. ambassador. His name, although all but forgotten in his hometown, appears in every Mexican history text: Henry Lane Wilson. Prior to the coup d'état of February 1913, Lane Wilson systematically opposed Madero. With the outbreak of the coup, he garnered the blessings of president Taft and secretary of state Philander Knox and shifted from diplomatic war to the diplomacy of war. The plan to depose the man who was known by Mexicans as "the apostle of democracy," was devised in the U.S. embassy and was known to the protagonists as the "Treaty of the Embassy." Thirteen days after the *cuartelazo* began, Madero was murdered. Several months later, an emissary of the new U.S. president, Woodrow Wilson, gave his own account of the events:

> Without the assistance provided by the ambassador of the United States to General [Victoriano] Huerta in formulating his traitorous plans against the president, the coup attempt would have failed. . . . President Madero was not betrayed and arrested by his own officials until there was no doubt that the American ambassador had no objections to such an ignoble event. The crime could not have been committed without his consent.

"History," Hugh Trevor Roper wrote, "is what transpired within the context of what might have taken place." If, instead of favoring Huerta, president Taft had supported exile for Madero, Mexican history would have been different. With the legitimacy and political experience that he previously lacked, Madero would have returned to Mexico to restore the democratic order and once again depose the dictator, Huerta. This restoration, supported by Wilson, would have been less bloody than the civil war that shook the country as a result of the presidential assassination.

Madero's new triumph could have permanently consolidated a democratic system in Mexico. Furthermore, the coincidence of the two progressives in power would have established a precedent of understanding and cooperation between the two countries. Unfortunately, this did not occur. What might have been a policy of actively promoting democracy became one of blockading a new dictatorship. In one of his first statements as president (and after Madero's death) Woodrow Wilson said, "I will not recognize a government of butchers." He also said,

Cooperation is only possible where there is due process and a fair government based on the rule of law, not on the use of force or arbitrariness. . . . We shall see to it that these principles form the basis of the respectful and fruitful exchange between us and our sister republics. We will utilize the full extent of our influence in order to see these principles advance, as we know that disorder, personal intrigue and challenges to constitutional rights weaken and discredit governments and hurt the people. . . . We cannot sympathize with those who seek to seize the power of government to advance their personal interests or ambitions. We are friends of peace, but we also know that no peace can last under such conditions.

Despite the pressure of key European governments and U.S. companies doing business in Mexico, president Wilson adhered to these moral principles and refused to recognize Huerta. In the end, however, Wilson ordered the occupation of the city of Veracruz. This maneuver lasted for several months and precipitated Huerta's demise. Despite the limited nature of the occupation, the triumphant constitutionalist revolution could not publicly recognize the help it had received from the U.S. occupation forces. The "good" Wilson was paying the price for the "bad" Wilson. All in all, Knight was correct when he said that the occupation took place against the deepest wishes of president Wilson; therefore, he cannot be grouped together with the "authentic interventionists." Any other president, particularly prior to 1916 or after 1919, would have gone to war. Plenty of people called for action, but Wilson would not hear of it. He believed that "the strongest forces in history are moral forces." This saying, which any political realist would find laughable, had direct and beneficial impact on his relations with Mexico. In addition, Knight concluded,

Wilson was no moralist simpleton obsessed with teaching the Mexicans how to do things right. Nor was he an instrument of Standard Oil. Wilson's policies combined a certain moral liberalism with long-term realpolitik: for individuals, as for the United States, short-term morality served more permanent interests. According to Wilson, only a representative government could ensure political stability and with it, capitalist development. One had to support representative governments, especially those which were struggling to free themselves from old, corrupt and dictatorial regimes. . . . Tolerating these regimes was, overall, both morally and strategically erroneous.

Despite the relative success of his policies toward Mexico, Wilson's example faded with his passing. His interest in seeing liberal and constitutional democracies in Latin America is remarkable in the history of the U.S. presidency. The good neighbor policy, the Alliance for Progress, and the human rights policy of president Jimmy Carter had their positive aspects and achieved a certain closeness with the countries to the south, but they lacked in their very essence the *purely democratic spirit* of the Wilsonian message.

Many years later, Daniel Cosío Villegas reflected on U.S. mistakes with Cuba and explained why he believed the so-called Wilson Doctrine did not take root. The earlier doctrine of (commercial) manifest destiny took precedence. Foreign-policy interests were subjugated to domestic commercial demands. He rightly believed that the twentieth century offered undeniable proof of this. Even the good neighbor, Theodore Roosevelt, had cabinet members with interests in Cuban sugar. President Herbert Hoover had declared that without U.S. exports the "great masses" of Latin America would wind up in barbarism. Years later the commercial credentials of John Foster Dulles were hailed as the epitome of diplomatic excellency. The other antidemocratic elements of U.S. foreign policy are all too well known: from the support of dictators who, like Marcos Pérez Jiménez in Venezuela, assured a "fertile climate" for U.S. investments to the deliberate policy of destabilizing a few democratically elected regimes (from Madero to Salvador Allende).

Cosío Villegas was a liberal in the classic sense, a student of John Stuart Mill. He hated the Soviet Union and admired many things about the United States. He saw events in Cuba as unfortunate for that country and for all the Americas. From those same liberal convictions, he tried to understand—not accuse or denounce—the Latin American distrust of the United States, which grew from the close relationship between U.S. politicians and businessmen. Cosío Villegas said this relationship was perceived as "perfectly abnormal" everywhere but in the United States and this "irreparably damages its people and its government." To the rest of the world this attitude had a simple and age-old name: greed. Its effect was generalized animosity and mistrust. He wrote these words with the bitterness of a prophet who has lived long enough to see his prophecies come true. In 1947 he wrote that if the American attitude continued:

> Latin America will seethe with restlessness and be ready for anything. Carried on a tide of desperation and fiery hate, these countries—apparently submissive to the point of abasement—will be capable of anything: of protecting and encouraging the adversaries of the United States, or converting themselves into the worst of all possible enemies. Once this occurs not even threats will quell them.

This argument implied that in its foreign relations, U.S. democracy put the political and moral values of its founders at the service of commercial interests; therefore, it was not worthy of emulation. The most powerful democracy in the Americas has not been the main obstacle to the growth of democracy in Latin America. The main obstacle has been the longtime irresponsibility of Latin American political life, leaders, and institutions. Nevertheless, one does not have to be a left-wing intellectual to acknowledge that, judging from its historical performance, the most powerful democracy in the Americas has in general not helped democracy in Latin America.

Edmund Burke's Rule

As a young man, Woodrow Wilson hung a picture of William Gladstone in his dormitory room. As president, he recalled the historic lessons of the English liberal tradition. Gladstone wrote in 1877, "India should rule herself."

It is time for principles to come down from the icy heights of political philosophy to the warmth of daily life as rules of practical living that limit our officials. . . . If not, we will be ill prepared to confront the growing Indian intelligence stemming from the process of political education that we ourselves have introduced into that country.

The processes of political education to which Gladstone referred began toward the end of the eighteenth century with the first translations of Sanskrit and Persian classics into English and the adoption of English as the language of the courts. Hindu College was founded in Calcutta at the beginning of the nineteenth century. There, many generations of intellectuals, journalists, lawyers, and teachers—the social actors in India's long transition to democracy—were taught.

That century saw the rise of such leaders as Gopal Krishna Gokhale—teacher, editor, patient social reformer, and politician—whom Gandhi considered his political guru. The key to Gokhale's success was his faith in the moral fiber of English liberalism. Nada Bhai Naoroji, another of the great masters of Indian nationalism and the first Indian member of the House of Commons, summarized this basic conviction:

The British are incapable of despotism. They may be—and in fact sometimes are—heavy handed, but their instinct and love of liberty, the constitutionalism with which they are born and is a part of them leads the Britisher—even in extreme situations—to abstain from the use of power lest he be perceived as incurring the disgrace of despotism.

Although the liberal reforms in India did not lead to the effective and responsible self-governance that Gladstone desired, the key actors introduced doses of administrative decentralization and economic reform. The schism in the ranks of liberalism that developed over the issue of Irish home rule and the rise of imperialism kept the more radical wing of liberalism from having a greater impact in India. Many liberals were opposed to Gladstone's form of democratic liberalism, which favored self-determination for Ireland and the farther flung colonies. Overall, the liberal message influenced several of the Raj viceroys who slowly incorporated Indian representatives into the councils and the judicial system.

Incidentally, one of the more fascinating aspects of the introduction of English democracy in India was the role of the theosophists. An unusual Scotsman named Allan Octavian Hume—retired officer, mystical reformer, and ornithologist—was the founder of the Congressional party and was its first British member. Even Gandhi had bet on the latent liberalism of British politics, though not without reservations.

How then was it possible that the

original Anglo-Saxon trunk gave root to democracy? An eighteenth-century Mexican historian and an English political reformer shed some light on this mystery.

Cosío Villegas, in his critique of the United States, repeated—perhaps unwittingly—the arguments made by Edmund Burke two centuries earlier in his famous suit against the East India Company. Around 1780 Burke compiled such great quantities of evidence of the company's arbitrary behavior that the House of Commons initiated an investigation into its principal architect, Warren Hastings. In describing the company as "oppressive, irregular, capricious, unstable, predatory, despotic and corrupt," Burke summarized his complaint in three propositions:

> First, in India there is not one prince or state, large or small that has a relationship with the Company that has not been corrupted. . . . Second, there is not one single treaty that [the Company] has made that it hasn't broken. . . . Third, there is not one prince or state that trusted in the Company that is not now in ruin. No one can be certain of succeeding beyond the limits imposed by his deep mistrust and irreconcilable enmity toward England.

The heart of the argument is simple. Burke recognized the commercial rights of the company, but he refused to compare them with or subordinate them to the rights of the nation, much less to the natural rights of man. In order to prove his point he invoked the original pact of English society:

> The Magna Carta gives the right to restrict power and to destroy monopolies. The charter of the East India gives it the right to establish a monopoly and create

power. Political and commercial power are not the right of man.

One must recollect that he who wrote these lines would, in just a few years, pen one of the most severe criticisms of the French Revolution.

Neither of the great empires—England in the nineteenth century and the United States in the twentieth—was ever motivated by philanthropic ideals. In the case of the former, however, the political philosophy on which it was based created certain limits. A map of the former British empire reveals a constellation of democracies. This is the philosophy that Burke invoked in his arguments against the East India Company and provided the basis for his earlier support of the independence of the American colonies. The very nature of that philosophy required its dissemination. In a renowned speech before Parliament in 1833 Thomas Babington Macaulay declared:

> It may be possible that the public spirit in India may expand under our system and take it one step further; that through good government we can prepare the Indians for self-governance; that having been educated in European culture they adopt, at some point in the future, European institutions. I don't know whether this day will come, but if it does, it will be the proudest day in the history of England.

After many centuries of living with democracy as the art of limiting power, the English understood the necessity of limiting their own power:

> Among the precautions against ambition, it may be worth taking precautions against our ambition. In all honesty I must say that I fear our own power and our own

ambition. I fear that we are too feared.

In contrast, U.S. history recognizes neither the notion of limits nor the pride of disseminating democracy beyond its borders. In its intellectual history, there is no Burke or Macaulay, and, in its political history, there is but one Gladstone. True, by saving Europe in World War II and by implementing the Marshall Plan, the United States saved European democracy. There is a subtle difference, however, in fostering the cause of democracy in times of peace and in times of war. The United States has done the big job but failed to do the little job—the one that needs patience, wisdom, and decades or centuries of effort.

Things have come full circle. The obstacles that the United States will encounter in its efforts to promote democratic ideas legitimately are set forth by its own Anglo-Saxon philosophic tradition. In order to formulate a new Pan-American Magna Carta, the U.S. government must adopt and propose the adoption of the original and very same Magna Carta that the nobles imposed on King John in feudal times.

Acknowledgement: Another version of this essay was prepared for the International Leadership Forum in Lisbon, Portugal, June 16-19, 1988, to accompany those of Carl Gershman and Larry Diamond (*TWQ*, 12:1). Another version was printed in the Mexican journal, *Vuelta*.

Bibliography

Villegas, Daniel Cosío. *Ensayos y notas*. Editorial Hermes. 1966.

Hale, Charles. *Mexican Liberalism in the Age of Mora, 1821–1853*. New Haven, Conn.: Yale University Press. 1968.

Huizinga, Hohan. *America*. New York: Harper. 1972.

Katz, Friedrich. *La Guerra Secreta en México*. Vol. 1. Era. 1982.

Knight, Alan. "U.S.-Mexican Relations, 1910–1940: An Interpretation." Monograph Series 28. San Diego, Calif.: University of California, Center for U.S.-Mexican Studies. 1987.

Link, Arthur S. *Wilson: The Road to the White House*. Vols. 1–5. Princeton, N.J.: Princeton University Press. 1947–1965.

———, ed. *Woodrow Wilson and a Revolutionary World 1913–1921*. Chapel Hill, N.C.: University of North Carolina Press. 1982.

———. *Woodrow Wilson and the Progressive Era 1910–1917*. New York: Harper. 1954.

Moore, R. J. *Liberalism and Indian Politics 1872–1922*. London: Edward Arnold Publishers. 1968.

O'Brien, Conor Cruise. "The Manifesto of a Contrarevolution." In *Reflections on the Revolution in France*. Edmund Burke, ed. New York: Penguin. 1983.

Quirk, Robert E. *An Affair of Honor: Woodrow Wilson and the Occupation of Veracruz*. New York: W. W. Norton and Company. 1967.

U.S. Political Parties Abroad

Joshua Muravchik

"I BELONG TO no organized political party. I am a Democrat." The point of this Will Rogers quip applies not only to the Democrats but to U.S. political parties in general. It is sometimes hard for outsiders to understand just how loosely structured U.S. parties are, that, for example, it is not possible to "join" the Democratic or Republican parties. To be sure, in many locales one may join a Democratic or Republican club, but only a few voters do, often those with political ambitions, and even such clubs have no organic links to the national parties. The national parties exist essentially in the form of the Democratic and Republican national committees, the members of which are selected by the national nominating conventions. The conventions in turn are composed mainly of delegates chosen in presidential primaries. The delegates represent the various contenders for the presidential nomination of their party rather than local party bodies.

Just as the parties have no membership, they also have no doctrine or ideology. They even have little in the way of party policy. True, each party adopts a platform every four years at its nominating convention, but the nominee essentially dictates the platform. It may lean left one election and

right the next. Or it may lean in no discernable direction at all, a recipe for a bland mush designed to offend as few voters as possible, seasoned only with a bouquet of special favors chosen to appeal to particular interest groups. If the nominee wins the presidency, no one regards him as bound by the platform, and, if he loses, the platform endures not a moment beyond the election.

In 1978 the Democrats broke precedent and convenend a national "issues conference." A pale imitation of European party conferences, the Democratic gathering made no attempt to adopt resolutions, limiting itself to panel discussions on various topics. Even this was too ideologically rich for American blood. The Republicans declined to hold any similar gathering, and the Democrats soon decided that airing their views or their discord put them at a competitive disadvantage, so they cancelled plans to hold future such talkfests every four years between presidential elections.

U.S. parties, in short, are loose electoral coalitions, held together in part by substantive affinities, in part by expedience, and in part by inertia. Even after a 25-year trend toward sharper ideological definition—toward liberalism for the Democrats and toward conservatism for the Republicans—roughly a fifth of the Democrats in the U.S. Senate are more conservative than roughly a fifth of the Republicans,[1] and the overlap in the House is probably at least as large.

Joshua Muravchik is a resident scholar at the American Enterprise Institute. His most recent book is *News Coverage of the Sandinista Revolution* (Washington, D.C.: American Enterprise Institute, 1988).

It is little wonder then that U.S. parties have abstained from the kind of international activities that are second nature to most European parties. Party internationalism, after all, is rooted in ideology. Its prototype was Marx's International Workingmen's Association, founded on his premise that "the working men have no country." That premise, and with it the successor Second International, was exploded by the outbreak of World War I and the decision of the various socialist parties to support their respective governments (with the notable exceptions of the Bolsheviks and the American Socialists). Nonetheless, the less radical notion that, in addition to bonds of nationalism, socialists or Christian Democrats or liberals or conservatives have important bonds with their ideological confreres across borders remains the essence of party internationalism. Such ideological affinities do not come easily to U.S. parties which, as Mr. Dooley said of the Democratic party, "ain't on speakin' terms with itsilf," much less with foreign parties.

Despite this background, during the past five years the two major U.S. parties have begun programs of international activities, and there is reason to expect that these will grow. This demarche is part of the renewed spirit of democratic idealism that has swelled in Americans during the last decade, the synthesis of Jimmy Carter's moralism and Ronald Reagan's nationalism. This spirit was given institutional form in the National Endowment for Democracy (NED), a Reagan administration creation that has enjoyed bipartisan congressional support. Indeed, it drew on some earlier proposals by such Democrats as senator Hubert Humphrey and representatives Dante Fascell and Donald Fraser.

The NED, like other government-supported endowments, is privately incorporated and governed only by its own board but relies on annual appropriations from Congress for its income. It is primarily a grant-making institution, offering support to foreign groups, the overseas programs of U.S. groups, and occasional scholarly undertakings, all with the aim of fostering the spread of democratic government around the world. The paradigmatic activity for the NED is to give a grant to a U.S. group for its work with a counterpart group abroad. The theory behind this is that strengthening nongovernmental organizations is essential to building democracy and that the most effective assistance to such elements comes from their U.S. equivalents. The model for this activity is the assistance that has been given for decades by U.S. labor unions to unions, or those trying to organize unions, in developing countries. Indeed, a big share of the NED's modest budget is earmarked for expanding such labor programs through the Free Trade Union Institute (FTUI) which was created for the purpose as a kind of companion or subsidiary of the endowment.

In addition to FTUI, three other companion institutes were founded along with the NED: the Center for International Private Enterprise organized by the U.S. Chamber of Commerce to promote entrepreneurship and civic action by Third World business groups, and an institute associated with each of the two major political parties, the National Republican Institute for International Affairs (NRI) and a similarly named Democratic body (NDI). It is easy to see the logic of making labor, business, and the two parties—four preeminent sectors of U.S. political life—the pillars of an effort to endow democracy abroad, but labor was the only one of the four with any such experience. Aside from its operational logic, a further reason for this arrangement may have sprung from domestic political considerations, namely, to try to vest enough interest in the endowment on the part of various constituencies to ensure that it itself would be endowed by Congress.

If this was the ulterior motive behind the founding of the Republican and Democratic institutes for international affairs, the ploy backfired. Congressional support for the endowment was shallow, and the party institutes were especially unpopular. Many legislators were loath to appear to be appropriating public funds to political parties. Some were also cyncial about the party national committees and worried that the two party institutes would just be used as slush funds for junkets and other self-indulgent or unfocused activity. "Meetin' an' eatin'," was how Senator Fritz Hollings, a strong opponent of the endowment, put it. Congress nearly abandoned the endowment in its second year of life, fiscal year 1985, and it cut off without a cent the party institutes. The following year, however, funding was restored, and since then congressional support for all these programs has been hardening gradually.

Like the NED, the Republican and Democratic institutes are each independently incorporated organizations, formally accountable only to their own governing boards which consist of prominent party members, about a dozen for the Republicans, twice that number for the Democrats. Although each has strong informal ties to the national committee of its party, no national committee officer may serve simultaneously as an officer of the NRI or NDI. Each institute is run by a president chosen by the board. Each

receives a budget of about $2 million a year appropriated by Congress through the NED and supplements it by raising a few hundred thousand dollars in private contributions.

Though similar in form and genesis, the two party institutes diverge sharply in philosophy and method. The Democratic institute defines its mission in a way that closely tracks the NED, encouraging democratic processes but usually avoiding taking sides between competing groups in the countries where it works. The Republican institute follows more closely in the tradition of party internationalism, seeking to cultivate ties with those foreign parties with which it feels an ideological affinity.

This difference is a product of differences in the internal dynamics of the two parties, as well as of the exceptional nature of the U.S. political spectrum. In Western Europe the parties that occupy the part of the spectrum equivalent to that of the Democrats are socialist parties. However, given the anathema attached to the word "socialist" in U.S. politics, the Democrats could ill afford to identify themselves exclusively with those parties. Moreover, the Democratic party, says Brian Atwood, president of the National Democratic Institute, is a "moveable feast when it comes to ideology." This is something of an exaggeration, because the Democrats in recent years have been dominated by their liberal wing,[2] but the party does still contain moderates and conservatives, too, and its liberals come in various stripes. To select a single ideological tendency as its interlocutor in its work abroad would be to invite internecine rancor in its ranks at home. Ergo, the Democratic institute follows what it calls a nonpartisan approach.

The term "nonpartisan" does not refer to the NDI's domestic status—it is of course affiliated with the Democratic party—but to the wide array of foreign political groups with which it works. NDI President Atwood sits as a member of the bureau of the Liberal International, while his institute also holds official observer status with the Christian Democrat Union and sends representives to gatherings of the Socialist International and the conservative International Democrat Union (IDU).

The Republican Institute, in contrast works almost exclusively with the IDU, of which the Republican party is a full member. One reason for the difference, says Keith Schuette, president of the Republican institute, is that "we are an ideologically more homogeneous party." It is the Republican National Committee, not the Republican institute, through which the party is affiliated with the IDU. Schuette has represented the RNC at the IDU so that the activities of these bodies meld neatly. Schuette sees his role as one of encouraging the IDU, which is made up mostly of parties from advanced industrial countries, to give more help and encouragement to conservative elements in the developing countries, which are the main focus of the NRI.

Some Democrats criticize the Republican institute for not mirroring their nonpartisan approach. The criticism is implicit in Atwood's remark that because the U.S. parties are "operating in a 'superpower' context . . . favoring of one side or another in a democratic setting could have the effect of distorting the political process, not strengthening it."[3] Schuette replies by pointing out that parties on the left side of the political spectrum, from extreme to moderate—Communist, Socialist, and Chistian Democrat—have long histories of international solidarity, with parties in rich

countries aiding those in poor. "Internationally, it is the conservative end of the spectrum that has suffered from the lack of a mutual support network." His work, he says, only redresses the balance, enabling conservative parties in Third World countries to compete on a more equal footing.

The Democrats, themselves, deviate from nonpartisanship, under certain circumstances, as they do not hesitate to acknowledge. In countries that are not democratic, in which the hope for a democratic transition seems to rest with a particular political grouping, the Democratic institute may seek to assist that group. As Atwood says, his institute "has not hesitated to work with single parties or coalitions which espouse democratic reform." The single most important example of such partisanship has been in Chile, where the Democratic institute supported the coalition of opposition parties that became the "command for the 'no'" in the 1988 plebiscite. In South Korea in 1985 and 1986, the institute worked with the New Korea Democratic party, then the principle opposition group pressing for democratization.

In its most notable deviation from nonpartisanship, the NDI has run an extensive party-building program with the Social Democratic and Labor party (SDLP) of Northern Ireland. The institute has helped the SDLP to create an affiliated foundation "to execute non-electoral functions, such as research, training and leadership development." It has brought three different groups of mid-level SDLP leaders to the United States for training in political organizing skills, and last year it held a series of eight training seminars for local party activists in various locales in Northern Ireland. Although Northern Ireland is not a dictatorship, the NDI defends its partisan role there on the grounds that the SDLP is the main party in the nationalist Catholic community seeking peaceful, democratic change in the status of Northern Ireland, and that, therefore, it constitutes the essential alternative to violent and authoritarian elements. And Atwood acknowledges that the NDI has a kind of special relationship with Northern Ireland as a result of the extraordinary efforts of several leading Democrats of Irish ancestry to dissuade Irish Americans from support of the Irish Republican Army and other violent sects.

With their modest budgets, and with democracy either absent or tenuous in most of the world, both party institutes have had to pick their shots. The Democrats' strategy is to "place . . . a priority on programs that, at critical moments in a nation's history, will make an important impact on the momentum of democratic development."[4] Thus, the institute has eschewed long-term development projects in countries where the prospects for democracy are remote, seeking instead to concentrate on three types of situation, "new democracies, societies in conflict and nondemocratic countries with strong democratic movements."[5]

In new democracies, the NDI has sought ways to nurture democratic roots. In Argentina, for example it has held conferences on constitutional reform and on civil-military relations. One of its goals is to strengthen legislative power in such countries as a makeweight to executive power. Toward that end it has sponsored a project in Brazil aiming to teach legislators there about the U.S. congressional budgetary process in the hope that this will help them to gain and wield greater power of the purse.

As for societies in conflict, the institute has assumed the part of election monitor in several transitional situations. Together with the Republican institute, the NDI sponsored a nonpartisan delegation that exposed the fraudulent means by which Philippine president Ferdinand Marcos attempted to misrepresent the results of the 1986 "snap election" in which apparently he was bested by current President Corazon Aquino. Given the United States' strong influence in the Philippines, this authoritative, bipartisan refutation of Marcos's claim was instrumental to the ensuing chain of events in which Marcos was forced from power and the Philippine electorate's choice was vindicated. Building on that experience, the institute also sent observers in 1988 to the national parliamentary elections in Pakistan and the plebiscite in Chile. One major failure in the election observation program was the effort of a bipartisan team sent to Haiti for the scheduled presidential election in 1987. The American observers were helpless to protect the electoral process against the violent elements who were determined to thwart it. The would-be monitors counted themselves lucky to have escaped without adding to the list of casualties as two groups of them became targets of gunfire.

The NDI's election observer teams are multinational in composition. One way that the institute tries to achieve its goal of abetting prodemocracy movements in undemocratic countries is by including members of these movements in its observers teams to third countries, in the hope that they will gain useful experience. Thus, for example, Paraguayans were among the observers sent to Chile. In addition, the institute has undertaken small programs of technical aid to opposition movements in Taiwan and Paraguay as well as those in South Korea and Chile.

Although the institute does not ordinarily sponsor scholarly research, it has undertaken one innovative project that aims at expanding the knowledge base for democratic progress or the intellectual arsenal of those fighting for democracy. It has sponsored a series of three conferences in and about countries where democracy is thriving although surrounded by a sea of dictatorship or instability—Botswana, Costa Rica, and Israel. Neither Botswana nor Costa Rica is radically distinct from its neighbors in cultural heritage or natural endowment, yet each is distinct in its happy political history. Israel of course is a cultural anomaly in its region; its democracy can be understood in terms of a cultural heritage that is more European than Middle Eastern. Yet the Israeli example is important because of the enormous role of the military in society, a situation that has bedeviled democratic progress in so many other countries. The conferences will eventuate in a forthcoming (1989) book. It aims to serve both an empirical and a normative purpose. The empirical purpose is to help explain how democracy succeeds in adverse circumstances. The normative purpose is to underline the fact that democracy can succeed under such circumstances, thereby blunting the arguments of those who would too readily excuse its absence.

Of the various projects so far undertaken by the Democratic institute, the one of which it is proudest, and for which outsiders give it high marks, is its work in Chile. Sending an election observer team to monitor the plebiscite was but the culmination of three years of work that may well have made a crucial difference in what now appears to be a major success story of the transition to democracy.

Early in 1985 the NDI sought to encourage dialogue among the varying parties in the Chilean opposition. Those same parties joined together later that year to sign the National Accord pledging united action to hasten the restoration of democracy. The NDI then worked to preserve this unity against centrifugal forces by bringing the 11 signers of the accord together in 1986 in Caracas, Venezuela, along with democratic leaders from other countries.

Early in 1988 the opposition made the crucial decision to campaign in the plebiscite for a "no" vote, rather than to boycott it. The plebiscite was of course unfair, forcing voters to say yes or no to Augusto Pinochet rather than having a choice of candidates. In addition, the government enjoyed a monopoly over the airwaves and the terms of the plebiscite provided that even if defeated Pinochet would remain as president for a year and as head of the armed forces for many more. The opposition fought for constitutional change to allow a more democratic election, but, when the government refused to budge, the oppositon faced a hard choice. Should it participate on these unfair terms, thereby risking legitmating Pinochet's rule? In hindsight, it is easy to say that it made the right choice by seizing the small democratic opportunity that was available.

However disadvantageous its terms, the plebiscite was susceptible to the one resource that U.S. political parties have in abundance: campaign technique. Democratic political professionals traveled to Chile under NDI auspices to teach voter registration methods. Through the sophisticated polling that the Americans brought, the opposition was able to calculate how many voters needed to be registered to maximize the chance for a victory for the "no." The polls also helped guide the choice of themes for the "no" campaign. The NDI's professionals helped the opposition to develop the television spots that it broadcast during the 15 minutes of nightly air time that each side was allotted during the last weeks of the campaign. A poll by a Chilean opinion research organization (which itself received considerable support from the Republican institute)

> showed that the effectiveness of the "no" media campaign far eclipsed that of the "yes." Chileans rated the "no" campaign highest in every category tested in the survey, including being "credible," "optimistic," "clearly understood," "dynamic," "motivating," and the "better choice," and in communicating its "capability in governing the country."[6]

The media whizzes of the "no" campaign even commissioned a campaign jingle that, by some accounts, became the most popular song in Chile at the time. In such a contest Pinochet and his fellow officers were out of their depths.

On polling day, the Chilean opposition used computerized sampling and tallying systems, with which the NDI also had assisted, to make its own calculation of the outcome of the vote. This capability proved crucial on election night. Shortly after the polls closed, government officials announced that the "yes" was ahead, then for several pregnant hours no further news came from official sources, apparently as the government absorbed the fact of its defeat. The junta convened behind closed doors at midnight, and at 2:30 a.m. officials confirmed that the "no" had won. The fact that the opposition was announcing accurate independent counts and the presence of international observers

probably helped to dissuade Pinochet from any tampering with the results.

Although the Republican institute does not share the Democrats' concept of nonpartisanship, it aims, according to its president, Keith Schuette, "first and foremost [to] promote the democratic process." However, he adds, "when we approach that task we work with those institutions with which we share the most common values." His brief list of those values includes "free market economics, individual liberty, rule of law, family values." "We can be most helpful to those who want to create in their own societies things like those we support here," he says. Hence, a large part of the institute's work revolves around the IDU, which *The Wall Street Journal* calls "the nonsocialist international."

In its method of operation, the NRI differs in another important way from the NDI. The Democratic institute is more of an action agency, carrying out its own programs and employing a relatively large staff. The Republican institute works more in the manner of the NED, serving primarily as a grantmaking body.

The Republican institute's grants aim to boost the work of affiliates of the IDU or likeminded elements, but rarely does the institute contribute directly to a political party. As a tax-exempt institution, the NRI is severely restricted in the political activities that it is allowed to carry out at home, and for reasons of prudence it has adopted the rule-of-thumb of partaking in no activity abroad that it could not do legally in the United States. As a result, it directs most of its grants to foundations that are affiliated with foreign parties rather than to the parties themselves. These foundations engage in research, publishing, polling, education, training, and the like, all of which are useful in pol-

179

itics, but they are supposed to avoid direct campaign work.

Most of the groups with which the NRI works are in Latin America. One, to which it points with special pride is the Bolivian Foundation for the Promotion of Democracy (FUNDEMOS) which is associated with the National Democratic Action party, now Bolivia's largest party. FUNDEMOS works to promote political participation and conservative policies. Bolivia, which today has an elected government, has in its history had a dearth of peaceful transitions of government. One aim of the work that the NRI supports, says Schuette, is to convince Bolivian conservatives, businessmen, and the military that their legitimate interests can be protected under democratic rule.

In Argentina, the NRI supports the Instituto de la Economia Social de Mercado, which is aligned with the Union Central Democratico (UCD) party. NRI funds underwrite the institute's four periodicals as well as various seminars and an essay contest for students. The UCD is Argentina's third largest party, and Schuette candidly volunteers that it enjoyed only 7 percent support in opinion polls not long ago. The party's electoral weakness, however, is of small concern to the NRI, although Schuette takes some pleasure in the UCD's improved showing in more recent polls. The important point is to nourish a conservative viewpoint (as distinct from an authoritarian-rightist one) that has been absent too often from Argentine political dialogue. They are not daunted by the prospect that that viewpoint may remain in the minority for many years.

One situation where the Republican institute worked directly with a political party was in Grenada in the wake of the U.S. invasion. Having toppled the Communist regime, the United States was eager to see power pass as quickly as possible to a new, elected government. For a time it seemed that the only organized political forces that could take advantage of the electoral opportunity were those loyal to Grenada Labor party leader Eric Gairy, the erratic former prime minister, and the Maurice Bishop loyalists among the followers of the New Jewel Movement. The NRI gave direct assistance to the prodemocratic Grenadans who organized the New Patriotic party which succeeded in winning 14 of 15 legislative seats and forming a new government.

Like the NED, the two party institutes continue to face some congressional opposition albeit less than a few years ago. Some, on the conservative side of the spectrum, are suspicious of the institutes' do-good agenda and of any expenditure of tax dollars that seems less than imperative. Their ranks include conservative Democrat Fritz Hollings who chairs the subcommittee that overseas appropriations for the endowment and the institutes. On the liberal side, some legislators shrink from assertions of U.S. influence in foreign countries. One of their most extreme number is Congressman Mervyn Dymally of California, who perceives "a fascist trend" in the United States and who believes that U.S. foreign policy is directed by a "monied, elite group of people who oppose humanitarian concerns in favor of the military, in order to resist the Communists and thereby safeguard their economic interests." Dymally has just become chairman of the House subcommittee that authorizes funds for the NED and related bodies.

These opponents probably do not have the legislative muscle to kill the institutes, but they may be able to keep them severely undernourished. Indeed, to accomplish this, they need do little more than resist any increase over the niggardly budget requests that the Reagan and Bush administrations have sent to Capitol Hill the last few years. This year's request for the NED (in which the party institutes' allocations are included) is about 40 percent lower in constant dollars than what it received when it began five years ago.

Politics not being a science, the work of these groups is inherently experimental. What works in one situation may not work in another. The most sensible way for them to proceed is by sponsoring many small projects and then expanding and sustaining the successful ones. Such a mode of operation, however, becomes almost impossible if the programs face real dollar cuts in their appropriations year after year. This congressional penny-pinching seems all the more short-sighted because the sums involved are so small. The entire budget proposal for this democracy-building work is equal to one-quarter of 1 percent of the amount President Bush proposes to cut from the Reagan defense budget this year. The accomplishments of the institutes in Chile, Grenada, and the Philippines alone are sufficient to justify this expenditure, and this is only a small part of the overall program of the NED and its affiliates.

One of the difficulties against which these bodies labor is that no definitive proof or measurement of their impact is possible. Who can say for certain what might have happened in any given historical situation if one element present had been absent, or vice versa? Perhaps, the future of Bolivia will be unaffected by the Republicans' efforts or that of Northern Ireland by those of the Democrats. Perhaps, even the fate of Chile, Grenada, and the Philippines will be no different than had the institutes not been involved,

although it seems likely that their efforts will have made a difference.

Conversely, perhaps Nicaragua would not have fallen to the benighted tyranny of the Sandinistas had its democratic elements been bolstered in the 1970s to the point of being able to lead the opposition to Somoza. The triumph of the Sandinistas was rather a close call—as was, to make the point more dramatic, Hitler's in Germany and Lenin's in Russia. How might history have been different had outside assistance been available to the Mensheviks and Constitutional Democrats and Right Socialist Revolutionaries during 1917 and the surrounding years? Or to the various democratic parties of the Weimar Republic during its tragic life?

One case in which such outside intervention almost surely was important was in Portugal in 1975 when leftist military officers came within a hair's breadth of delivering the country to the Communist camp. Portugal's Socialists, led by Mario Soares, played a key role in pulling the country back from the brink, and they in turn received widely reported assistance from the German Social Democrats and other Socialists in Western Europe. This assistance from fellow democrats counterbalanced the assistance that Portugese Communists were receiving from their comrades in Moscow.

This example points to one of the most basic motivations for the work being undertaken by the party institutes and the NED, namely that democracy's most potent enemies, the Communists, have long invested large sums and energies in international work designed to foster Communism. Is it not natural, if not imperative, that democrats try to respond by working to foster democracy? Indeed, should not such political competition, as opposed to military, be the chosen battleground of the democrats? Ironically, with communism today writhing in the deepest crisis since its birth, the question looms of what can be done by the West to nurture democratization in the Communist world itself. That is the ultimate challenge facing democratic internationalism.

Notes

1. This calculation is based on the voting scores of legislators issued annually by the liberal Americans for Democratic Action.

2. See Joshua Muravchik, "Why the Democrats Lost," *Commentary* 79:1 (January 1985), pp. 15–26, and "Why the Democrats Lost Again," *Commentary* 87:2 (February 1989), pp. 13–22.

3. Memorandum, to the chairman, the board of directors and the senior advisory committee of NDI, from J. Brian Atwood, re NDI policies and objectives, September 23, 1988, p. 6.

4. J. Brian Atwood, Foreword to a report, *National Democratic Institute for International Affairs Activities 1988* (Washington, D.C.: NDIIA, n.d.), p. 3.

5. Ibid., Foreword to a report, *National Democratic Institute for International Affairs Activities 1984–1988*, (Washington, D.C.: NDIIA, n.d.), p. 5.

6. National Democratic Institute for International Affairs, *Chile's Transition to Democracy: The 1988 Presidential Plebiscite* (Washington, D.C.: NDIIA, 1988), p. 42.

Assisting Elections in the Third World

Marilyn Anne Zak

TELEVISION AND FRONT-PAGE coverage of Third World elections often provide vivid pictures of fraud, intimidation, and administrative foul-ups. When there is a major U.S. role in or concern with a foreign election, as in the cases of El Salvador in 1984 and the Philippines in 1986, American press coverage is extensive. The holding of free and fair elections in countries striving toward democracy is a favorite topic of the media.

Free and fair elections in Haiti, South Korea, Pakistan, and Chile may be a desirable objective, but given the flagrant fraud and abuse in the Panamanian elections in 1984, and then again in Mexico and the Philippines in 1986, what can we realistically expect? What do we know about Third World elections and the criteria for determining a free and fair election? Who now makes these determinations? What is the role of the international observer? Given past U.S. assistance efforts and experience, how do we safeguard against fraud and abuse?

Elections for political office in West-

ern democratic nations are an inherent part of the political and cultural system. This tradition is in marked contrast to the Third World, where citizens are generally unaccustomed to choosing their representatives and leaders by elections. Where choice is available, election systems are often institutionally weak, seriously flawed, or downright fraudulent. Third World nations that have received U.S. election assistance have yet to become models of democracy.

Each country's election is a unique situation, and success in one country does not necessarily ensure a universal formula. Before we can consider the impact of external assistance, we must first understand the historical development of the election process, including the role of international observers. We must recognize the inherent problems resulting from a lack of agreement about what constitutes a free and fair election, the differences between congressional views and executive branch opinions regarding the results of specific elections, and what Third World election officials have set as their own agendas. We must recognize the problems of our past assistance efforts, and we must, above all, understand the limitations of U.S. or any other outside assistance to ensure free and fair elections in another country. With these qualifications, I still put forward the view that it is possible for U.S. elec-

Marilyn Anne Zak, a career officer with the Agency for International Development, is currently deputy office director of the Office of Caribbean Affairs at AID. This paper is an expanded version of a research paper written while Ms. Zak was a student at the National War College, Class of 1986. The views expressed in this article are her own and do not necessarily reflect the views of AID or the Department of Defense.

tion assistance to make a positive contribution to the development of free and fair elections and democracy in the Third World.

Furthermore, the quality of an election system is not the determinant factor for a free and fair election. The determinant factor is political will. No matter how bad the election system is, if the political parties want to have a free and fair election, they can have one. The converse is also true: no matter how good the system is, if the political parties, especially the party in power, do not want a free and fair election, it will be very difficult to hold one. In addition, no system has yet been devised that eliminates the advantage of the incumbent government in reelection.

Background

Elections are a fundamental element of representative government. Major international human rights documents call for periodic and genuine elections, universal and equal suffrage, and a secret vote. Beyond this, there is little agreement among governments and election experts as to what constitutes a genuinely democratic election.

Elections are an ever evolving process. There is no perfect model. Even advanced developed countries have fraudulent elections. The rules and regulations governing elections are many and varied throughout the world. The American system of elections is very different from Third World systems, and even from those of other industrialized democracies.

The evolution of the modern electoral system, according to the *Encyclopedia Americana*, produced three innovations during the nineteenth and twentieth centuries: "(1) broadening of the right to vote or the franchise, (2) equalizing the basis of representa-

tion, and (3) standardizing electoral procedures." The standardization of procedures has included all phases of election administration from registration, balloting, tabulation of votes, and certification of winners. Such measures became essential when the vote was expanded to formerly dependent socioeconomic groups. These procedures were meant to eliminate intimidation and pressure from previously dominant groups. The secret ballot, originally developed in Australia in the 1850s, is considered one of the most important innovations.

U.S. Election Experience

The United States has a long involvement in assisting foreign elections. From 1900 to 1940, elections throughout Central America and the Caribbean (specifically in Costa Rica, Cuba, the Dominican Republic, El Salvador, Guatemala, Haiti, Honduras, Nicaragua, Mexico, and Panama) included U.S. involvement ranging from general observation to complete administration of elections. In some instances, U.S. military officers and troops were assigned to help administer the foreign elections.[1] During this period, U.S. presidents, secretaries of state, and diplomatic and military officers experienced considerable frustration in administering elections. The problem of designing an election process from election law through final vote tabulation in Central America and the Caribbean was frequently compounded by widespread fraud. At times the U.S. government's involvement was clearly unwelcome; on other occasions, U.S. supervision was sought as the only means of assuring the political parties of a fair election. Local political parties frequently saw any U.S. involvement as favoring only one side, and in many cases this was a valid observation.

The early years of U.S. election activities in Central America and the Caribbean, however, did result in some relatively fair elections. Some U.S. goals were accomplished in the short run, such as helping the local government to stop a pending revolution or to maintain political stability albeit temporarily. The United States historically has employed a wide variety of policy tools in the process of supporting Third World elections, including diplomatic representation and protest, nonrecognition of newly installed governments, mediation by special mission, and the threat and use of military force.[2] Overall, there has been no institutionalization of representative government nor any lasting assurance of genuine and periodic elections in targeted countries in the Western Hemisphere as a result of U.S. involvement and assistance to elections.

During the 1940s, U.S. election assistance reemerged in Europe. Free elections were made implicit in the Atlantic Charter in 1941 and explicit in the Yalta Declaration of Liberated Europe in February 1945.[3] Free elections in Eastern Europe were sought by the same techniques used by the United States in Latin America: nonrecognition, the creation of coalition governments, diplomatic protest, and election observance and supervision.[4] Post-World War II election activities marked the end of U.S. foreign election assistance until the late 1960s when South Vietnam became a major U.S. policy issue.

In June 1982, President Reagan announced in his speech to the British Parliament that his administration would promote the "infrastructure" of democracy, including elections. The Report of the National Bipartisan Commission on Central America in 1984 called for the promotion of democratization, including the right of self-determination through free and fair elections. Under the Reagan administration, two principal rationales have emerged for U.S. election assistance: the desire to ensure free and fair elections as an integral part of the democratic process, and the recognition of the high financial costs for any government to hold a national election.

U.S. government election activities are presently funded by the Agency for International Development (AID). AID election activities come under section 116(e) of the Foreign Assistance Act of 1961 (as amended), which requires AID to promote the observance of human rights. Election assistance must be impartial. A provision in section 116(e) states that human rights funds "may not be used directly or indirectly, to influence the outcome of any election in any country."

U.S. election assistance since 1980 has often been an *ad hoc* response to an urgent request. What focus there has been in bilateral election assistance has concentrated on providing election materials and limiting fraud, rather than on long-term institutional development of election systems.

The recent reemergence of large-scale U.S. assistance to elections began in El Salvador. The Reagan administration's interest in promoting democratic development in El Salvador and its concern that the March 1982 constituent assembly election be seen as free and fair, led the United States, through AID, to partially fund international observers to the Salvadoran elections. An unusual element, particularly in present-day Latin America, was the willingness of Salvadoran officials to permit the United States to have a major and visible role in their election process. For the

March 1984 presidential elections and subsequent runoff in May, AID provided a $3.4 million grant for computers, software, and technical assistance for an electoral registry, and partial funding of international observers. An additional amount equivalent to $4.2 million in local currency from AID-generated counterpart funds owned by the government was used to support local election activities. The total cost of the two elections to El Salvador and the United States was equivalent to $14.8 million. The 1985 Salvadoran elections for the legislative assembly and municipal councils in El Salvador cost an equivalent of $8.9 million of which AID provided $4.6 million in local currency, $400,000 for international observers, and $100,000 for technical assistance for the registry.

There was extraordinary interest by the United States in the 1986 Philippine election, but there was no request for U.S. assistance from the Philippine government nor from the locally organized poll watching group, NAMFREL. AID did, however, fund two groups of international observers, one each from both the Democratic and the Republican Institutes of International Affairs, and provided some indirect support for training poll watchers, educational publications on the elections, and quick reporting of election results.

For the 1985 Liberian election, the U.S. government contemplated large-scale assistance, but as the election process progressed serious problems arose. Opposition parties found it exceedingly difficult to register for the election. There was also detention of opposition party leaders. As a result, the United States provided minimum assistance. The United States was prepared to fund a major program to improve the election registry in Bolivia for the 1985 presidential election, but

internal opposition to the U.S.-funded project made the Bolivian government withdraw its request.

For the 1985 presidential elections in Guatemala, AID funded the purchase of security ballot paper and provided a grant for the training of 21,000 election workers. For the 1985 Honduran presidential election, AID funded election materials, such as ballot paper and indelible ink, and financed the international observer program. Through a regional election institute, AID is supporting a voter education campaign in Haiti during 1987.

Election Observation

Although election observation has existed for more than a century, it is a very loose, unstructured aspect of outside involvement with elections. How does one handle an election where some—but not all—opposition is permitted? Is a semi-competitive election better than no election at all? How free is free and how fair is fair? And who should make these judgments? Although some academics have tried to identify criteria for determining what is free and fair, there is little agreement on what constitutes a genuinely democratic election.

The first official observance of an election began with the Divans of Moldavia and Wallachia in 1857. Since 1948, the number of elections held under international auspices has increased both in terms of quantity and geography.[5] In the past 40 years, governments, intergovernmental organizations, and nongovernmental organizations have increasingly sponsored missions to observe elections. The United Nations and the Organization of American States (OAS) have been the principal international organizations involved in election observance and assistance. The United States has been the principal country providing election assistance and sponsoring international observation missions to Third World elections.

Elections have also been observed and commented on by local embassies, journalists, and academics. It is now generally accepted practice to have governments invite official delegations to observe controversial or transitional elections.[6] However, there are some governments, such as Mexico, that neither send nor invite observers. Sweden does not send observers even to countries where it has provided technical assistance (e.g., Nicaragua in 1984). Since the early 1980s, the United States has sent official missions to observe elections in El Salvador, Grenada, Guatemala, Honduras, and the Philippines.

With AID funding, the International Human Rights Law Group developed *The Guidelines for International Election Observing*. The guidelines list minimal conditions for a free and fair election:

1. The following conditions should exist in a country holding an election: no unreasonable limitations placed on a citizen's ability to participate in the political process, including the right to a secret vote and the right to be elected to office; and respect for the rights of freedom of expression, freedom of association and freedom of assembly for a period adequate to allow political organizing and campaigning and to inform citizens about the candidates and issues.

2. For a free and fair election, it is also necessary that the integrity of the balloting process be respected, including consideration whether the candidate or party that receives the proportion of the vote prescribed by law is allowed to assume office and power.[7]

Sometimes one can agree to a set of standards but dispute the application. This problem is compounded when an election observation mission consists of a potpourri of individuals, a few having extensive experience with foreign elections, some limited experience, and the rest none. The short time frame usually given to observe an election, the lack of stated standards being used to make judgments, and subsequent absence of written public statements or reports on the election by most observer missions make for a difficult election process. It is also difficult for an official governmental mission to be critical of a friendly government's election process.

Congressional Involvement

Increasing congressional involvement has added a new dimension and complexity to U.S. foreign election assistance. In the last several years, Congress has passed certain legislative provisions that condition U.S. economic and military assistance on the holding of free and fair elections. The first such provision related to economic assistance to Nicaragua in 1980. Since then, Congress has passed similar provisions for both military and economic assistance for El Salvador, Haiti, Liberia, Mozambique, and the Philippines. Legislated policy goals for Lebanon and Uganda have also mentioned the holding of free and fair elections. The Authorization of the International Security and Development Cooperation Act of 1985 has numerous references to the holding of free and fair elections. The Act contains two statements of congressional policy which relate U.S. assistance to a nation's holding a free and fair election—

187

Section 807 on Liberia and Section 901 on the Philippines. For military assistance to Mozambique, Congress went beyond a nonbinding provision and required actual certification.

The 1985 election in Liberia raised serious issues of whether the United States should reduce or eliminate assistance if an election is not free and fair. The Liberian election also raised the issue of who decides if an election is free and fair.

On December 18, 1985 the Senate passed Resolution 271 which listed the improprieties characterizing the Liberian election. These entailed the lack of participation by the major opposition parties and a secret vote tally after an earlier tabulation gave the results to another candidate. The State Department has not officially declared whether the Liberian elections were free and fair. No official U.S. observation mission was sent to Liberia, although U.S. embassy personnel did observe the election. The incumbent, Samuel K. Doe, was reported by the Liberian Election Commission to have received 50.9 percent of the vote. U.S. Assistant Secretary of State for African Affairs Chester A. Crocker, in testimony before the Senate Subcommittee on African Affairs on December 10, 1985, acknowledged clear problems with the Liberian election. However, he pointed out some positive aspects to that election: the incumbent claimed only a narrow victory, instead of the 95 to 100 percent usually claimed in Africa; four political parties competed for voters' support; newspapers and radio stations provided campaign coverage of all parties' activities; voter turnout was enormous; and the authorities extended the polling hours until 11 pm to encourage widespread voting.

Following the flawed election, the Liberian government faced an attempted coup and arrested a number of opposition political leaders. Assistant Secretary Crocker later testified on January 23, 1985 to a joint House Foreign Affairs Committee session of the Subcommittees on Africa and on Human Rights and International Organizations that on election day U.S. embassy observers had found heavy support for the opposition, but that majority support for each of the parties varied at different polling places. The embassy could not conclude who had really won since its observers' sample was too small.

In the case of the Philippines, Congress took a more assertive role and passed Concurrent Resolution 232 on November 14, 1985, calling for steps to be taken for a free and fair election. These included the appointment of an impartial election commission, timely accreditation of the independent citizens election monitoring organization, official access to all polling places, adequate access to the media for the democratic opposition during the campaign, and neutral conduct by the Philippine military. In addition, the Senate Foreign Relations Committee requested the Center for Democracy at Boston University to visit the Philippines on behalf of the Committee in order to take an active role in overseeing the election.

The executive branch sponsored a congressional observation mission to the 1986 Philippine election, and AID funded international observers sponsored by the Democratic and Republican Institutes of International Affairs. There was eventually widespread agreement among the observers, including the official U.S. observer mission, that the election was fatally flawed and did not reflect the will of the Philippine people.

The Liberian and Philippine elections raise many questions. Had the fraud in the Philippines not been as blatant as it was, how would the observers have judged the systematic disenfranchisement of voters, the government domination of the media, and voter intimidation? Would the observers still have concluded that the results were fatally flawed? What accounts for the different treatment by the U.S. government of the fraudulent elections in Liberia and the Philippines? Is it due to the lack of a U.S. official observer mission to Liberia and the media's awarding substantially less attention to the Liberian election? Whatever the factors, it can be expected that future critical elections, whether assisted by the United States or not, will receive more attention by Congress and the media.

Election Officials' Views

In the last several years I have had many discussions with election officials from Latin America. A common theme among them is how to correct the particular election fraud and abuses that have created the most problems in their country. In Latin America, most constitutions or election laws require an official list of voters, frequently based on a civil registry of all citizens. This registry of either all citizens or eligible voters has been a source of innumerable problems. False and duplicate entries are frequently cited as a major reason for fraud. The costly involvement of the United States in the 1984 elections in El Salvador resulted from the election tribunal's insistence on having a valid computerized registry. A "clean" registry was considered a prerequisite to the election.

Given the economic resources required to develop and maintain an ac-

curate and up-to-date civil or an election registry, and the institutional weaknesses in Third World countries, one would expect to find enough serious problems in simply creating a registry apart from any problems related to fraud. I have found in only one country a strong commitment to the institutions needed to have an accurate registry. Costa Rica not only has the best civil registry in Latin America, but also one of the world's best election systems; no observer comes away unimpressed. For a country to maintain an accurate voter registry, considerable infrastructure is needed, and an accurate and up-to-date civil registry of births and deaths is crucial. Vital statistics are frequently missing in the Third World. Where they exist at all, election registries are out of date within a few years without a major commitment of resources. There are no quick fixes. However, a registry is not a prerequisite for an election (e.g., Zimbabwe in 1980).

There are differences between the current and past political environments in which the United States is providing election assistance. Today, one principal factor in the Western Hemisphere is the willingness of Latin American and Caribbean countries to work together in support of free and fair elections. In 1982 the foreign ministers of the hemisphere proposed the creation of an advisory body to provide technical advice and promote elections. In 1983, in response to the declaration, the Center for Electoral Promotion and Assistance (CAPEL), under the Inter-American Human Rights Institute in San Jose, Costa Rica, was established. CAPEL developed a research, publication, and training program, and trained election workers and poll watchers for the 1985 Guatemalan elections. In Haiti, CAPEL is running a voter education program. (AID provides funding to CA-PEL for administrative support and some of its specialized programs.) A number of election tribunals in Central America and the Caribbean have formed an association, with CAPEL as the technical arm. Both initiatives represent efforts to institutionalize honest and impartial election systems in this region. But while this sharing of information and experiences among election officials during the last three years has been very positive, this interest, unfortunately, is not apparent in other developing regions of the world.

Specific Election Experience

From my research and election observation, I offer the following personal comments on the five elections I have observed in El Salvador, Guatemala, Honduras, Costa Rica, and the Philippines. Two other elections—in Panama and Mexico—are worth discussion because of widespread reports of fraud.

El Salvador. Under El Salvador's constitution, a run-off is required if no presidential candidate receives an absolute majority of the vote. This provision and the results of the March 1984 election required a runoff. Had it not been for the runoff election in May, U.S. election assistance would have been very different. The March election was an administrative disaster. Because there was an opportunity for a second try in May and because the Salvadorans learned some lessons, the 1984 elections are considered a success.

The problems in March 1984 were due to the following factors: the politicization of the Central Election Commission (CCE); the setting up of an election system so determined to avoid election fraud that it was complex, cumbersome, and rigid; the lack

of financial support from the government of El Salvador; the late passage of the electoral law; the Salvadoran government procurement regulations which slowed delivery of election equipment and materials; the many problems with the registry list; the ineffective dissemination to the voters on the changes in the system and where to go to vote; the problems in the timely delivery of election materials to the polling sites; the insufficient number of national polling places for voters outside their home districts; the polling sites not being equipped to handle large number of voters; and the power outages caused by the guerrillas the night before the election.

What impressed me most during election day and made up for the administrative breakdowns was the behavior of the people of El Salvador. With few exceptions, the election workers and poll watchers put aside their passionate political differences and tried their best to help the voters vote, and the voters were determined to vote.

The CCE was made up of representatives of the political parties. No decision was final until the CCE had voted twice. In deciding a particular issue, members often reflected their party's position. The inability to make decisions was most apparent at the beginning of the official vote tabulation. AID had provided eight computer terminals and had trained one technician from each of the eight political parties to enter the official results of the elections on his own terminal. The computer terminals and party technicians were all at the election center of the CCE. One member of the CCE at the stadium where the ballots were being delivered decided that it was necessary to read out loud the results of every ballot box before the results were to be officially entered into the computers. There were over 7,000 ballot boxes. This new interpretation of the election law brought a halt to the official tabulation. The election law was checked, discussions were held by other members of the CCE, but nothing was changed. Five days later the official results of each ballot box were still being read out loud. The eight computer terminals sat unused on election night. Fortunately, since each official party observer had been given a copy of the tally at each ballot box, the parties, by late evening of election day, knew the results.

Was the election free and fair? Some 150,000 voters were prevented from casting their votes because of the problems mentioned. The total vote was 1.4 million. Some fraud and intimidation was observed by others. I did not see fraud. What I saw was administrative and logistical failure. My conclusion is that despite the failures in the election system, the vote reflected the will of the people. It was my observation that the best deterrence to fraud was the presence of party poll watchers at all polling and tabulating sites and of election workers representing different political parties at each ballot box.

The major U.S. election program in El Salvador did provide critical elements needed for an election—such as a list of eligible voters, ballot boxes, and indelible ink—and helped established a system capable of providing honest elections in the future. The system, however, after credible elections in 1982, 1984, and 1985, is still fragile. The registry used in 1984 and 1985 still does not meet the constitutional requirement that such a registry be under the control of the CCE. AID has been requested to help finance a new election registry under the CCE. The CCE is now composed of representatives from each of the three main political parties. Although the political division continues to dominate the CCE operations, there is slow progress to a less politicized entity.

Guatemala. The perceptions of election fraud in Guatemala resulted in increasingly smaller voter turnout for elections prior to 1984. Thirty three percent of the registered Guatemalan electorate abstained in the 1958 election, and the percentage grew over the years, peaking at 64 percent in 1978.[8]

The 1984 election for the constituent assembly was generally considered fair. The major problem in the election was the large number of null and blank ballots totalling 22 percent of the overall vote. In some districts the nulled vote was higher than that of the winning candidate. Typically, the null vote was around 10 percent. Guatemalan election officials believed that these high numbers were not due to protest, but rather to poor voter education and untrained election workers.

For the November 1985 election in Guatemala, the Supreme Election Tribunal (TSE) was determined to undertake a major training program. CAPEL, with AID funding, trained 21,000 election workers, and with funds from the National Endowment for Democracy trained party poll watchers and organized a TV public educational campaign. The training for the party poll watchers was less successful than that for the election workers because of an internal power struggle in the local organization handling the training. The party poll watchers, however, were given a pocket guide that listed the voting procedures and methods to resolve problems and disputes.

Overall, the election went smoothly. I flew by helicopter to a remote region and saw the same election procedures being used by election officials there as those used in Guatemala City. The problems with the 1985 election were minor. Out of 1.9 million votes, 12 percent were null or blank. Sixty nine percent of the registered voters turned out compared with 78 percent in 1984.

One provision in the Guatemalan election law was troubling. Voter registration is required for all literate citizens, while registration is optional for illiterates. Given the history of Guatemala, where the Indians have been historically disenfranchised because of illiteracy, the law was unequally applied. Eighty four percent of literate Guatemalans registered to vote. Fifty six percent of illiterate Guatemalans registered. Voting was conducted only in municipal areas and not in villages or estates, which had frequently been the sites of election fraud. Voting sites were assigned by voter registration number, and not on the basis of voter residence. The rural population, almost all Indians, had to walk far to a polling place. Some Indians reported walking 12 miles to a polling site. While this is not unusual in rural areas in the Third World, it does discourage voting among the rural population.

The Guatemalans took great care in establishing the TSE as an organization independent and autonomous from the state by giving it full authority over the entire election process. A special commission was formed to nominate 20 candidates for magistrates of the TSE. The Supreme Court then chose five magistrates and five alternates. The magistrates have the qualifications, immunities and salaries of a Supreme Court justice. This procedure effectively establishes an impartial election commission focused on the efficient running of an election, and not on party politics.

Honduras. The November 1985 election was the first election in 60 years that transferred power from one

elected civilian government to another. There were such strong divisions among the political parties that the Hondurans used the Uruguayan election system for their 1985 election, whereby the primary and general elections are held at the same time. The party receiving the most votes is declared the winner and the candidate within that party who receives the most votes becomes president. Therefore it is possible, as did happen in Honduras in 1985, that the candidate with the highest number of votes is not the winner. This election system was in conflict with the Honduran constitution, which calls for the president to be elected by a simple majority. It was not until the night before the election that the National Election Tribunal (TNE) upheld the use of the Uruguayan ballot on a four to one vote along party lines. While all the presidential candidates had committed themselves to abide by the new system, the National Party continued to state that it would challenge the outcome of the election.

The TNE is composed of five members—one nominated by the Supreme Court and one representative from each of the four legal parties. Only one member of the TNE had previous administrative election experience. There was no professional staff. The TNE did not always vote along party lines. On one major vote (on whether to hold the election) the president of the TNE voted against his own party's position.

The major administrative problem on election day came from the indelible ink used to mark a voter's finger. The resulting stain marks a person as having already voted. (As in the Salvadoran elections, AID supplied the ink.) After dipping the finger in the solution, the finger had to be exposed to natural light for a few minutes before the stain was visible. In most voting places, the rooms were dimly lighted and at 6:00 am sunlight was limited. Election workers were not told by the TNE about the time needed to make the stain visible, and there were no instructions available at the polling site. Subsequently, many polls remained closed for up to an hour until the apparent problem with the ink was resolved. Ink supplies ran out at some polls because of the earlier experimenting. Voting was then held up until additional ink was obtained. There were further problems with the ink in the afternoon when one of the political parties informed the TSE that the ink stain was not indelible and could be easily removed from the finger with a local solution. A quick test by some of the observers, including myself, confirmed the charges. In the 1984 elections in El Salvador, there had also been problems with the use of the ink, but no reports that the stain came off.

While not the smoothest election, the Honduran election did succeed. The voters were cooperative, patient, and supportive. This was especially true in rural areas where long walks or rides to polling places were not uncommon. While the TNE conducted a decent election despite its lack of experience, without a professional staff and an impartial attitude among the TSE members, institutionalization of a reliable election system is still in the future. The TNE has requested further AID assistance to help improve the registry and develop its organization.

Costa Rica. The election system in Costa Rica is a marvel. It is so because there has long been a commitment to ensuring that it is an honest and fair system. The Supreme Electoral Tribunal (TSE) has developed into a unique institution. It is a fourth branch of government and has complete control of the election. The magistrates are selected by the Supreme Court and must have the same qualifications as a Supreme Court justice—a law degree and 10 years of legal experience. One magistrate has 30 years of experience in running elections. The TSE is internationally respected and widely believed to be responsible for helping to maintain Costa Rica's democratic system. There is confidence in the system by the citizens that any election in Costa Rica will be free and fair.

In Costa Rica the election system is based on the civil registry. The TSE controls the civil registry, the only election tribunal I know that has this dual responsibility. Within two weeks of birth or death an entry is made in the civil registry. Individual files also include data on residency, marital history, education, and occupation.

Election ballots are printed on regular paper, the ballot boxes are cardboard, and the election materials are distributed up to several weeks prior to the election with no special security precautions. Many Costa Ricans told me that not even a pencil had been lost over the years. The key to the system is the participation of a large number of people of all ages. Children, wearing party colors, greet voters at the polling sites. The TSE holds elections at the universities and schools for student offices. The same election system is used. Under the sponsorship of CAPEL, two schools in San Jose were used for children to vote in a mock election for president, and parents in great numbers took their children to vote. It is hard to describe the joy, pride, enthusiasm, and good-natured spirit of the Costa Ricans during election eve and election day, regardless how bitter the political campaign.

Three times during election day the TSE lists the names of all voters who have cast ballots. The political parties, if organized, can then check their list of party members and know who to call or bring to a polling site. The victorious National Liberation Party had personal computers located near the polling sites with a program to check names. I believe this organization and efficiency made the difference in what was to have been a close election.

The Philippines. Oddly enough, despite a long history of massive election fraud and abuse, the election system in the Philippines is basically sound. Improvements may be needed in the system, but the election code is detailed and provides for many safeguards. The major flaw in 1986 was that the election registry had not been cleaned up from the abuses of the 1984 election. The Philippine election experience makes the important point that a good election system may be useless unless the administration of the election is honest and fair.

Because of intense media coverage, the problems with the presidential election on February 7, 1986 became evident to the whole world. I was informally attached to an international mission to observe the election in Tarlac Province, two hours north of Manila. Tarlac is the home territory of then-opposition candidate Cory Aquino, and residents there experienced some of the worst intimidation, violence, and fraud.

Fraud and abuse problems in the 1986 election went far beyond normal for the Philippines. The problems involved improper campaign practices; unequal access to the media; intimidation and harassment; disregard for safeguards, such as using indelible ink to mark the voter's finger; disenfranchisement of 3.5 million voters, principally in provinces with strong opposition support; "flying" voters who voted in numerous voting sites; ghost precincts; counterfeit ballots; vote buying; denying access to official poll watchers; theft of ballot boxes; major discrepancies in all phases of the vote count; and a lack of an impartial legislative body to certify the results.

One aspect of the registration process for new voters illustrates how the election system can affect what kinds of voters register. The Philippine election law requires that each new voter submit four photographs when registering. In the rural areas this is both difficult and expensive. In Tarlac province, 5,000 individuals submitted registration applications. At the time of registration only 400 had photographs. Of the remaining 4,600 individuals, only 200 later submitted photographs.

The most interesting aspect of the election was the role of NAMFREL in monitoring the election. The election code permits official poll watchers of the candidates and "other" watchers with prior approval of the election commission, COMELEC. NAMFREL, organized by private citizens with the tacit support of the Catholic Church, had 100,000 volunteers to monitor the 1984 elections. NAMFREL volunteers covered 40 to 60 percent of the 90,000 precincts. In 1986, 500,000 volunteers were present at 80 percent of the polling stations. But despite this massive effort, NAMFREL could not deter fraud, it could only observe and report it. NAMFREL's own count of the vote illuminated the discrepancies with the official count.

COMELEC has nine members appointed by the president and was clearly under the control of Marcos loyalist. Two openings were left unfilled until just before the election. A lot happened on election day, but the disenfranchisement of voters was clearly planned and undertaken well before the election. It was deliberate, and with the involvement of COMELEC. To commit the disenfranchisement and much of the other fraud that occurred, one had to be in charge of the election machinery.

When COMELEC and NAMFREL began publishing their election results, the magnitude of the fraud became obvious to both foreign and domestic observers. In 1984 there were 4 million registered voters in Metro Manila, an area of strong Aquino support, compared with 4.2 million in 1986. The total vote was 3.4 million, with 86 percent of registered voters casting their ballots in 1984. In contrast, in 1986 the total vote by the NAMFREL count was 3 million with only a 72 percent voter turn-out. Even recognizing problems with the 1984 vote in Metro Manila, there is no reasonable explanation that in such an important election and in an area where Aquino support was the strongest, 400,000 fewer people voted in 1986.

The fraud was massive. That the election system was technically sound was totally irrelevant. There is no deterrence to fraud when it is as pervasive as it was and done with the active participation of election officials.

The completion of a clean registry was the highest priority item for the February 1987 constitutional referendum. The question for future elections is whether there will be impartial administration through the entire Philippine election system.

Panama. The May 1984 election was the first presidential election since 1968. Special efforts were undertaken by the Election Tribunal to prepare a clean registry, to establish elaborate procedures for ballot counting at polling sites, and to have nonpartisan and party observers at all polling tables. In addition, international observers were also present. After a delay of almost two weeks the Electoral Tribunal's official tally gave the election to Nicolas Barletta of the governing party by 1,713 votes over Arnulfo Arias of the National Democratic Unity party. There were considerable irregularities in the vote count and the handling of challenges. Although there were opposition poll watchers present, they were poorly trained. When problems did occur, the poll watchers were unfamiliar with the election law and did not know how to formally file challenges. The law required challenges to be filed by a lawyer within 24 hours of the polls closing. Many challenges were thrown out on technical or procedural grounds. Observers saw tally sheets crudely altered to favor Barletta. Apparently, the government party did not expect the vote to be so close, and its tactics to ensure victory became blatant during the vote count. The general view is that the election should have gone to Arias by a slim margin. There has been a popular saying in Panama over the years, "He who counts the votes elects."

Mexico. Voter apathy reflected by sharply increased voter abstention in the 1970s led the government to institute political and electoral reforms in 1977. The reforms increased the role of the opposition parties and liberalized some of the rules governing elections at the federal level. The important changes in 1977 permitted conditionally registered opposition candidates to name representatives to the supervisory committees at each polling place. The committee members had the authority to challenge the election process at any time. The reforms also provided access to documentation on vote counts.

Over the years, electoral fraud has

included stuffing ballot boxes, voter intimidation, violence against opposition parties, disenfranchisement, and invalidation of voting results by the government-run election commission when opposition candidates do win. For its political legitimacy, the Institutional Revolutionary Party (PRI) not only must win, it must win by a large margin. This in itself puts pressure on PRI local officials to deliver a decisive margin of victory.

President Miguel de la Madrid made it known for the 1982 elections that he wanted them to be free of fraud. Relatively speaking, for the most part, they were, especially in urban areas. In the rural areas, problems continued to exist, especially the stuffing of ballot boxes. Victories by opposition candidates in some local elections in 1982 and 1983 led the PRI to resort again to widespread fraud in the elections in late 1983 and 1984. In December 1985, the PRI changed the election law in the largest Mexican state, Chihuahua, where the National Action Party (PAN) had the strongest support, so that its own representatives would tally the vote. It is with this background that the July 1986 election in Chihuahua took place. A nonpartisan civic group monitored the elections.

PAN poll watchers were thrown out of a number of polling places and were replaced by impostors in others. Ballot box stuffing was reported in many districts, and ballot box theft in others. PAN voters reported not finding their names on the registry. There were reports from some polling sites that, at the close of voting election, officials voted for everyone who had not voted and that expertly forged vote tally sheets changed the actual vote count. One hour after the polls closed, the PRI declared a landslide victory. PAN

and the other observer groups called the election a complete fraud.

The number and placement of polling places can favor one side or the other. In one opposition neighborhood in Chihuahua City, there was a polling site for 4,000 registered voters while there were many polling sites in PRI neighborhoods. Long waits, sometimes up to 10 hours, were discouraging to voters in opposition neighborhoods.

It will take a major political commitment by the PRI to assure honest elections in Mexico. As long as PRI dominates the election machinery in all phases of the election, no reforms can guarantee fair elections. There are few problems in districts where the PRI wins honestly by wide margins. In the districts on the northern border, where PRI dominance is challenged, there will likely be continuing problems with election fraud.

Determinant Factors

The distinction between fraud and poor administration is often vague during the election. Administering an election requires complex logistics that can be a tremendous challenge to the government of a developing country. Planning, organizing, and delivering a careful series of operations on a timely basis are needed. Even with an established election system, it is difficult for a developing country to hold a major election in a short period of time.

Elections are tremendously costly in both financial and human resources—elements frequently lacking in the Third World. Commodities such as security ballot paper, ballot boxes, and ink often need to be imported, using scarce dollar resources. AID's funding of commodities for the Guatemalan and Honduran elections was the result of a lack of dollar resources by the two Central American governments to pay for imports. Assistance to Liberia was based on the need to provide the resources to the election process that the Liberian government could not, or would not, commit.

Fraud often can be difficult to detect. It usually has to be fairly blatant to be readily apparent to observers. Most blatant fraud affecting the outcome of an election usually happens after the polls close, when ballots are being counted and transported. This is especially true when the party in power finds itself behind as voting closes.

The way an election is structured and administered, such as the codes and by-laws, the registry, and the like, can also influence an election so significantly that it is not necessary to commit fraud to win. Impartial administration by the election commission is of vital importance. Frequently, election commissions are composed of political party representatives. The elections studied here demonstrate that while such representatives have been known to vote against their parties' position, they mostly represent their party's interest which often times complicate election implementation.

Sophisticated or systemic fraud and manipulation can take time to detect. Detection generally requires analysis of election results. Comparisons must be made with previous voter registries, results by election districts, and voting turnout. Publication of this type of analysis usually takes time.

The U.S. wanted free and fair elections in Liberia and the Philippines and made that known in Monrovia and Manila. These two elections have again demonstrated that despite strong U.S. diplomatic pressure on a govern-

ment to hold a fair election, the local government determines its own course. This reconfirms our past election experience from 1900 to 1940 in Central America and the Caribbean.

Overall, AID's assistance has been helpful and generally has been seen as impartial. Specific elections have benefited from our support. The *ad hoc* nature of the requests and of our response has not institutionalized stronger election systems. But it is a start. AID can now provide expertise on what types of election materials are effective and obtainable at a reasonable cost. CAPEL's work, supported by AID, is a positive step to a longer term approach for Latin America.

Components of a Model Election System

Although there is no perfect election system, experience suggests what the components of a model election system should be. These components, listed below, highlight the complexities of the election process. No system has all these elements, and all are not needed to develop a system which has the voter's confidence. Each country will emphasize one area or another given its past history with either administration problems or fraud and abuse. What is important is that a combination of elements can lead to free and fair elections.

Legal Basis.

- The drafting of the election law is nonpartisan.
- The election commission is to provide competent administrators who are able to administer the system in an impartial manner.
- An impartial body interprets the election law.

- The election laws or codes are published and made readily available on a timely basis.
- The election law provides easy and rapid means to challenge irregularities in the system.
- Voting districts are established in an impartial manner.
- Regulations on political parties and campaigns encourage all political parties to form and compete on roughly equal terms.
- There is no legal basis that results in any segment of the society being denied the right to vote.
- The certification of the election results is made by an impartial body.

Administration.

- The election commission functions in an impartial manner with competent officials.
- All election workers are provided adequate training on specific duties.
- The system provides adequate safeguards against fraud and abuse, such as multiple voting, ballot stuffing, and theft of ballot boxes.
- The system allows sufficient time to plan and implement the required logistics.

Observers.

- Representatives from all parties observe the functioning of the election, specifically voting and tabulation.
- If foreign observers are permitted, they are given visas for sufficient time for adequate observation. Ready access to election officials and all aspects of the election process are required.

Registration.

- If registration is required, the process is impartial.
- The registration procedure does not create hardships for the voter nor

disadvantage any segment of the population.

- If registration is not required, a method of ensuring against double voting, such as marking the voter's finger, is used.
- The registry is published sufficiently in advance to provide an opportunity for individuals and parties to check it for errors or irregularities.

Voting.

- Access to voting places should be equitable for all segments of voters. Rural voters should have access to neutral transportation to and from voting places.
- Physical facilities are provided for secrecy of vote.
- Voters can decide how to vote—or even spoil their ballot as a protest—without difficulty or external pressure.
- The voter is not denied the right or access to voting based upon the voter's level of literacy.
- Ballot design is neutral for all parties and candidates.
- If absentee balloting is permitted, adequate safeguards exist.
- Provisions are made so that no segment of society is denied the right to vote. The one exception would be limiting the military from voting during a transition from military to civilian rule. This may be necessary to ensure neutrality by the military (as was done in El Salvador and Guatemala), but it should be only a temporary measure.
- If voting is compulsory, fines should be minimal.

Tabulation.

- Procedures are sufficient to provide for the accounting of all ballots in an accurate and timely manner that can be verified.

- Recognized poll watchers receive an official copy of the results from each voting box.
- Transportation of ballots is under secure and reliable methods.

U.S. Assistance to Elections

The following are suggested guidelines for determining which elections in a foreign country should receive U.S. election assistance, and the types of U.S. election assistance that are effective to help ensure free and fair elections. One condition governing all bilateral assistance should be that it be approved by all major political parties in the country to receive the assistance. If these guidelines are followed, U.S. assistance can be a positive contribution toward democratic development.

Elections that are transitional, such as those from military to civilian rule, or those that offer critical choices, will inevitably be of interest to the United States and should receive support. In addition, countries with democratic traditions that have demonstrated interest in improving their election administration should also be considered for assistance. Countries that cannot afford to ensure the security of the election process should also be candidates for assistance. The important decision factor should be whether there has been progress from the previous election. Is the process more free and fair? Does the election support democratic development? Is there more competition in semi-competitive elections? If the answer is yes, then assistance should be given to that country.

U.S. assistance should be conditioned on the receiving government providing guarantees for a free and fair election. Each election must be analyzed for the key components necessary to make for a credible election. If a government does not want U.S. election assistance or is unwilling to provide sufficient guarantees, then it may be desirable to provide assistance to a coalition of political parties or a private nonpartisan group to monitor the election.

A vital element in free elections is the ethics of the major political parties involved, including the government in power. Given the limited ability of outside assistance to ensure free and fair elections, a judgment must be made about ethics before assistance is given. The judgment should take into consideration these factors:

- willingness to establish and implement impartial election law and an administrative body;
- acceptance of party poll watchers and international observers throughout the election process;
- acceptance of security measures to guard against fraud and abuse;
- the willingness of the country to use resources to develop and institutionalize an honest and efficient election system;
- the assurance of adequate time for the entire election process; and
- the existence of guarantees to provide equal freedom for the political parties to organize, register, and campaign.

The types of assistance appropriate for an election should depend on whether assistance is intended for one election or the improved administration of the election process. All assistance must be carefully reviewed in order that it in no way affect the outcome of an election. Details must be known concerning how the assistance will be used for careful implementation so that the assistance is used in a neutral manner.

Rather than focusing exclusively on bilateral assistance, U.S. assistance should also be available for less direct types of election activities, such as to CAPEL and associations of election commissions. Assistance from regional or international organizations (UN or OAS) should be encouraged, and the United States should be able to work jointly with these groups.

The presence of party poll watchers at all polling and tabulating sites during the election is the best means to detect and possibly deter fraud. Assistance for the training of poll watchers and their presence at all polling sites should be a priority. Short-term training of election officials is also a priority. Commodities such as secure ballot paper and indelible ink should be eligible for funding. Assistance for international election observers should also be eligible. Observer programs should be structured according to the already existing guidelines. Educational programs for the voter should receive support. Assistance to design and implement major election registry projects should be reviewed to make certain the local support and financial resources will be available. This assistance should be part of long-term election administration assistance. When the focus is on one election, usually the time frame is short. This in itself will preclude assistance for improved institutional performance that is a requirement for establishing and maintaining a registry.

Assistance aimed at the long-term improvement of election administration has the best chance of ensuring both free and fair elections on a continuing basis. All components of an election system should be considered possible areas of assistance. Assistance should not be solely concentrated on the administrative structure, but should also be aimed at educating the

voter. Both are needed to institutionalize an honest, impartial, and effective election system.

The key component to this assistance is the willingness of a country to provide the needed financial resources and competent and impartial administrators to run the system. The largest amount of financial resources required for any element in the system is that of a computerized election registry. Before a decision is made to finance the establishment of a new registry or improve an existing one, there must be strong evidence that the needed infrastructure is there or will be there. Providing expensive equipment, such as computers, should be based on what improvements the equipment can add to the system in comparison to less expensive and technical means, and what infrastructure is available to support it.

Local, regional, and international efforts that encourage contacts, exchanges, training and research on elections and election systems should be supported. Election officials should be exposed to election systems other than their own. Experiences should be shared by election administrators. There has been little research done on election systems. In-country research on elections and elections systems should be supported. Further efforts to improve the international observance of elections should also receive support.

The development of contacts and exchanges among election officials helps strengthen existing expertise. Exchanges and contacts among election observers should help toward defining more clearly the elements of a free and fair election. These activities can and should be supported.

We should not forget that there are countries in the Third World that have been able to provide credible elections

after years of military rule without outside assistance. Argentina, Brazil, and
Uruguay are recent examples. There
are also countries that will not want
outside assistance in their election process, even if their needs are great.

If perceived to be impartial, the
United States will continue to find opportunities for providing assistance. It
is doubtful, however, that there will
be a major or extensive role for the
United States throughout the Third
World. Our bilateral election assistance will continue to be primarily to
countries with close ties to the United
States.

Notes

1. Theodore P. Wright, Jr. *American Support for Free Elections Abroad* (Washington, D.C.: Public Affairs Press, 1984), pp. 139-149.

2. Ibid., p. 139.

3. Ibid., pp. 113, 119.

4. Ibid., p. 120.

5. Dennis J. Amato, "Elections Under International Auspices, 1948-1970," unpublished dissertation, Johns Hopkins University, 1971, pp. 2-9.

6. Larry Garber, *Guidelines for International Elections Observing* (Washington, D.C.: The International Human Rights Law Group, 1984), pp. 1-4.

7. Garber, p. 18.

8. Hector Rosada Granados, *Guatemala 1984 Elecciones para Asamblea Nacional Constituyente* (San Jose, Costa Rica: Centro de Aseroria y Promocion Electoral, 1985), p. 41.

Human Rights and International Security

Brad Roberts

THERE WAS A time, not very long ago, when all one needed to know about the connection between human rights and international security was captured in the single word, linkage. Linkage conveys the idea that a state's human rights behavior should be connected somehow to certain benefits provided by the international community, such as trade, aid, or diplomatic recognition, an idea that came to be embodied in the Helsinki Agreements of 1975 and the so-called Jackson Amendment. That time is passing, along with the passing of the postwar era. Nothing better illustrates this point than the outdated nature of a human rights strategy for Eastern Europe designed to encourage incremental improvements in freedom of travel, association, etc., while the human rights map of Europe is redrawn with the dismantling of the Iron Curtain.

This is not to argue that the concepts and lexicon of the human rights movement are irrelevant today; rather, new circumstances and new opportunities compel a rethinking of both the means and ends of human rights policy, writ large. At the intersection of issues of human rights, international security, and democratization, we find

a large gap between conventional wisdom and new realities as well as renewed questioning about the kind of leadership the United States wants to provide.

Competing Western Traditions

To update the human rights agenda for the 1990s, it is useful first to go backwards. Specialists in human rights, like policy specialists generally, tend to treat their subject as if it has no history—as if the philosophical and policy debates being joined today are without useful precedent in past experience. It is not possible to see clearly where the human rights issue is headed without a better sense of where it has come from.

History has given us two traditions with respect to the connection between human rights and international security. One enshrines state interest as the central tenet of foreign policy and prudent pursuit of that interest as the cornerstone of security. This tradition has its genesis in the classic international system as it emerged in post-Renaissance Europe, which embodied the idea that states are fully self-contained, independent, and, above all, sovereign entities whose domestic affairs are to be protected from any outside interference. Although citizens of one state might express a moral preference about the actions of another state, there is not, according

Brad Roberts is editor of *The Washington Quarterly* and a research fellow in international security studies at the Center for Strategic and International Studies.

to this tradition, a tangible connection between the human rights practices of one state and the security of another. Security depends upon the respect of the principles of sovereignty and non-interference and on an overall balance of power among the states in the international system.

The purview of international politics always has extended beyond the state system, however, and this classic model never has captured fully the competing principles and myriad additional factors of international security. With the founding of the American republic in the late eighteenth century, a different ethic began to emerge: that a people living in freedom has a moral obligation to encourage the spread of liberty, and that, in the long term, a world order based on shared liberty would contribute to international peace, as well as to the security of the United States. Hence, a second tradition emerged, one that enshrines ethical principle and public purpose as the cornerstones of foreign policy.

The sense that human rights are universal extends today well beyond the United States. The nineteenth and twentieth centuries have proved the appeal of democratic governance to a growing number of nations. No longer seen as a form of government particularly American or Western in nature, democracy has emerged as a significant international force. The heresy of the eighteenth century has become a nearly global conviction in the twentieth century—that the way a state treats its citizens is the legitimate concern of all. This view embodies the belief that any person has the right to a system of government that respects and protects his or her rights, and anyone denied that right deserves the assistance of those who find themselves in more fortuitous circumstances.

Only in the middle of this century, with the creation of the United Nations, has the world community acted to universalize and legalize this notion in the Universal Declaration of Human Rights. In the Helsinki Final Act, this tradition was carried one step further, providing states party to the agreement a legal basis to concern themselves with and challenge the human rights practices of others.

These two traditions coexist uneasily in today's interdependent, nuclear world. Nothing better illustrates this point than the recent debate with the leadership of the People's Republic of China about U.S. interference in Chinese domestic affairs. China drew an extremely narrow conception of proper U.S. behavior, insisting adamantly on principles of noninterference. Its stridency rang hollow and anachronistic, however, and appeared driven more by self-serving expediency than political principle; after all, that leadership is more than happy to suffer the consequences of the "interference" of Western trade and technology.

The Passing Postwar Era

In the post-World War II era, now receding at breathtaking pace, the emergence of profound ideological conflict between East and West, together with a significant military dimension, reshaped thinking about the connection between human rights practices and international security. The entrenchment of Stalinist regimes in Eastern Europe and elsewhere, which were predicated on the subservice of the individual to the vanguard of the working class and were openly contemptuous of human rights as understood in the West, sharpened the choices confronting the West. The only meaningful action Western leaders could take to support democratic reform in the East was to join with those seeking to overthrow Stalinist or Soviet control; to make such a choice, however, meant risking war with the Soviet Union, a choice the West proved unwilling to make when tested in Hungary in 1956 and Czechoslovakia in 1968. The hands of the West effectively were tied by the need to promote peace. Henry Kissinger was hardly the first to point out that, in a nuclear era, peace has become the fundamental human right.[1]

So long as there seemed to be so little that the West could do to promote human rights practices in Eastern Europe and the Soviet Union, Westerners sought to catalog human rights and instrumentalize agreements with regard to freedom of family contact, belief, emigration, etc., by incorporating them into the larger process of East–West bargaining. Efforts to secure some Communist bloc commitment and limited compliance were embodied in Basket Three of the Helsinki Final Act. Throughout the 1970s and most of the 1980s, however, human rights practices in the Communist world changed only incrementally and at the margins.

The East–West conflict also has had ramifications for human rights issues elsewhere. The Western effort to contain the spread of communism often led to a U.S. preference for strong local governments in strategically key, pro-American Third World states. Although many of these states were democratic, at least in form, dictators emerged to run them as fiefdoms. In the late 1970s, Jeane Kirkpatrick sought to distinguish between authoritarian and totalitarian forms of government according to their significance for U.S. foreign policy, arguing that authoritarian regimes may transform themselves into democracies whereas totalitarian regimes cannot.[2] Taken by many as an argument to coddle up to dictators, Kirkpatrick's views were deemed by her critics to be symptomatic of a United States too tolerant of human rights abuses in the name of security and too willing to equate pro-American sentiment and domestic stasis with a desirable or, at least, necessary international security framework.

To a very striking degree, this postwar era has disappeared. New factors are reshaping the thinking about the place of human rights on the international security agenda and about whether and how to promote these rights. Happily, new circumstances offer greater congruence between the moral values of the United States and its security interests. Also, the idea that stability can be had at the cost of acquiescence to authoritarian or totalitarian rule has been largely discredited.

What defines the end of the postwar era? Only in part does it have to do with a mellowing of the U.S.–Soviet relationship or the easing of the division of Europe—these are symptoms, in the author's view, not causes. The end at hand is not the end of history, but the end of ideology.[3] To be sure, ideology remains a force, but as the major force driving regional and global politics throughout the twentieth century, it is being devalued steadily. In closed societies in Europe, Asia, Latin America, and even Africa, stagnation has given new weight to pragmatism. The ideas sweeping the world today are not the grand metaphysical constructs of ideologues, but the wisdoms of pragmatically minded problem-solvers. The world seems to take its inspiration from Lech Walesa's bloodless revolution in Poland, Hernando de Soto's answer to Marx found in the informal sectors of the Peruvian economy,[4] and the power of people as expressed vividly from Manila to Prague. What binds them together is a belief in the pragmatic virtue of participatory forms of economics and politics.

For all of the talk of the democratic revolution in world politics, as yet there has been no sweeping institutionalization of liberal democracy. This should not blind us, however, to the historic delegitimization of authoritarian and totalitarian forms of governance. Who outside of Havana and Managua still believes that these systems are relevant to the problems of political community in the late twentieth century? Political communities the world over seem to be experiencing the same kinds of needs: for prosperity, for national identity, for governments that respect the dignity of the individual, and for politics that generate, on a self-recreating basis, the legitimacy and authority to cope with fundamental social and technological change. Democracy has established itself firmly as a means toward these ends.

In the past, the appeal of democracy tended to be largely idealistic. If democracy were admired widely as a form of governance consistent with liberty, it also was considered by many to be less effective than other forms of governance at meeting basic social needs. Today, its appeal has merged with a pragmatic one.

How has this transformation shaped thinking about the connection between human rights and international security?

In the developing world, the 1970s and 1980s put to the test the view that dictators were necessary to preserve regional stability and to extend U.S. influence. The peace of the dictator proved unstable: domestic instability

mounted, human rights abuses increased, and outsiders intervened seeking to exploit the ensuing conflict for ideological benefit.

By the end of the 1980s, a tenuous consensus seems to have emerged in the United States that the only path to a stable and prosperous Third World lies through the difficult and time-consuming business of building participatory political and economic institutions capable of generating legitimacy and, hence, the authority to manage change. The focus of U.S. policy has shifted from working with authoritarian regimes to facilitating democratic transitions. The debate about human rights in the Third World has become a debate about what the United States can and should learn from political change in places like Iran and the Philippines, and about how and how not to nurture democratic political transitions.[5]

Human rights concerns vis-à-vis the Communist world are undergoing a similar transformation. To be sure, the linkage-related agenda as defined by the Helsinki process remains relevant, especially in those corners of the Communist world where the rule of law and the legitimacy of popular consent have been slow to emerge, as in the Soviet Union and China. Dramatic change in Eastern Europe has challenged Western human rights thinking and outdated badly the selective Western focus on specific human rights. In that volatile region, the building of political systems that embody and guarantee human rights as a moral norm and pragmatic need is the primary concern of new leadership groups responding to public compulsion. Within reach now are forms of political organization in Eastern Europe that not only honor but guarantee human rights. Western human rights strategy should not ignore the larger plums that have moved within its reach.

Democracy and Peace

With change in the developing and Communist worlds, the human rights agenda of the postwar era has been subsumed in the larger topic of the connection between domestic political order and peaceableness, and of the security of international systems composed of democratically minded states. This brings us directly to the question: is democracy good for peace?

Democracy possesses a number of attributes that lend themselves well to the business of peace. Thomas Jefferson pointed to one: "Reason and free inquiry are the only effectual agents against error. They are the natural enemies of error, and of error only."[6] In short, democracy is an instrument compelling states to act more like the rational actors so beloved by social scientists. For those working inside the Washington beltway, it seems comic, if not foolish, to describe U.S. democracy as rational; the point, however, is that democracies, for all their inefficiencies, do a commendable job of focusing public policy debate on costs and benefits.

Democracies possess other attributes relevant to their international behavior. Because they depend on popular consent for their legitimacy, they only can make wars that are perceived by the public to be just. Wars of aggression or punitive wars waged by or among democracies are rarities in the modern era. Similarly, given that democracies are based on the domestic exercise of public principle, their leadership is less apt to look at the larger world in raw power political terms than the leadership of states that are concerned domestically only with the distribution of coercive power.

This is not to argue that democracy is a perfect instrument of peace. Indeed, its shortcomings are well known. As Alexis de Tocqueville observed,

Foreign politics demand scarcely any of those qualities which are peculiar to a democracy; they require, on the contrary, the perfect use of almost all those in which it is deficient. Democracy is favorable to the increase of the internal resources of a state; it diffuses wealth and comfort, promotes public spirit, and fortifies the respect for law in all classes of society: all these are advantages which have only an indirect influence over the relations which one people bears to another. But a democracy can only with great difficulty regulate the details of an important undertaking, persevere in a fixed design, and work out its execution in spite of serious obstacles. It cannot combine its measures with secrecy or await their consequences with patience. These are qualities which more especially belong to an individual or an aristocracy; and they are precisely the qualities by which a nation, like an individual, attains a dominant position.[7]

In a world where the balance of power tradition remains relevant and where not all states share a common commitment to basic values and rules of the international system, the pacific inclination of democracies sometimes may be a liability. As Jean Francois Revel has observed, "Democracy...is not basically structured to defend it-

Brad Roberts

self against outside enemies seeking its annihilation."[8]

However, as Leszek Kolakowski has observed,

> Among Europe's uncountable wars, big and small, there has not since 1919 been a war between democratic countries. This is not to imply that democratic countries have always behaved impeccably. Some did revolting things to their dependencies; others displayed an abominable cowardice toward despotic regimes; but they have not waged war against one another.[9]

Recent research tends to support this line of argument. For example, a study recently published in *The Journal of Conflict Resolution* concludes that "The proportion of democratic dyads in the system has a negative effect on the number of wars begun and on the proportion of disputes that escalate into war."[10] Of course, such statistical analyses of the connection between democracy and peace are open to criticism about definitions and criteria.

This predisposition of democracies against war-making has contributed greatly to the post–World War II peace. To be sure, there have been other factors: the geostrategic coincidence of Western and Asian democracies mutually confronted by a powerful Soviet Union, technological change that has brought both the nuclear bomb and far-reaching economic interdependence, and shared cultural traditions and values. Nevertheless, the importance of these factors only makes harder the task of defining the salience of democracy—it does not diminish that salience.

It is useful to think of two kinds of peace—that of the armed truce, such as we have seen in East–West relations, and that of a community of

shared interests and values, such as we have enjoyed in West–West relations. One is fragile, the other is durable. Democracy is relevant to both. For the first, it is probably a necessary, but not sufficient, condition for peace. For the second, it is the foundation of justice upon which durable peace can be built.

The German philosopher Immanuel Kant provided some careful thinking on this subject that has not been outdated by two centuries of experience: states disposed to respect the rights of individuals would respect the legitimacy of other countries similarly governed and encourage rather than restrict mutually satisfying trade relations, leading to the gradual emergence of a so-called zone of peace.[11]

Democratization and Peace in the 1990s

It is tempting to conclude, as many have, that the current wave of democratization in the Second and Third Worlds means that basic problems of U.S. security have been solved or will be shortly. This conclusion requires, however, that one overlook that, generally speaking, democratization is a long and complicated process, and that it has proceeded more quickly so far in the hearts and minds of people than in the emergence of stable and mature institutions of democratic governance. The security and human rights agendas have changed—but nirvana is not yet at hand. To illustrate the point, it is useful to examine both East–West and North–South relations.

Clearly, the prospect of war between East and West has diminished as Communist leaders have acknowledged the failures of their system and sought a breathing spell to rebuild their societies or regenerate the socialist model. To the extent that regeneration leads to the creation of permanent institutions of civil power that are sensitive to the need to avoid international conflict, Western and global security interests will be well-served by continued reform. Soviet dissident Andrei Sakharov made this point repeatedly throughout the 1970s and 1980s in arguing that true security would not be possible until the passing of totalitarianism in the Soviet Union.

Peace is by no means assured, however. The path to posttotalitarianism is an uncertain one, and although the events of 1989 in Eastern Europe have been heartening, new problems of prosperity and domestic politics are emerging forcefully. Furthermore, 1989 was a year to demonstrate the varieties of Communist reform, and the fact that a Soviet Communist Party clinging to one-party rule and a restoration of Leninist principles or a Chinese Communist Party willing to take the lives of hundreds of its citizens to preserve its ideology have quite different goals from reformers in Eastern Europe.

The crisis of communism too readily could become an international conflict. The scope and pace of change are unprecedented and ultimately may create fully democratic societies, but in the short-to-medium term, the chance for violence, retrenchment, or merely cosmetic change is still great. Old power structures will pass away reluctantly, as vividly demonstrated by continuing reports of political prisoners in the Soviet Union.[12] The transition itself to a new security structure is fraught with unknown dangers. Furthermore, if reform leads to the disintegration of the Soviet empire, the West must be careful not to precipitate crisis as it supports reform.

Military power accumulated by the Soviet Union cannot remain irrelevant to Western thinking about political re-form. The passing of totalitarian communism will not necessarily mean the passing of the Soviet empire or of its fundamental security dilemma. In fact, it is equally easy to imagine heightened Soviet insecurity in an era marked by disappointing economic performance, more vocal national movements, and an East European longing for West European prosperity. Soviet military power will not remain inconsequential to these factors. Soviet power remains important in another way: there is no historical precedent to illuminate the ways in which a nuclear-armed state will sustain unprecedented ideological transformation and perhaps disintegration.

Some are fearful that the easing of the East–West stalemate in Europe and possible German reunification necessarily will release long-standing instabilities in the continent arising from unsettled geographic claims, ethnic conflict, and disequilibria in balances of power.[13] These concerns are legitimate. They also will test the relevance of democracy and interdependence to peace in Europe. History suggests that European divisions can be superseded by new historical circumstances—the bitter division between Germany and France, which repeatedly plunged Europe into war, has faded away. The ingredients of that transformation seem to be the emergence of fully democratic institutions in both societies and the gradual emergence of public sentiment vested in common interests and peace, rather than domination by elites beholden to an unworkable ideology or simple self-aggrandizement. If the Europe of the turn of the twenty-first century will look something like the Europe at the turn of the twentieth century in terms of the resurgence of local problems, the differences will be important as well. A fully democratic Germany and a highly integrated, prosperous continent will bring new strength to the resolution of old problems.

In North–South matters, democratization draws us again to think anew about problems of international security. In his essay on *The End of History*, Francis Fukuyama has posed the issue starkly:

> This does not by any means imply the end of international conflict per se. For the world at that point would be divided between a part that was historical and a part that was post-historical. Conflict between states still in history, and between those states and those at the end of history, would still be possible. There would still be a high and perhaps rising level of ethnic and nationalist violence, since those are impulses incompletely played out, even in parts of the post-historical world. Palestinians and Kurds, Sikhs and Tamils, Irish Catholics and Walloons, Armenians and Azeris, will continue to have their unresolved grievances. This implies that terrorism and wars of national liberation will continue to be an important item on the international agenda. But large-scale conflict must involve large states still caught in the grip of history, and they are what appear to be passing from the scene.[14]

This gloomy assessment of conflict in the Third World gets gloomier yet if one thinks about the many obstacles along the path of democratization likely to pitch a country into civil war: the failure to address effectively the problem of minority rights in democracy, failure to address the more participatory economic agenda that goes along with participatory politics, failure to find a proper place in society for instruments of authority, and a failure

to manage transfers of power from one leader to another.

Some believe that the problem of anarchy in the world will be met effectively by U.S.–Soviet cooperation on regional security problems. Let us hope that common interests will lead to effective joint political engagement in conflicts in the Middle East, Asia, and Africa. However, a superpower condominium, bantered about by some, seems extremely unlikely. To a significant degree, the passing of the postwar era is also the passing of the superpower era. The growing military and economic power of developing states, the emergence of a multipolar international system, the growing disutility of military power to the resolution of conflicts (and the escalating military and political costs of projecting U.S. power abroad), combined with a Soviet Union that, for years if not decades to come, will look more like the poor man of Europe than a robust global actor, render quaint and outmoded the notion of superpower condominium.

Anarchy in the developing world will be constrained by other factors, however. We can anticipate that the salutary benefits of democratization will counterbalance the risks cited above, at least in many places, compelling a search for common interests with erstwhile competitors. We can anticipate that growing interdependence also will contribute to more stable international relations. Further, we can anticipate that a world propelled forward by the economic integration of the European Community in 1992, by the boom economies of the Pacific Basin, and by the opening of closed societies in the Communist world, will spur many states in the developing world to seek settlements to old disputes in order not to be left behind economically and politically.

There is one last important spur to democratization, often overlooked in Western debate. Global weapons proliferation is centrally relevant to global democratization. States acquiring massively destructive military capabilities will be forced by the power inherent in those weapons to learn to possess them wisely. Above all, this requires of leaders in the developing world that they act like the rational actors assumed in all deterrence models. If the experience of nuclear or near-nuclear powers in the developing world is any indication, such leaders will encounter increasing international pressure to explain when, how, and why such weapons might be used. Such pressures also emerge domestically, as more sectors of society are mobilized by the awareness of the risks of misusing weapons of mass destruction. This reinforces the trend toward democracy as a form of pragmatic governance described above. By promoting democracy abroad, the United States also will be promoting the long-term amelioration of the instabilities wrought by the proliferation of weapons of mass destruction.

U.S. Human Rights Policy

The human rights and international security policy choices before the United States seem ever more difficult in today's rapidly changing and highly complex world—hardly the stuff of the benevolent managerialism envisioned by Dr. Fukuyama. It is foolish, however, to think that it is possible not to shape the choices made by others—and not to want to—in an era of growing interdependence and mutual nuclear vulnerability. Looking to the 1990s, what are the implications of the foregoing analysis for U.S. human rights policy?

First, the United States should maintain the policy agenda embodied in the Helsinki accords. The posttotalitarian transformation of Eastern Europe and the Soviet Union is still incomplete. Linkage remains a useful and legitimate instrument of policy, so long as human rights are contested anywhere that U.S. actions count.

Second, the United States should support the continued growth of the democratic principle in world politics with a more variegated strategy. The U.S. National Endowment for Democracy should constitute the beginning of the work of the United States on democratization, not its culmination. In part, this is a question of money: the endowment has stayed relatively even in its four years of operation rather than expanding five-fold, as originally planned. However, this is also a question of community: the established democracies have done very little to work together to support the emergence of democratic institutions. Above all, the United States must lead by example—the symbolic value of American democracy has not been lost on democrats abroad: individuals such as Lech Walesa begin speeches to the U.S. Congress by quoting the Constitution of the United States. The American experiment in democracy is a continuing one, and the health of the domestic polity is ignored at peril to the broader democratic cause.

Third, in advancing its commitment to democratization, the United States should not forget that democracy cannot be exported. Democracy can be encouraged and assisted; but it cannot be imposed. The generation of self-recreating political authority and of political institutions that enjoy popular legitimacy is something that can be done only by the political community itself. The twentieth century provides an abundance of evidence to suggest

Brad Roberts

that the only stable political institutions and values are democratic ones arising from the historical circumstances unique to each political community. Democracy and respect for human rights have emerged in so many different countries because they fulfill, better than any other political form, the pragmatic need for effective governance, as well as basic human aspirations. This is not a caution to stand by idly: indeed, the twentieth century includes examples where democracy has been nurtured fervently, as in many decolonizing states and the defeated fascist powers. However, this history requires that Western efforts to nurture democracy accommodate the necessity of indigenous maturation.[15]

Fourth, the United States must seize the opportunity to do what it can to make change in the Soviet Union irreversible. The West has relatively few means at its disposal to ensure that Communist reform outlives the wishes of any particular generation of leadership. Arms control agreements provide an opportunity to ensure that Mikhail Gorbachev's *peredyshka* (breathing spell) lives on in a future era of peaceful exchange and cooperation by structuring the choices of future Soviet leaders about the disposition and use of military force. By no means can arms control ensure lasting political freedom and peace; but by institutionalizing strategic stability, the West limits the ability of the Communist leaders to impose their will by force or exploit international instability for domestic benefit.

Finally, the United States must stay engaged. Its leadership remains relevant to the problems of human rights and international security in the 1990s and beyond. Such engagement is by no means certain. From Alan Tonelson's "new nationalism" in the Democratic Party to the plea of Republican

Patrick Buchanan that "when the Cold War is over, America should come home," the isolationist impulse is certain to be piqued in the years ahead.[16]

Tonelson and Buchanan seem to preach a policy mix of realpolitik and benign neglect. Such a mix would prove very costly in a world where U.S. isolation is neither economically, technologically, nor politically feasible. In the area of human rights alone, to abandon leadership now would be to squander opportunities to consolidate democratic gains and could nourish a sense of abandonment of people in struggling societies—something that would augur badly for the future foreign policy of the United States. Furthermore, the American public never has shown itself to be a great fan of a narrow realpolitik foreign policy—in this democracy, at least, such a policy would lack support, legitimacy, and longevity.

Isolationism is not the only problem, however. Leadership will be difficult to sustain for other reasons. Senior policymakers have watched as interested bystanders the events in Eastern Europe, applauding the collapse of communism seemingly without truly understanding its source. That source derives from the place of human values in politics and the fundamental, pragmatic necessity of systems of governance that honor the deepest impulses of humankind and embody its highest aspirations. Leaders in the United States so far have shown themselves to be unable or unwilling to speak to these deeper impulses, choosing instead to downplay the human rights agenda for a more sterile diplomacy with the Soviet Union and the People's Republic of China. Unless the leaders of this democracy are able to recapture the moral basis of public policy and the U.S. world role, they may find that

212

they have accelerated the decline of U.S. influence at the moment of its greatest victory.

An earlier version of this essay was presented to a U.S. Department of State colloquium on "Human Rights in an Era of Democratic Transition" on December 7, 1989.

Notes

1. Henry Kissinger, *American Foreign Policy* (New York: Norton, 1977), p. 125.

2. Jeane Kirkpatrick, "Dictatorships and Double Standards," *Commentary* 68:5, November 1979, pp. 34–35.

3. See Daniel Bell, *The End of Ideology* (Cambridge: Harvard University Press, 1988), and Francis Fukuyama, "The End of History," *The National Interest* 16 (Summer 1989). Although such prognostications are treated skeptically, the debate sparked by Fukuyama usefully has rekindled interest in Bell's earlier thesis.

4. Hernando de Soto's *The Other Path*, written as an answer to the radicalism of Peru's Shining Path guerrillas, is a global best seller. For a condensed version of his arguments, see "The Informals Pose an Answer to Marx," *Washington Quarterly* 12:1 (Winter 1989).

5. See Hans Binnendijk, "Authoritarian Regimes in Transition," *Washington Quarterly* 10:2 (Spring 1987), and Larry Diamond, "Beyond Authoritarianism and Totalitarianism: Strategies for Democratization," *Washington Quarterly* 12:1 (Winter 1989).

6. Thomas Jefferson, *Notes on Virginia*, in Saul K. Padover, *Sources of Democracy: Voices of Freedom, Hope and Justice* (London and New York: McGraw Hill, 1973),

p. 157. Citation from introduction from forthcoming book by Stanley Kober on values and power in U.S. foreign policy.

7. Alexis de Tocqueville, *Democracy in America* (New York: Vintage Books, 1945), vol. 1, pp. 243–244.

8. Jean Francois Revel, *How Democracies Perish*, trans. William Byron (New York and London: Harper & Row, 1983), p. 3.

9. Leszek Kolakowski, "Forty-Four Years Late: Peace in Europe," *Wall Street Journal*, September 1, 1989.

10. Z. Maoz and N. Abolali, "Regime Types and International Conflict, 1816–1976," *Journal of Conflict Resolution* 33:1 (March 1989). Also of interest is: M. Small and J. D. Singer, "The War-Proneness of Democratic Regimes, 1816–1965," *Jerusalem Journal of International Relations* 1:4 (1976). Both studies are synopsized in L. Starobin, ed., *World Peace Report* 5:10 (August 1989).

11. Immanuel Kant, *Prolegomena to a Perpetual Peace*.

12. Frank Wolf and Chris Smith, "Don't Forget Those Still in the Gulag," *Washington Post*, November 28, 1989.

13. Andrew Goldberg, "Soviet Imperial Decline and the Emerging Balance of Power in Europe," *Washington Quarterly* 13:1 (Winter 1990).

14. Fukuyama, "The End of History," p. 18.

15. Diamond, "Beyond Authoritarianism."

16. Alan Tonelson, "On Democrats," *The National Interest* 16 (Summer 1989). Patrick Buchanan, "Messianic Globaloney," *The Defense Democrat* (November 1989). See also George Weigel, "That New, Improved Ready-for-Prime-Time Isolationism," *American Purpose* 3:8 (October 1989), pp. 60–61.

Authoritarian Regimes in Transition

Hans Binnendijk

IN THE 1970s, political change in countries previously controlled by authoritarian governments often led to defeats for U.S. foreign policy and to tragedy for the nations involved. The 1973 military coup against Ethiopia's Haile Selassie radicalized the ruling Derg and enhanced Soviet influence in the Horn of Africa. After the shah fled Iran in 1979, Shi'ite fundamentalists executed thousands, reversed that nation's economic progress, and persisted in a devastating war with Iraq. Marxists soon dominated the Sandinista revolution in Nicaragua and allied themselves with the Soviet Union. Successive Soviet-backed coups in Afghanistan in 1978 and 1979 led to a Soviet invasion and six years of brutal warfare. These events created the impression, by 1980, that authoritarian regimes, if toppled, would probably beget totalitarian regimes.

Today, the prospects seem to have improved for healthy and democratic political change in countries ruled by authoritarian governments. During the 1980s, Brazil, Argentina, and numerous other Latin American countries shed authoritarian regimes for democratic alternatives. In the midst of civil

Hans Binnendijk is director of studies at the International Institute for Strategic Studies in London. He was formerly director of the Center for the Study of Foreign Affairs at the Department of State's Foreign Service Institute. The views in this paper do not necessarily represent the views of the Department of State.

war, El Salvador conducted internationally supervised elections that brought the moderate José Napoleon Duarte to power. The Turkish military, under pressure from NATO governments, restored nominal civilian rule. In the Philippines, a strong centrist coalition ousted Ferdinand Marcos' regime, and President Corazon Aquino embarked on a democratic path. And in Haiti, President Jean-Claude Duvalier's departure paved the way for a transitional government that has set a timetable for democratic rule.

As domestic pressures build in Chile, South Korea, Pakistan, and elsewhere, analysts are now sifting through the events of the past 15 years to search for clues that might help prevent future Irans and encourage future Spains. Key questions are being asked. Why do dictators fall? What are the warning signs? How do transitions differ? Why do democracies develop? What is the Soviet role? What should the United States do?

The Foreign Service Institute's Center for the Study of Foreign Affairs recently conducted six symposia to explore these questions. More than 50 prominent scholars and government officials analyzed 11 different cases of success and failure in transition from autocratic rule.[1] No general theory emerged from these case studies, but patterns are discernible and some lessons can be learned.

Hans Binnendijk

The Period of Decline

The decline of an autocrat generally begins with a long period of unrest. At a particular point he loses legitimacy with key elements of society, thereby triggering a second, much shorter, period of rapid decline. This, in turn, is followed by the final events of the transition. It is crucial that U.S. policymakers recognize which of the three stages exists when U.S. policy is formulated.

The period of unrest prior to the fall of an authoritarian regime can last five to ten years or longer. In retrospect, it is often easy to mark the event that created serious internal tension. In the case of Iran, the shah's decisions in the early 1970s to expand regional security commitments, pursue the Westernization of social and economic policies, and persecute religious leaders who opposed his policies all began a process that later tore apart the social fabric of the country. In 1970 there were no politically motivated bombings in Iran; by 1972 there were 13. By 1974 there were student riots at Pahlavi University, bread riots in South Tehran, and a clear resurgence of fundamentalist Islam. Anti-Americanism was prevalent by 1977, and a cycle of violent demonstrations became common in 1978. The shah was in exile in Panama by 1979.

In Haiti the period of unrest started in 1980, a year marked by financial crisis, an abrupt political crackdown, and Jean-Claude Duvalier's marriage to Michelle Bennett, a light-skinned beauty from a wealthy family who came to epitomize the conspicuous corruption of the regime. During the latter 1970s, the Haitian economy grew at an average rate of 4 percent, there was modest political liberalization, jails were gradually cleared of political prisoners, and violence was at a minimum. After 1980, these favorable trends were replaced by rising political patronage, increasing political arrests, firing of able technocrats, and rigging of elections. A steady decline continued until Duvalier's exit in February 1986.

Similarly long gestation periods are evident elsewhere. In El Salvador, a decade of unrest was triggered in 1972 when José Napoleon Duarte was elected president but denied office, thus causing society to polarize between the oligarchy's death squads and left wing guerrillas. In Nicaragua, Somoza triggered open expressions of widespread discontent in the early 1970s by misappropriating international funds meant for earthquake relief. And in Argentina, the dirty war against that nation's left wing, which started in the mid-1970s, laid the groundwork for the regime's fall in 1983.

The demise of the autocrat is not inevitable during these long periods of unrest. If he continues to maintain tight control over the basic instruments of power, such as the military and the economy, he may survive despite the unrest. But if the situation continues to deteriorate, he may lose his legitimacy with those who control the instruments of power in society. Once this happens he will go into a second period of steep decline.

Loss of effective legitimacy generally tends to take place from three to eighteen months prior to the actual transition. The shah's indecisiveness during the cycles of violence in 1978 cost him legitimacy with the army. The assassination of opposition *La Prensa* editor Pedro Joaquin Chamorro and Eden Pastora's successful capture of the National Palace in 1978 highlighted both Somoza's faults and his vulnerabilities. For the Argentine junta, legitimacy disappeared when the Falkland Islands war was lost. Duvalier probably lost his final measure of legitimacy as a result of his wife's million dollar European shopping trip in the fall of 1985 while the country was in economic turmoil. And Marcos lost legitimacy in stages, first by rigging the trial of senior officials accused of assassinating Benigno Aquino and months later by rigging an internationally supervised election.

Once an authoritarian leader has lost legitimacy with key elements of power in a society, his demise becomes almost inevitable. Rapidly moving events tend to dominate everyone's thinking, and the authoritarian leader, although he may not know or admit it at the time, may have no choice other than to try to negotiate a peaceful transition and find a safe haven. A military crackdown by the autocrat might be effective during earlier stages, but when large coalitions form against him and the military's reliability is in question, violent repression generally results in an even more tumultuous transition, as was the case in Iran and Nicaragua.

At this point, a final event or set of events can trigger the transition. In 1986, the final chapter came for Duvalier and Marcos without a great deal of violence. It came for Duvalier because riots spread from outlying areas, where loyal Ton Ton Macoutes were prepared to kill their countrymen, to Port-au-Prince, where the army was in charge and unwilling to massacre civilians. Secretary of State George Shultz's suggestion that Duvalier's time was up simply reflected reality and prompted Duvalier's final departure soon thereafter. Similarly, the defection of senior military leaders in the Philippines was the coup de grace for Marcos, and his subsequent phone conversation with Senator Paul Laxalt (R-Nev.) brought home this reality.

In both cases, the autocrat had already lost legitimacy, and his fall was inevitable. Had the United States failed to expedite the departure of either Marcos or Duvalier, a more violent and less successful transition most likely would have taken place.

Warning Signs of Decline

There are seven warning signs that analysts should watch for during periods of unrest in an autocratic society. Not all seven factors were present in each case study, but several in combination generally formed a critical mass that destroyed the leader's legitimacy and led to a period of rapid decline.

Probably the most important warning sign of decline is the physical health and mental capability of the leader himself. Signs that the leader may not be in control in the long run affect the attitudes of others and can hasten the leader's demise. The most extreme examples are the deaths of Antonio Salazar in Portugal and Francisco Franco in Spain, both long-time autocrats who retained their legitimacy until their deaths but whose form of government died with them. Somoza's heart attack and Marcos' kidney problems each left an impression of vulnerability that tended to undercut their authority. Haile Selassie's senility plus the crown prince's stroke left a vacuum to be filled by the professional military. Daoud's apparent senility contributed to the success of the pro-Soviet coup in Afghanistan in 1978. Even the Shah of Iran, who kept his cancer secret from his family and allies, was probably more indecisive because of his illness. An autocrat's ill health generally becomes public information, but when it is successfully hidden, it can distort U.S. policy. In any deteriorating political situation involving an autocrat, the temperature and temperament of the individual leader is crucial.

Often transitions of government follow military defeats, a second critical warning sign. Governments based upon military authority derive legitimacy from their alleged ability to defend the national interest. For example, the Argentine military junta, like the Greek colonels, fell after humiliating defeats over contested islands. The Portuguese government refused to modify its policies after losing ground in three simultaneous colonial wars in the early 1970s, undercutting its legitimacy with junior military officers. During this same period, the Ethiopian Army failed to suppress the rebellion in Eritrea, causing dissension among junior military officers. And the Philippine insurgents of the New People's Army made significant progress under the militarily inept leadership of President Marcos' friend, General Fabian Ver. When autocrats lose wars or are perceived as poor managers in military situations, they lose both legitimacy and power.

Economic problems are another strong indicator of trouble ahead. In the most egregious case, the famine of the early 1970s in Ethiopia took millions of lives and demonstrated the basic incompetence of Haile Selassie's government. Every other transition reviewed was also characterized by economic woes. All transitions studied took place in a period of economic decline, with negative or near negative growth rates that generally were accompanied by high rates of inflation. Iran is a typical example. Its real Gross Domestic Product dropped from 10.7 percent in 1976 to minus 5.3 percent in 1978. Just prior to the transition in Argentina, inflation ranged between 100 and 350 percent. In most cases, the country was in the second or third year of economic decline that followed

several years of significant growth. Rising public expectations for a better life frustrated by disappointing economic results is a common phenomenon just prior to the period of steep decline.

The fourth warning signal is the development of deep social tensions that divide the autocrat from the people and eventually undercut his position. For example, in 1974 bookstore owners in Tehran claimed that 60 to 70 percent of the books they sold were on religious subjects, but the shah was trying to discourage strong religious ties and Westernize Iran. Similarly, Duvalier's marriage to a wealthy mulatto increasingly exacerbated social divisions with Haiti's predominately poor, dark-skinned people. In both cases the autocrats became completely identified with social forces that ran against the grain of their societies, and eventually their rule was overwhelmed by these differences.

The impression of widespread abuse of power can also contribute to an autocrat's demise when linked with other factors. The corruption of the Marcos, Duvalier, and Somoza families continued for years and only gradually became an important political factor. Similarly, torture used by SAVAK (the secret police) in Iran and by the junta in Argentina alone did not bring those regimes down, but, in combination with other factors, the abuses accelerated the process. The assassination of key political opposition figures by the autocrat's regime can have even more serious consequences for the regime. For example, the murders of Senator Benigno Aquino in the Philippines, Ayatollah Reza Saidi in Iran, and Pedro Joaquin Chamorro in Nicaragua, created martyrs whose deaths came to signify all that was wrong with the government.

Most transitions develop only after

widespread resistance occurs and loose coalitions emerge that are united primarily by a common desire for a change in government. This warning sign has repeated itself in Iran, Argentina, the Philippines, and Haiti, among others. The middle class and business class of society are hurt by economic stagnation and organize for change. Opposition parties unite long enough to agree to oust the autocrat. Religious leaders, be they mullahs or Catholic bishops, join the struggle, bringing moral authority to the cause. Students and youth groups lead the charge in the streets, but generally do not control events. Finally, when large elements of the military begin to join the coalition, the autocrat's time is up.

The seventh and final warning sign of decline is the disposition of the military. Faced with economic crisis, military defeat, or unpopular orders to shoot their fellow citizens, military establishments tend to protect their own institution above all else. How they try to do this differs widely. In some cases, such as Portugal and Ethiopia in 1974, groups within the military removed the autocrat by coup d'état. In other cases, such as Brazil in 1985, the military handed power over to a civilian government to avoid being blamed for the country's troubles. In Argentina the military sought in vain to avoid unrest with a foreign adventure. In the Philippines and Haiti, the military protected itself by shifting allegiances and allying itself with the new coalition government. When the military fails to protect itself during a transition, it may shatter, as was the case in Iran and Nicaragua. The attitudes of those who control the guns are crucial during a transition.

An autocrat, like any other leader, is most likely to remain in power if he stays healthy and decisive, avoids military defeats and deep social divisions among his people, and produces an economic performance with slow but steady growth. If he allows or fails to control abuses of power, those abuses will magnify his problems. And once problems reach a critical mass, the autocrat runs a high risk of losing legitimacy when coalitions of opponents to his rule form and the military abandons him in order to save its own power and cohesion.

Types of Transitions

Once enough critical problems coalesce to work against the autocrat, the transition process will soon begin. The nature of this process is important in determining the form and orientation of the next government. While all transitions are unique, they can be loosely categorized into four types.

The first type of transition is uncontrolled revolutionary collapse, in which most institutions of the old society collapse along with the autocrat. The transition generally is violent, with guerrilla forces or mob rule overwhelming existing military forces. The new leadership is highly ideological and has little experience governing. Interim governments may be formed immediately following the collapse, but the revolutionary leadership, ruthless and single-minded, eventually takes over. Moderates are purged. In cases where the previous regime was friendly toward the United States, there has been a high degree of anti-Americanism. The revolution continues to drift in an extreme direction. The demise of the Shah of Iran and Somoza in Nicaragua are modern examples of revolutionary collapse.

The second transition possibility is revolutionary restructuring. Transition in a revolutionary situation need not always lead to a complete collapse of society. Once the autocrat is off the scene, a transition can bring a restructuring of government within the institutions of the old society. This type of transition generally promotes a more stable outcome in the long-term and can in fact lead to strengthened ties with the United States.

The revolutionary restructuring model generally includes street confrontations between supporters and opponents of the autocrat, but the transition itself is usually relatively bloodless. The autocrat usually flees the country or is arrested. Many of the existing economic, social, and political institutions remain basically intact. New political leaders emerge to run the government, and elements of the former military leadership either share power or acquiesce in civilian leadership. The new leadership is more pragmatic than ideological, less inclined to seek or hold power through violent means, and generally has some governmental experience. Recent examples of the revolutionary restructuring model include Argentina after the junta, the Philippines after Marcos, and Haiti after Duvalier.

A third type of transition is revolution by coup d'état. This kind of transition usually occurs in relatively underdeveloped societies in which the military is the dominant political institution and military coups offer the only possibility for political change. The ease with which a few officers can dominate government often results in a series of coups and countercoups until a dominant figure appears. Sometimes there is a good deal of bloodletting between factions of the military, resulting in dramatic political reversals. Such transitions can be difficult for the United States to influence. Personal relations and rivalries, hard to divine from the outside, often play a significant role. The nation that maintains strong ties with key individuals can sometimes influence the outcome however. For example, in both Ethiopia and Afghanistan the Soviets managed to develop close ties with coup leaders and to benefit from the coup. Yet the Soviets, though they knew key players, failed to capitalize on the coups and countercoups in Portugal in 1974.

A fourth type of transition is the managed transition, a process through which authoritarian leaders themselves see the need for a peaceful transition of government and plan for it. Their motives are varied and the process is not always fully under their control, but such transitions are generally successful. In the case of Brazil, the military in the early 1970s began a process of gradual liberalization called *abertura* or opening. The insurgents were defeated and the economy prospered, thus making it difficult for the ruling military junta to justify continued military rule. So the military leadership slowly liberalized society, formed alliances with technocrats, and developed their own political parties. When economic problems developed in the mid-1980s, the Brazilian junta lost control of the process—at least temporarily—but they nonetheless allowed a peaceful transition to occur in 1985. Similarly managed transitions have taken place in Spain and El Salvador. In Spain, Franco had the foresight to prepare for events after his death by naming Juan Carlos as king, who in turn carefully planned a transition to democracy. In El Salvador, it took a great deal of pressure from the United States and the courage of José Napoleon Duarte to begin the transition to democracy. In both cases, the military still retains considerable influence in government.

Of these four types of transitions, U.S. interests appear to fare best with the revolutionary restructuring and managed transition models. In fact, every case reviewed in these two categories has furthered the foreign policy interests of the United States. The common denominator in both types is that actions are taken by some groups within the old regime to soften the blow of the transition and prevent a complete collapse of social institutions. On the other hand, the revolutionary collapse and the military coup transitions pose serious challenges to U.S. foreign policy. Only in isolated cases such as Portugal did democracy prevail. The extent to which key government officials see a transition coming and take timely steps to modify its impact is critical to the orientation of the next government.

Determinants of the Outcome

Why does one country end up with totalitarian rule while another develops a democracy? Part of the answer, as we have seen, lies with the nature of the transition itself. The rest of the answer lies with the interrelationships among three variables: the existence of a democratic tradition or a supportive role model, the institutional foundation for the development of democracy, and the orientation and capabilities of the nation's new leadership.

A history of democratic values and traditions obviously is important in determining the direction of a posttransition government. Argentina, Brazil, and the Philippines each reverted to democratic traditions in their past.

What has been less obvious is that these democratic values can be reinforced and in some cases created by social contacts with other democratic countries. Both Spain and Portugal, for example, emerged from decades of one-man rule with strong ties to the rest of Europe. The German Social Democratic Party and other European political parties had made concerted efforts to develop and encourage the Socialist Parties in the Iberian Peninsula. They had provided money, political advice, and moral support to fledgling political institutions that otherwise might not have survived. A decade later, the Spanish and Portuguese successes inspired the Spanish- and Portuguese-speaking peoples of Argentina and Brazil. Similarly, the United States encouraged the development of democratic institutions in the Philippines and El Salvador, nations with close social and economic ties to the United States. The existence of a supportive role model can make an important difference in the outcome of a transition.

Democratic heritage and support from democratic nations are the cornerstones of democracy, but they must stand on a firm foundation—the institutions and institution-building capacity of the nation itself. The existence of centrist institutions such as opposition political parties, the Catholic church, and a free press bode well for democracy after a transition. In countries such as the Philippines and Argentina, where these institutions coexisted with dictatorial rule, democracy tends to prevail.

In other countries where opposition political parties were repressed during authoritarian rule, the emergence of a large middle class can serve as a sound basis for the development of such institutions. In Spain and Portugal, for example, political parties were built almost from scratch on the basis of a new middle class with a centrist political orientation. In both countries the Catholic church became an independent institution working for reform.

Prospects for democracy were not good, however, in countries where autocrats did not allow opposition parties to exist, where the middle class was small, or where religious and military institutions held extremist rather than centrist views. The shah, Haile Selassie, and Anastasio Somoza were all hereditary leaders who saw ruling as their divine right and tried to limit any organized opposition. Few centrist institutions were in place when they and their heirs left the scene. Those that were in place in Nicaragua and Iran either were limited in scope or destroyed by the new governments. Wealth was concentrated and no significant middle class could step in with newly developed political institutions. The political scene was highly polarized and ideologues had few credible centrist forces blocking their path to power. Thus, transitions in Third World countries formerly ruled by dynasties do not have a good chance of yielding democracies.

Strong personal leadership is a final ingredient in the recipe for the development toward democracy after a transition. Building a democracy takes time and can be a dangerous process for those attempting it. In Spain, for example, the transition was carefully planned by King Juan Carlos and Prime Minister Adolfo Suarez and social dynamics were conducive to democracy, but it still took the prestige of the king to prevent a military coup in February of 1981. In El Salvador, where the setting was less conducive for democracy than in Spain, President Duarte had the ability and courage to nudge democracy along in a divided society, convince the U.S. Congress to support him, and operate under constant threat of assassination. In Argentina President Raúl Alfonsín had the political skill to avoid a polarizing Peronist victory and the political courage to punish military officers guilty of abuses.

In sum, democracy tends to prevail after a transition from dictatorship when a country has a relatively orderly transition of power, a supportive role model, a society that can support moderate political institutions, and competent leadership dedicated to making democracy work.

The Soviet Connection

During the past decade, superpowers have seldom controlled the events that lead to a transition from authoritarian rule. Usually the most they can hope to do is establish relationships with key actors, react to indigenous events, and then try to help stabilize the new situation if it is in their favor. In fact, many transitions take place with no major input from the superpowers.

In cases where there is superpower interest or influence, the Soviets start with a few potential advantages over the United States. First, they usually do not have close ties with the incumbent authoritarian regime and so they are not tarred with whatever excesses the dictator or his regime may have perpetrated. Second, they have an ideology that emphasizes the destruction of the old system. And third, the Soviets are prepared to be ruthless and brutal if necessary. Despite these advantages, however, they have come out ahead in only a few instances.

The Soviets are selective when committing themselves to major overt involvement in a country's transition process. Several criteria appear important to their decision, including the following:

- the country's location, both for its strategic value and its military supply potential;
- an apparent U.S. lack of interest, which limits the risks of superpower confrontation;
- the existence of a relatively

closed society with potential for manipulation of small ruling groups;
• and strong encouragement by local Marxist leaders.

The opportunities in Ethiopia and Afghanistan met these criteria. Each country is of great strategic value to the Soviet Union. Ethiopia is dominant on the Horn of Africa, controls access to the Bab el Mandeb Straits, and can be supplied by direct airlift and by sea. Afghanistan borders on the Soviet Union's Islamic provinces and provides a potential Soviet base for operations against Pakistan and the Persian Gulf, and it can be supplied by ground and air.

The United States appeared to abandon its interest in each country, thereby reducing any risk of direct superpower confrontation for the Soviets. In the mid-1970s, the United States withdrew from its previous heavy involvement in Ethiopia because its communications facility at Kagnew station became redundant, and because it could not tolerate the brutality of the Derg. By 1977 Congress had prohibited further U.S. military aid to Ethiopia. The United States also rejected military aid to Afghanistan in the 1950s and appeared unwilling to challenge the Soviets on their periphery.

Both countries had closed societies in which small revolutionary groups could be influenced by the Soviets. Haile Selassie destroyed all Ethiopian institutions that could compete with the military, and after 1973 the radical Derg controlled the military. The Soviet-oriented Communist Party of Afghanistan controlled much of the Afghan military, even during Daoud's rule.

And in both cases, local Marxists felt threatened and therefore strongly encouraged Soviet involvement to secure their revolution. In Ethiopia the Derg saw threats to Ethiopia's sovereignty from Eritrea in the north and from Somalia in the west. In Afghanistan the Daoud government threatened the Communist Party in 1977–1978 by creating one official party that excluded them.

Nicaragua does not fit these criteria as precisely as Afghanistan and Ethiopia, and the Soviet commitment there has been more limited. Nicaragua has strategic value for the Soviets because it can serve as a base for insurgency operations elsewhere in Central America. The Sandinistas also formed a fairly closed group that felt threatened by the United States and sought help from the Soviets. But the Soviets cannot count on risk-free intervention in Nicaragua because of its proximity to the United States.

The Soviets usually become heavily committed only after the initial transition has taken place. The 1973 coup against Haile Selassie, the April 1978 coup against Daoud in Afghanistan, and the 1979 revolution by the Sandinistas all involved key people influenced by the Soviets, but the Soviets left few fingerprints. In each case the plotters carried out the transition by themselves, without overt Soviet help.

Once a Marxist-oriented regime is established, however, the Soviets often commit themselves to large overt support. Over 100,000 Soviet troops invaded Afghanistan to suppress, with brutal methods, widespread opposition to the Marxist regime in Kabul. Over $4 billion in military aid and thousands of Cuban troops were sent to Ethiopia to prop up the government and end Somalia's effort to annex the Ogaden. And over $500 million in military aid has been provided to the Sandinistas.

The Soviets, therefore, have been

selective in their initial involvement in transitions from authoritarian regimes, relying primarily on covert operations and surrogates until a Marxist regime takes over. Once this happens, however, they make a major commitment of resources to sustain that new Marxist regime. They have succeeded in the past decade in gaining influence in several countries including Afghanistan, Ethiopia, and Nicaragua. But despite their advantages, they have failed to influence most other transitions during the past 15 years. They also have paid a price for their limited successes by contributing to the demise of U.S.-Soviet détente.

The U.S. Connection

The United States traditionally has faced several disadvantages in dealing with transitions. The United States has global security commitments and commercial interests that often require it to deal with autocrats simply because they are the heads of government. Ties develop and sometimes U.S. policymakers resist change, either because of loyalty to the autocrat or because of fear of the unknown. So U.S. involvement in a transition can become difficult to avoid. At the same time, the United States is associated with the autocrat in the minds of the opposition.

These problems often are further complicated by inadequate intelligence and lack of ties with opposition leaders. In Iran, the shah, like many other autocrats, strongly discouraged U.S. diplomatic contact with his opponents. Most U.S. intelligence came via SAVAK, the secret police. U.S. analysts, lacking critically important information, failed to see the extent to which his legitimacy had eroded. Americans also were unable to form close ties with potential successors and make realistic judgments about their strengths and their political orientation.

With incomplete intelligence in Iran, U.S. policymakers were unable to reach policy consensus. Excessive use of force, which the Soviets might have suggested had they been in our place, was inconsistent with American values. The shah, dying of cancer while watching his dynasty crumble, turned to the United States and got mixed advice. He froze long enough for Ayatollah Khomeini and his forces to tear down the few groups in Iranian society, such as the emerging business class and the technocrats, that might have sustained a limited form of democracy. The United States joined the shah in his fall from power in Iran.

There are, however, other patterns that have turned out to be more successful for the United States. In Brazil the United States chose to support a managed transition from the sidelines rather than become directly involved. In Argentina the United States distanced itself from the regime during the late 1970s, which put it in good stead with the opposition when it came to power in 1983. In Portugal, in the mid-1970s, Ambassador Frank Carlucci developed a substantial aid program for the Portuguese military while West Germany helped strengthen the nation's political parties. In Spain Ambassador Wells Stabler disregarded warnings to the contrary and nurtured a working relationship with the opposition in 1975 and 1976. Each strategy worked well, in part because the United States maintained close ties with the opposition and could distinguish between Social Democrats and Communists.

Recently, the developing transitions in Haiti and the Philippines created concern about a replay of the Iranian revolution. But the dynamics of the situation in the United States were different. In each case reasonably good intelligence assessments based on ties with opposition groups gave policymakers an adequate appreciation of the deteriorating situation. U.S. policy was more unified, with relatively little backbiting and few press leaks. In addition, wavering autocrats proved willing to take U.S. advice and were given safe haven.

Through these experiences the United States has overcome some of the disadvantages it previously had in dealing with governments in transition. A unified policy based on good intelligence assessments and a willingness to support change when necessary provide a new formula with which the United States can compete successfully with the Soviet Union in dealing with political transitions.

Lessons to Be Learned

There are a number of foreign policy lessons to be learned from this review of authoritarian regimes in transition. They include the following:

- Internal factors dominate most transition processes. While the role of the superpowers is generally limited, there are critical moments when their actions can make a difference.
- Democracies tend to emerge after a transition from autocracy if the nation has a democratic heritage, a democratic role model, institutions that can support democracy, and strong leadership that promotes democracy. Dynasties have few of these characteristics and thus present particular problems during a transition. The United States could enhance the long-term prospects for emerging democracies in most cases by making greater use of the National Endowment for

Democracy and similar institutions to strengthen these criteria.
- The decline of an autocracy passes through various stages, and it is important that U.S. policymakers understand in which stage a particular transition is. Timing is critical to successful U.S. policy during a transition. Withdrawing U.S. support too soon or maintaining support for too long are equally dangerous. An intelligence assessment, unfettered by an autocrat's prohibitions or by a misplaced sense of U.S. loyalty to an autocrat, is crucial to this effort.
- At a certain point in the process an autocrat can lose his effective legitimacy with power centers in his country. After this happens his ultimate demise is generally inevitable. There are seven danger signals discussed in this paper for analysts to watch. The autocrat will lose legitimacy when a critical mass of these combine against him.
- U.S. interests are best served when a transition is managed by senior elements of the old government and when the previous autocrat is given a graceful exit. The greatest danger to U.S. interests has historically developed when a revolution destroys the middle class institutions in society or when ideological military officers initiate a coup. U.S. policy during a period of pending transition should be to encourage the former and prevent the latter.
- The United States has suffered in the past from divided and uncertain policies toward governments in transition. These divisions have complicated the transition process and enhanced the prospects for a foreign policy failure. When a consensus exists within the U.S. government, the prospects for helping to facilitate a successful transfer are much greater.

- The Soviets have been selective in their involvement in transition processes. Once they become involved, however, they make a major commitment to sustain their allies. While they enjoy some potential advantages over the United States in trying to influence the transition process, the record shows that these Soviet advantages can be overcome.

In conclusion, history shows that the alternative to authoritarian government need not be totalitarian rule. Democracy can prevail and the United States can play a constructive role during a transition from autocratic rule. The United States must deal with autocrats around the world, but we need not tie our interests to their fate. While a foreign autocrat is in power, the United States should make every effort to support those institutions in his society that can form the basis for a future democracy; develop close ties with leaders of the democratic opposition, if they exist; and gather intelligence necessary to gain early warning of a potential transition.

Transitions can be managed if the process is started in time by senior members of the old government working with the moderate opposition. The United States should actively encourage such managed transitions once warning signs indicate that a transition is likely. Failure to manage a transition in time can lead a nation like Iran or Nicaragua down a sad path. But successful management of a transition can bring at least a form of democracy to a nation and can in the process enhance U.S. foreign policy interests.

Notes

1. Many of the conclusions in this review are based upon the assessments of these analysts, which will appear in a forthcoming book to be published by the Foreign Service Institute. The eleven case studies provide a diverse look at this complex subject matter. Seven cases featured transitions that thus far have evolved toward more democratic forms of government: Spain and Portugal in the mid-1970s, Argentina in 1983, El Salvador in 1984, Brazil in 1985, and the Philippines and Haiti in 1986. Three cases featured heavy Soviet involvement in the posttransition period: Ethiopia's transition from Haile Selassie, Afghanistan's transition from Mohammad Daoud Khan, and Nicaragua's transition from Anastasio Somoza. The last, the revolution in Iran, ended with a victory for radical Islamic fundamentalism.

Beyond Authoritarianism and Totalitarianism: Strategies for Democratization

Larry Diamond

THE WORLD OF the 1980s is a world of democratic ferment, struggle, and promise. The breakdown of Western Europe's last three dictatorships in the mid-1970s appears to demarcate a new and important phase in what many view as a global evolution beyond authoritarianism and totalitarianism. Since the transitions to democracy in Greece, Portugal, and Spain in the 1970s, most of the bureaucratic-authoritarian states of Latin America have followed with transitions of their own (back) to civilian, constitutional government. More recently, the democratic tide has begun to sweep through Asia, unraveling authoritarian regimes of long standing in the Philippines and South Korea, and bringing significant (and perhaps inadequately appreciated) democratic progress in Taiwan and Pakistan. Even in insular Burma, a rigid and long-standing one-party dictatorship is reeling.

Larry Diamond is a senior research fellow at the Hoover Institution, Stanford University. He is the author of *Class, Ethnicity and Democracy in Nigeria* and numerous articles on democracy and political development in Nigeria, Africa, and the Third World. This essay is revised from a paper prepared for the conference on "Pluralism, Participation and Democracy: Prospects and Prescriptions into the 21st Century," sponsored by CSIS and held in Lisbon, Portugal, June 19–21, 1988.

In the Caribbean, the corrupt and brutal dictatorship of the Duvaliers in Haiti was finally terminated in 1986, and now one of Latin America's most venal and wily autocrats, General Manuel Noriega of Panama, is under pressure. Less progress has been visible in Africa; however, ruthless dictatorships have been displaced in recent years in Uganda and Guinea, Sudan now has an elected civilian government, and an imaginatively planned transition to a third democratic republic is now well underway in Nigeria. Even among the communist states, pluralist thinking and mobilization in civil society are increasing, and so are the constraints on the ability of the communist parties to resort to the totalitarian formulas of the past in order to maintain their hegemony.

Viewed in this way, there appears to be a kind of global zeitgeist for democracy, even an inevitable trend toward democratic growth in the world. After all, democracy is the only form of government that commands widespread and deep legitimacy in the world today. The great competing ideologies of the twentieth century have largely been discredited. Fascism was destroyed as a vital force in World War II, and the appeals of Marxism-Leninism have visibly declined with the harsh repressiveness, glaring economic failures, and loss of revolutionary idealism of the existing communist regimes. In addition, international attention to human rights conditions has increased dramatically within the past two decades, gradually compelling communist and authoritarian regimes to become more accountable before a growing network of international treaties, institutions, and public opinion forums. Incremental improvements, however small, in respect for elementary rights of conscience, expression, and organization create space in which citizens can mobilize for further liberalization of their regimes.

Yet if this picture is bright, it is also partly illusory. Most of the independent states of the world today are governed less than democratically, and a great many allow virtually no space at all for opposition and dissent. Raymond Gastil's invaluable survey, "Freedom in the World," counted little more than a third of the independent states of the world as "free" (which can be roughly interpreted as democratic) in 1987.[1] A disproportionate share of these were microstates of less than one million, and mostly less than a quarter million, people. Furthermore, the total number of democracies in the world has not changed much since the survey began in 1973.[2] This is not because political regimes have been stagnant since then; as noted above, there has been a good deal of movement. The problem is that movement has been in both directions. Although 15 countries that were under authoritarian rule at some point in the past 15 years are democratic today, 12 countries that had democratic government in that period do not have it today.

The frequency of democratic breakdowns in this century—and the difficulty of consolidating new democra-cies—must give serious pause to those who would argue teleologically for the inevitability of global democratization. There is nothing inevitable about the progress, or the stability, of democracy in the world. The intrinsic openness and competitiveness of democracies imply a certain element of fragility, and, outside the deeply institutionalized polities of the industrialized West, this fragility has been acute. As a result, those concerned about how countries can move "beyond authoritarianism and totalitarianism" must also ponder the conditions that permit such movement to endure. To rid a country of an authoritarian regime or dictator is not necessarily to move it fundamentally beyond authoritarianism.

Some Conceptual Starting Points. It is symptomatic of the international momentum of democracy in the world that so many different kinds of regimes strive (and strain) to define themselves as democracies and that democracy is the term used to signify so many different visions of the "good" society. This is one source of conceptual confusion. Another is that many people conceive of democracy as not only a political but also a social and economic system, while others believe that a free, open, and competitive form of government is a valued goal in and of itself.

For various normative and scientific reasons, it is important to conceive of democracy purely as a political form of government, however much it may be enhanced by, or even to some degree dependent on, particular social and economic structures.[3] Thus, democracy is defined as

a system of government that meets three essential conditions: meaningful and extensive *compe-*

tition among individuals and organized groups (especially political parties) for all effective positions of government power, at regular intervals and excluding the use of force; a highly inclusive level of *political participation* in the selection of leaders and policies, at least through regular and fair elections, such that no major (adult) social group is excluded; and a level of *civil and political liberties*—freedom of expression, freedom of the press, freedom to form and join organizations—sufficient to ensure the integrity of political competition and participation.[4]

Between totalitarian and authoritarian regimes—which allow little or no meaningful political competition, participation, and freedom—and democracies, a large number of regimes fall somewhere in the middle. Hence, semidemocratic are

> those countries where the effective power of elected officials is so limited, or political party competition is so restricted, or the freedom and fairness of elections so compromised that electoral outcomes, while competitive, still deviate signficantly from popular preferences; and/or where civil and political liberties are so limited that some political orientations and interests are unable to organize and express themselves.

At the most extreme end of the continuum opposite democracy lies totalitarianism. These regimes are distinct in the degree to which they control the lives of their citizens and eliminate all potentially competing sources of thinking and action in civil society. Building on the work of Zbigniew Brzezinski, Carl Friedrich, and others, Juan Linz defined totalitarian regimes

by the following components: a highly centralized, monistic structure of power, in which the ruling group "is not accountable to any large constituency and cannot be dislodged from power by institutionalized, peaceful means"; an exclusive, elaborate (totalist) ideology that legitimizes the regime and infuses it with a sense of historical purpose; the active mobilization of the citizenry for political and social tasks through a set of monopolistic institutions, including a single, mass mobilizational party, which together crowd out virtually all autonomous forms of social and political organization.[5] Thus, society becomes totally politicized, and the boundary between the state and civil society disintegrates.

Authoritarian regimes may have some of the above elements. Generally, however, they do not have an elaborate and guiding ideology. They allow some but still very limited and controlled pluralism of political thinking, expression, organization, and action, even semiopposition. They otherwise do not so totally dominate the lives of their citizens, nor so thoroughly and organically control the social and economic infrastructures of civil society, such as productive establishments, labor unions, schools, voluntary associations, the mass media, and the church. Totalitarian regimes demand active demonstrations of loyalty to the party and state; authoritarian regimes are content to have their citizens not actively oppose them. At the same time, however, authoritarian regimes do not permit effective competition for political power, nor meaningful and widespread popular participation in the formulation of public policies, through elections or other means. Nor do they allow substantial levels of civil liberties.[6]

Sources and Facilitators of Democracy

To determine how societies can move beyond authoritarianism and totalitarianism, one must understand the variety of social, cultural, economic, and political factors that encourage, facilitate, and sustain democratic government. Thorough consideration of these factors is well beyond the scope of this essay, but a brief review may highlight some issues particularly salient to the problem of regime transitions.[7]

Historical Sequences and Democratic Transitions. The historical development of democracy in the advanced industrialized democracies and the transitions to democracy of the past decade or so have many unique and distinctive features, but most of these cases also share some common characteristics. These follow from the nature of democracy as a system of institutionalized competition for power. For such competition to become stable, some measure of mutual trust and confidence is necessary among the various contenders for power, a settled respect for the rules of the game, what Robert Dahl called a "system of mutual security."[8]

Historically, this type of mutual confidence and tolerance among power contenders was most likely to develop gradually, at first within a restricted political arena. Hence, the most successful path of democratic evolution was a sequence in which political competition first developed within a relatively small circle of opposing elites, then gradually expanded to incorporate an increasing proportion of the population as legitimate participants.[9]

Although legal limits on the extent of the franchise and other participatory rights are no longer feasible in a competitive polity (as Dahl noted), the role of gradualism and sequencing in the development of democracy remains a salient lesson. Widespread political freedom, participation, and competition for power involve risks for the contending actors and for other established forces in society. To the extent this competition can be phased in gradually so that contending parties and candidates can learn to tolerate and work with one another—and so to trust that defeat will not mean elimination, that victory will be limited by accountability, and that power will be wielded responsibly—these risks and uncertainties can be diminished, and the prospects for a stable, nonviolent democracy increased.

This is not an argument for extending the lives of authoritarian regimes that have lost all legitimacy and are ripe for replacement. Quite often, the only way to arrive at—or return to—democracy is to rid the country of the authoritarian rulers and institutions quickly and decisively. This casting off occurs either because internal and perhaps external factors have converged to present a unique moment of democratic opportunity, or because the authoritarian regime has no sincere intention of relinquishing any degree of effective power and would use the promise of a democratic opening to frustrate the movement for democratic change and perhaps to identify then destroy its democratic opposition. The latter game is one that Mobutu Sese Seko has played repeatedly in Zaire.

The typical situation, however, is one in which the authoritarian regime more or less determines the timing, pace, and structure of its own exit, and in which a puritanical insistence by democratic forces on immediate and humiliating abdication will likely abort the prospective transition. As Linz wrote, "The strategy of a clean break is only viable in a revolutionary or potentially revolutionary situation."[10] Thus, a recent study of transitions to democracy in southern Europe and Latin America pointed to "a sequence of piecemeal reforms" as the most likely path of successful transition and emphasized the need for democratic oppositions to be willing to play within the initially very restricted games allowed them by authoritarian regimes early in the sequence, while seeking a negotiated solution and avoiding "widespread and recurrent violence."[11]

The frequent necessity of such a gradualist, sequential approach is illustrated not only by recent European and Latin American transitions but by the one now unfolding in Nigeria. The Nigerian transition may be seen as a model of how power can be gradually transferred from authoritarian to democratic, elected figures at successively higher levels of authority. The elaborately sequenced, 5-year program began in 1987–1988 with the election of (nonpartisan) local governments and the formation of a constituent assembly to draft a new constitution. In 1989 the ban on political parties will be lifted, then new local governments will be elected on a partisan basis. In 1990 state legislatures and governors will be elected. In 1991 a national census is to be conducted (for the first time in 20 years), then in the fourth quarter local government elections are to be held once more. Scheduled for the the first half of 1992 is the election and convening of a national assembly, to be followed later that year by the election and inauguration of a civilian president, marking the final stage in military withdrawal from power.

The value of this approach is that it gives competing political forces some time to gain experience with the risks and requirements of democratic elections and the responsibilities of democratic governance before the entire state structure is opened to political competition. Thus parties have a chance to form and mobilize in the open before they have to contest, and civilian politicians have some time to govern and compete at the state and local level before national power is contested. This more closely approximates the gradual opening of monarchical and other autocracies in Europe (and also the development of democratic mass parties and self-rule in such colonies as India and Sri Lanka). However, those democratic openings occurred over decades and generations, whereas this will take place within five years.

The issue of time represents one of the great dilemmas of the transition from authoritarianism. Democratic parties need time to develop their identities, leaderships, principles, and organizations, free from the pressures of an imminent election in which everything will be at stake. As mentioned above, they also need time to develop among them the relationships of mutual tolerance and trust and respect for law that can only emerge gradually, through years of competition and cooperation and repeated elections. The less the previous experience with democratic parties and elections and the less favorable the social and economic conditions that promote democratic tolerance and restraint (see below), the greater the need for time.

Some countries cannot afford the luxury of time; the democratic opening appears as a brief moment of imperative that must be seized. In other instances, there may be no particular moment of authoritarian vulnerability or breakdown, but neither is there any inclination or capacity on the part of authoritarian rulers to envisage, permit, or implement a carefully staged transition to democracy. Even when such a democratizing or liberalizing vision does exist, it may sour when the authoritarian regime realizes the full implications of what it has begun and tires of having to tolerate dissent and be held accountable by democratic forces in society and at lower levels of power. In still other instances, those authoritarian regimes that might in principle be willing to manage a gradual, phased institutionalization of democracy cannot sustain popular consent for such a lengthy period of continued rule at the top echelons of power. Moreover, once they have conceded that democratic rule is the preferred outcome of political evolution, ultimately the most legitimate form of government for the country, authoritarian rulers have undermined a major basis of their own legitimacy.

In the contemporary world of mass communications and rapid international diffusion, no highly mobilized and politically aware population seems willing to wait several decades for a regime to implement a long-term plan of democratization. Probably one reason why Nigeria's military regime has compressed so many phases of democratic transfer into so few years (five elections in three years) is that the country would not have stood for a significantly longer transition.

There are several steps that can be taken to attenuate these problems. An important one is to introduce, even into the authoritarian regime, institutions of democratic accountability and restraint of power. Particularly fundamental in this regard is the rule of law, which requires a professional, independent judiciary and police and autonomous institutions to monitor, check, and punish political corruption at any level. Associated with this but going beyond it is a relatively high

degree of civil liberty—freedoms of speech, the press, association, assembly, movement, and religion; freedom from terror, torture, degrading punishment, unjustified imprisonment, and unreasonable search and seizure. As O'Donnell and Schmitter noted, such individual and group liberties can exist alongside fairly authoritarian structures of power, and the process of liberalization seems almost invariably to precede or lead the democratization of power.[12]

An initial focus on liberalization may be a compelling strategy for three reasons. First, it is inherently desirable in its own right and often involves the termination of the most repugnant and appalling aspects of authoritarian rule. Second, it does not directly and immediately involve the transfer or surrender of power; hence, the risks to established interests of liberalization are significantly less than of democratization. Third, liberalization provides the citizenry with the legal space and means to push the process of transition forward to the transfer of power as well. In some situations,

> the opening of certain avenues for autonomy of the society—like some forms of collective bargaining, lower level trade union elections, free elections in professional associations, political activity in the universities, protest by neighborhood associations, the support by the churches of certain forms of protest, a relatively autonomous cultural life, etc.—create . . . opportunities for opposition leaders and sometimes illegal parties to achieve a certain presence and basis of support.[13]

Two other principles can also attenuate the politically unpalatable nature of an extended transition to democracy. One is rotation of leadership. Among the most objectionable features of authoritarian rule is its frequent personalization. The more personalized is a regime, the more it tends to be abusive, corrupt, and unaccountable. The longer a political leader remains in executive power, the more personalized, intolerant, unanswerable, lawless, and self-serving does his or her rule tend to become. To the extent that power rotates in a predictable and orderly fashion, even in an authoritarian regime, it will tend to be less abusive and more subject to checks and constraints, as the recent experience of Brazilian military rule suggests. Rotation of leadership can thus represent the first step on the road to constitutional government, while also setting a precedent for subsequent civilian heads of government.

A final principle that might increase the acceptability of a lengthy transition from authoritarianism, and in any case enhance the likelihood of eventual democratic success, is decentralization of power. The more people have control over their own immediate institutions and resources, the more inherently democratic is the society. In addition, decentralization of power promotes government responsiveness, ethnic tranquility, civil peace, and political system legitimacy. Hence, to the extent that the transition from authoritarianism begins not simply with a formal transfer of power at the local level but also with a meaningful and effective one, people may be more willing to abide the persistence for a time of undemocratic or semidemocratic rule at the center, and local government officials and politicians will gain more substantial experience with democracy.

All of this suggests that in many countries, a lengthy transition to democracy might well be more conducive to long-term democratic stability and success than a rapid one. Semi-democracy can serve as a way station on the road to the full democratization of power at every level of government. Expansion or restoration of civil liberties and the rule of law and creation of powerful, elected local government structures can be early steps. Creation of effective arenas of elective power at the provincial, regional, or state level can be a later step, requiring in some countries significant devolution of power from the center. An elected national legislature can serve for some time alongside an executive still effectively controlled by the military, as in Indonesia or to a great extent Thailand.

Where the military remains firmly in control, openly or behind the scenes, negotiating with it a plan for gradual democratization of political institutions may offer the best hope for committed democrats. The situation may be more delicate and intractable in countries like Mexico or, to a more extreme degree, the Soviet Union, where the hegemonic party has spun a vast network of patrons, bosses, and bureaucrats whose statuses, careers, and livelihoods (and not infrequently huge fortunes) would be threatened by democratization and who would therefore fight it desperately.

Whatever the type of authoritarian regime, a crucial issue is what will press it to continue the transition. As in Turkey, the driving force may be a talented leader firmly committed to the process, such as Mustafa Kemal Ataturk or, after World War II, president Ismet Inonu.[14] Such visionary leadership is rare, however, and rarely is it enough. Typically, the ruling structure in an authoritarian or semi-democratic regime includes many elements and interests firmly opposed to a transfer of effective power—"hard-liners" in the language of O'Donnell and Schmitter.[15] Their resistance will not be overcome, and often a transition may not even be launched, without the convergence of enormous pressure from below, in civil society and perhaps from outside, in other countries.

Social Pluralism and Associational Life. One of the most striking findings to emerge from the Diamond, Linz, and Lipset study and other recent studies is the vital importance for democracy of a pluralistic, vigorously organized civil society, featuring a dense network of intermediate groups and voluntary associations independent of the state. This pluralism may take many forms: business and producer groups, trade unions, peasant leagues, cooperatives, student and professional associations, women's organizations, self-help groups, religious institutions, ethnic and tribal associations. They may pursue economic, social, and cultural goals or more explicitly political (though nonpartisan) ones, such as protecting civil liberties, guarding against electoral fraud, and educating and turning out voters.

Voluntary associations perform many functions in a democracy. They constitute, in addition to political parties, an alternative channel for articulating interests and making demands upon the government. Through their internal structure and functioning, they may serve as training grounds in democracy, increasing the political efficacy and capacities of citizens, recruiting new political leaders, stimulating participation in the larger political system and enhancing citizen commitment to democracy. Perhaps most important, such autonomous associations check the relentless tendency of the state to centralize and expand its power and to evade civic accountability and control. In this sense, they may constitute (as the press and broadcast media, the plural-

ism and autonomy of which are equally important to democracy) an informal branch of government in their capacity to provide alternative channels for political expression and additional checks on executive or legislative power.

Not surprisingly, then, virtually everywhere movements for democratization exist, there is an explosion of interest group organization and mobilization, what O'Donnell and Schmitter term the resurrection (although in some instances it is really a fresh evolution) of civil society. The forms this may take include:

the resurgence of previous political parties or the formation of new ones to press for more explicit democratization or even revolution; the sudden appearance of books and magazines on themes long suppressed by censorship; the conversion of older institutions, such as trade unions, professional associations, and universities, from agents of governmental control into instruments for the expression of interests, ideals, and rage against the regime; the emergence of grass-roots organizations articulating demands long repressed or ignored by authoritarian rule; the expression of ethical concerns by religious and spiritual groups previously noted for their prudent accommodation to the authorities;

as well as a testing early on of the limits of cultural dissent by artists and intellectuals; and the defection, much later, of economically powerful and privileged groups.[16]

The catalyst for this efflorescence of associational life may be a decision on the part of the authoritarian regime to expand civil liberties or a more subtle process of gradual liberalization. As noted above, one reason why liberalization is such an important first step in the transition beyond authoritarianism is that it enhances the capacity of social groups to organize for their own interests and in opposition to political repression and injustice. Even more is this so with a transition from totalitarianism, where the establishment of even very limited freedoms of expression, association, assembly, and privacy of the person and home enable nascent democratic groups to take the first tentative steps toward the reconstruction of a boundary between the state and civil society. Once this line begins to be redrawn, the struggle for independent, mass-based interest groups, such as the Polish trade union, Solidarity, becomes the driving wedge of the quest not only for freedom but for democracy.

Nevertheless, a political initiative by the authoritarian regime is not the only possible source of this invigoration of civil society. It may also be spawned, and more lastingly, by economic and social changes that give rise to new interests which demand voice and recognition.

Legitimacy and Socioeconomic Change. Authoritarian regimes, particularly military regimes, face intrinsic difficulties in legitimating themselves. If the source of their legitimacy is the traditional nature of their authority, the customary ties of obeisance to the king—and to various lower order patrimonial authorities—dissolve with the spread of education, communications, foreign contact, and modern doctrines of popular sovereignty. If authority is legitimate only by virtue of its charismatic nature, it will dissolve when the charismatic ruler passes from the scene, and often long before then unless he or she takes steps to rationalize and institutionalize personal authority. Rational-legal authority in turn presupposes rationality, legality, due

process, and other impersonal criteria that authoritarian regimes tend to contradict (although Max Weber did not mean to equate this form of authority with democracy per se).

To some extent, all regimes depend for their legitimacy on their record of performance, but democratic regimes also derive legitimacy from the democratic character of their rule and the identification of their citizens with democratic values. By contrast, authoritarian regimes appear unable to legitimate themselves durably through the same intrinsic political features. This is because few citizens in the world identify with and cherish authoritarianism per se. They do not value inherently the monopoly of power by a narrow party or bureaucratic elite. They do not applaud as fundamentally good and just the limitation and repression of basic civil and political liberties. Rather, they may accept these as necessary for the achievement of some higher good— economic growth, socialism, communism, the Islamic society, utopia. When utopia does not come, but rather the lack of constitutional and social restraints leads to an increasingly arbitrary, abusive, and decadent exercise of power, the legitimacy of the authoritarian or totalitarian regime (such as it may have existed) crumbles.

To the extent that the regime may, in a totalitarian fashion, control all the means of ideological reproduction, it may in the short run be able to manipulate its own legitimation far more powerfully than the supposedly mythicizing "bourgeois democracy" condemned in Marxian theory. However, as recent events in the Soviet Union and China so dramatically demonstrate, all regimes must ultimately answer for their performance. Regimes that cannot, over the long run, deliver social and economic progress to the bulk of their citizens—or at least avoid deterioration in the quality of life—will encounter problems of legitimacy. These may eventually become so severe as to force those regimes to reform or risk collapsing under the weight of their own inertia.

The problem for authoritarian regimes, especially those that lack some institutional means for legitimation, such as a ruling party and mass-mobilizing ideology, is that socioeconomic progress and reform carry their own risks. As Samuel Huntington demonstrated a generation ago, "modernity breeds stability, but modernization breeds instability."[17] "Social and economic change—urbanization, increases in literacy and education, industrialization, mass media expansion—extend political consciousness, multiply political demands, broaden political participation."[18] As the traditional ties of peasant to lord, client to patron, and subject to ruler weaken, new and independent interests are generated, and new political and organizational capacities are acquired at the individual and group level.[19] Demands proliferate both for the right to participate politically and for tangible and symbolic benefits. Political institutions must expand and adapt to make room for these new entrants or risk breaking down.

Democratic regimes often have their own rigidities, but their open and competitive political institutions provide a means and stimulus for adaptation to change. Authoritarian regimes tend by nature to be rigid in their scope for meaningfully incorporating new political demands for participation and influence. In time, these proliferating demands and expectations may congeal into a broad popular campaign for democratization. A classic instance is South Korea,

where two decades of extraordinary economic growth fashioned profound social changes—dramatic growth in education and literacy and in the size and political consciousness of the middle class; a more pluralistic, organized, and autonomous civil society; increasing circulation of people, information, and ideas; and much denser linkages with the industrialized democracies—that facilitated and fueled the transition to democracy. Many of the same processes and effects are apparent now in Taiwan and even to some degree in Pakistan.

These (and other) cases demonstrate the generic vulnerability of contemporary authoritarian regimes, particularly military regimes. Lacking strong legitimating principles, their "support is based on more unstable considerations, like the self-interest of those sustaining or accepting them."[20] Thus, they face a legitimacy contradiction, a kind of catch-22. If they do not perform, they lose legitimacy because performance is their only justification for holding power. However, like South Korea or Peru (under Velasco's reformist military rule), if they do perform in delivering socioeconomic progress, they tend to refocus popular aspirations around political goals for voice and participation that they cannot satisfy without terminating their existence. Similarly, if they succeed in meeting the critical threat or challenge (e.g., subversion, terrorism, political violence) that justified their seizure of power, they become dispensable, just as the generation of new challenges and interests with the passing of time makes them, with their inability to adapt, irrelevant.[21]

For democrats, the policy implications are not as obvious as they seem, if one recalls Huntington's warning that the process of modernization can be destabilizing. However, this is not an argument against socioeconomic development, rather it is an appeal for simultaneous attention to political development—institution building. For socioeconomic development is not only an end in itself, not only a means to improve the physical quality of life. There is also considerable evidence that it fosters democratic changes in attitudes and values. It tends to make citizens more concerned about political and civil liberties, more demanding of government, more pluralistic in their organizational capacities and impulses, more hungry for free information, more opinionated and independent in their thinking, and less willing to abide authoritarian—not to mention totalitarian—rule.

Strategies for Democratization

Focused as it has been on the problem of transitions, the above review has considered only some of the factors that may affect the possibility for stable democracy. It has treated political culture and legitimacy as products of social and economic change and regime performance, but these also have roots in the cultural traditions and deep historical experiences of a country. It has not considered such important factors as the management of ethnic and religious cleavages, the relationship between the state and the economy, the constitutional structure and party system, the international environment, or the judgment, skill, and democratic commitment of political leadership. The latter two factors will come into sharper focus, however, as more tangible measures to move countries toward democracy are considered.

Domestic Political Actors. Obviously, the most favorable development for democratization is a firm and forceful commitment to the process on the part of a country's political leadership. The experience of Nigeria from 1975–1979 under the leadership of generals Murtala Muhammed and Olusegun Obasanjo demonstrates the overriding influence that skillful, dedicated leadership can exert. General Obasanjo's faithful execution of the military regime's 4-year timetable for transition—following the tragic and potentially explosive assassination of Murtala Muhammed in a failed coup attempt only five months after the transition had been announced—must rank as one of the great examples of democratic statesmanship in recent times.

To begin with the obvious: the authoritarian rulers themselves have more scope than any other set of actors to move their country toward democracy. To the extent they are fundamentally committed to the process, firmly in control of the regime (in any internal conflict with hardliners or backsliders), and far-sighted in designing a realistic program and timetable for transition, the transition is more likely to bear fruit and to endure.

Without reviewing earlier suggestions about the structure and timing of the transition, one can note here the importance of building a political consensus around the framework of the transition. This is inherently a political problem; therefore, it requires skills of which authoritarian, particularly military, leaders may be short. Respected intellectuals, scholars, and religious and interest group leaders should be involved and consulted, and popular participation in the design of the new system should be encouraged. To the extent that a democratic constitution results from a broad process of popular debate, consultation, and participation, it is more likely to fit the country's sociocultural context and to be widely accepted from the beginning as legitimate. This suggests that the membership of any constitutional drafting body should be openly announced, representative, and not only technically skilled but also politically sensitive to popular aspirations and concerns. It also argues strongly for a predominantly elective constituent assembly and sufficient freedom of expression to permit the open airing of individual and group views on constitutional issues. These features have characterized both Nigeria's previous transition to democracy and its current one.[22]

The problem, of course, is that authoritarian rulers are typically, at best, reluctant democratizers and often thoroughly unwilling ones. Thus, various groups in civil society—and, among those countries trying to restore democracy, in the previous party system—must craft strategies for democratization that overcome or neutralize resistance from the regime. This problem is far better addressed elsewhere than here.[23] From the preceding discussion, however, two lessons are apparent. First, popular pressure is crucial in inducing a reluctant or unwilling authoritarian regime to launch a democratic transition and to stick to it. Second, each situation is unique in its balance of political forces within and between the state and the society. Hence, the extent and forms of popular pressure most likely to be effective vary from country to country and invariably (unless the regime is about to collapse) must be balanced by a willingness of opposition forces to negotiate with the regime in some coherent way. Here again the skill and judgment of political leaders (in both the regime and the opposition) emerges as an important and, in some cases such as the Spanish transition, possibly a decisive variable.[24]

The distinctiveness of political alignments in each country and the need for negotiations in turn imply several requirements for the democratic opposition. A crucial one is effective organization. Broad and sustained popular mobilization for democracy requires that individuals be organized into a number of groups that can gather resources, channel communications, coordinate action, inspire members, and recruit support. Another is effective leadership. Leaders of democratic organizations must be able to discern when the moment demands forceful demonstrations of public opposition to authoritarian rule—protests, petitions, marches, general strikes, civil disobedience, peaceful assemblies (but never violence)—and when the moment is ripe for negotiation or pregnant with the risk of backlash.

This implies something of a contradiction. Much of the value of civil associations lies in their provision of democratic experience, training, and socialization. However, effective mobilization *for* democracy requires that organizational leaders have sufficient command over their followers to control the level of popular action quickly and decisively. The more precisely democratic leaders can mobilize and demobilize the movement for democracy, the more effective they will be in negotiating the regime's withdrawal. The more that elements of the movement resist such coordinated direction, the weaker will be the negotiating hand of the democrats and the greater will be the risk that violence and chaos induce a backlash against democratization by hardliners in the regime, with the support of many elements of society whose fear of disorder is greater than their desire for democracy. To some extent, organizational leadership that is democratic (elected, or at least representative and responsive, with provisions for some kind of collective, deliberative decision making) can in principle command this type of loyalty from its following. Nevertheless, the problem is very real. In the form of militant and often violent student protest, it came close to derailing the transition in South Korea and remains a source of difficulty for the democratic opposition to Pinochet in Chile.[25]

This problem reflects as well a third condition for democratic organization: that it be coherent. The value of multiple, diverse associations is that they incorporate a broader range of society. The more numerous and diverse they are, the greater are the sociopolitical costs for the regime (not to mention the tactical difficulties) of repression. This diversity must have some coherence and coordination if it is to be effective; otherwise, competing organizations will pursue different strategies with different tactics (as in Chile), and the regime will be able to play one group off against another.

To summarize, then, democrats in civil society must strike a balance between passion and prudence, between militance and moderation, between creative participation and the demands of organizational loyalty and coherence. Across different authoritarian situations, as well as over time, the balance may change. Although the impetus for the transition must come from civil society, success depends on shrewd and able leadership and dense and resourceful organization. The former is a product of domestic culture, politics, and chance, but much can be done from abroad to aid the latter.

International Actors. No aspect of the struggle for democracy provokes more intellectual and political controversy than the role of international actors. There is spirited debate over both the desirability and the possibility of effective international assistance for democratization. Although these normative and empirical issues are often intertwined in argument, they are separable.

Much of the normative opposition to international intervention begins with the assumption that it will do more harm than good. To be sure, official bilateral aid from such established democracies as the United States always serves a range of motives and interests, of which the promotion of democracy has typically not been a leading one, and often not one at all. Too often the United States has been content to support an authoritarian regime generously and uncritically (inter alia, those of the shah of Iran, Somoza, Marcos, Mobutu, Noriega) because it seemed to serve immediate, geopolitical U.S. interests. U.S. policies (both overt and covert) have sometimes served to undermine democracy, perhaps wittingly through economic sanctions and political pressure in Chile under Allende and at least unwittingly by vastly strengthening military and security establishments elsewhere in Latin America. The latter effect does not follow invariably from military assistance, rather from a level of aid that disproportionately inflates the resources and power of the military in relation to civil and political institutions and from a Cold War doctrine that disproportionately emphasizes the containment of communism and revolutionary insurgencies over the promotion of democracy and protection of civil liberties.[26]

These objections argue not against international assistance but for a reorientation of it around democratic objectives. However, a more sophisticated approach maintains that even well-intentioned democratic assistance is unlikely to be effective. This may

239

be because it taints and delegitimates the individuals and organizations that receive it or because the dependence on such aid undermines the necessary process of citizens empowering themselves and defining and waging their own struggle for democracy, without which no resulting democratic regime can be authentic and enduring. Embedded in this argument are certain value assumptions that cannot be refuted, but empirically it is difficult to reconcile with historical or contemporary realities.

One consideration is that economic assistance can make a difference to new and struggling democracies. International assistance, especially generous U.S. support under the Alliance for Progress, helped keep the Colombian economy afloat during the difficult early years of the new regime in the late 1950s and early 1960s. Economic assistance also helped Costa Rica consolidate economic growth and democracy in the decades after 1946.[27] Democratic Botswana's vibrant economic development has been boosted by the highest level of per capita development assistance in sub-Saharan Africa. To be sure, unending aid dependence has serious long-term costs for the recipient country, but aid that is structured specifically to nurture a country through difficult straits or to help lay the foundation for self-sustaining growth can benefit both development and democracy.

Similarly, external political initiatives and diplomatic pressures can have a democratic impact. Given the importance of improving civil liberties as a first step toward democratization and an end in itself, one can certainly applaud the human rights initiatives of the U.S. government under president Jimmy Carter. In Argentina, for example, such pressure did not force the withdrawal of the military, but it

"saved many victims of indiscriminate repression in the late 1970s, and was a factor in the international isolation of the military regime."[28] In the 1978 elections in the Dominican Republic, political pressure from the Carter administration blocked a blatantly fraudulent attempt by the right-wing party to remain in power.[29] During the Reagan administration, shrewd and forceful, if decidedly tardy, diplomatic initiatives also helped to hasten the departures of Ferdinand Marcos from the Philippines and Jean Claude Duvalier from Haiti with a minimum of bloodshed and may have helped dissuade president Chun Doo Hwan from unleashing a possibly bloody and disastrous wave of repression against the recent popular mobilization for democracy in South Korea. In Europe, the democratic condition for membership in the European Economic Community (EEC) provided substantial long-term pressure for democratic transition and consolidation in the less developed south European countries (Greece, Spain, and Portugal), which had been "suffering a sense of exclusion" under authoritarian rule.[30] More recently, pressure from the EEC has helped to persuade Turkey to lift martial law and institute stronger protections for human rights.[31]

Thus, external efforts can aid the process of democratization, but they can also frustrate, retard, or subvert it. It matters greatly what type of entity the external actor is, what its real objectives are, how they are perceived within the recipient country, what form the aid takes, and to whom in the recipient country it is directed.

From decades of mixed experience and certain elements of an emerging normative consensus in the world, the following principles for international action may be advanced:

1. It is in the legitimate interest of

all democratic nations to have as many democracies in the world as possible and to have countries that are not fully democratic be governed as democratically as possible. This is so because freedom is more secure in one country when it is firmly planted in others (political regime trends and ideologies do diffuse across borders) and because "no two liberal societies have ever fought each other."[32]

2. It is the legitimate business of all nations to be concerned about the status of human rights in any of them. The experience of genocide and other massive human rights violations in modern times compels a reconceptualization of the notion of sovereignty. At a minimum, a Hitler or Pol Pot or Idi Amin should be morally unacceptable to the community of nations, and another nation (such as Tanzania in the case of Amin) should be morally justified in aiding the citizens of a victimized country to resist and overthrow barbarous oppression.

3. True sovereignty resides not with the regime in control of the state of a country but with its people. When the people clearly indicate their rejection of the ruling regime, democratic governments and organizations are justified in offering them assistance to realize their political aspirations. This is not carte blanche for democracies to overthrow regimes they fear or dislike. Rather it is an argument for popular legitimacy as the fount of sovereignty and for reading unambiguous signals of the illegitimacy or delegitimation of an authoritarian regime as due cause for no longer according it the full respect and privileges of sovereignty.

4. Official external efforts to move a country toward popular sovereignty and democracy should place increasing emphasis on coordinated, multilateral efforts for at least two reasons. Multilateral initiatives will be less likely to

be distorted by the particular economic and geostrategic interests, beyond democratization, of any single powerful country. Because of this, multilateral projects will be less suspect as self-serving and neoimperialist within the recipient country. Where a democratic superpower has long been suspected and resented for its actions in the region—as with the United States in Latin America and Japan in East Asia—the advantages of multilateralism are particularly obvious and compelling. This may argue for creation of a new joint institution of the industrialized democracies to function, alongside the existing aid-giving organs of individual governments, to dispense economic and political development assistance. Certainly, it emphasizes the value of coordinating democratic assistance between the U.S. Agency for International Development (USAID) and its counterparts in Australia, Canada, Europe, and Japan.

5. For many of the same reasons, more politically autonomous and nongovernmental efforts are needed to aid democratic organizations and movements in authoritarian or newly democratizing countries. Aid that comes from nongovernmental organizations is less likely to be politically tainted or suspect and more likely to create enduring bonds of democratic cooperation across countries along functional lines: among journalists, intellectuals, bar associations, human rights organizations, women's organizations, student and youth groups, independent trade unions, business associations, and political parties of broadly similar orientation. In its brief five years of existence, the National Endowment for Democracy (NED) has done an outstanding job of fostering such linkages and supporting creative and often valiant efforts to strengthen demo-

cratic pluralism and to open closed societies. Other examples of important nongovernmental efforts, on very different scales, include the work of the Socialist International and the Committee to Protect Journalists.[33]

6. There is an urgent need for a new form of international organization representing exclusively the democratic governments of the world. Such a club of democracies would not supplant the United Nations or various regional organizations but would provide an institutional mechanism for the provision of multilateral assistance and the fashioning and coordination of multilateral strategies to foster democratization around the world. Further, it would provide a forum for democracies to study and discuss their common problems of consolidating, maintaining, and deepening democracy; extending it to other realms of society, such as the workplace; and improving democratic accountability, responsiveness, and openness. Finally, it would provide, through an increasingly dense network of cultural and political exchanges, a framework of mutual support and a medium of international status from which countries might regret to be excluded. Although there are reasons to be cautious in tying membership to economic benefits, such as freer trade and more generous aid, the more tangible the benefits of membership, the greater the incentive of countries to satisfy the political conditions for membership. At a minimum, creative means can be found to accentuate the special international status accorded to those countries with democratic political systems. The nature and scale of this organizational task are such that it could only be launched through the personal commitment of the elected leaders of major democratic countries in the world.[34]

Strategies and Targets of International Assistance. From these diverse sources, international assistance may pursue several strategies for democratization. First and most important, aid efforts should focus on fostering pluralism and autonomy in organizational life and the flow of information. This is particularly important because it builds the social and cultural foundation for democracy without dictating to a country what its constitutional structure should look like. Because it is one step removed from the distribution of state power, it is less immediately threatening, thus somewhat more palatable, to authoritarian rulers than explicit demands for their withdrawal from power. Anything that is done to increase the capacity and resources of the people to organize themselves (for a diverse range of purposes) independently of the state strengthens the democratic prospect. The same can be said for any initiative that improves access to objective information and reporting; fosters independent ideas, scholarship, and artistic expression; facilitates critical commentary and opinions; and encourages open debate between competing perspectives on issues. When such initiatives emerge from the grass roots of an authoritarian society—as with Solidarity in Poland, Charter 77 in Czechoslovakia, Radio Nanduti in Paraguay, or the black trade union movement in South Africa, or the Bangladesh Society for the Enforcement of Human Rights—they deserve material, technical, and moral support from the established democracies.

Second, external democratic actors need to encourage efforts to strengthen the rule of law in authoritarian regimes, as well as in transitional regimes, such as those in Central America or the Philippines, where judicial systems still suffer the scars of authoritarian rule and due process is not secure. This involves supporting human rights organizations that monitor and expose abuses, aid the victims of torture and violence, provide them legal assistance, and educate the people about their rights; training judges, magistrates, court clerks, lawyers, paralegal workers, and human rights educators; supporting programs for legal outreach, legal aid, and various forms of non- or quasi-judicial conflict conciliation; funding legal schools, libraries, institutes, and professional societies; and training prosecutors and police in professional, democratic methods of law enforcement.

Most of the aforementioned activities and organizations feature prominently in the democratic assistance efforts of the National Endowment for Democracy and the U.S. Agency for International Development.[35] Indeed, a scholarly assessment of these two institutions' programs, in light of the growing accumulation of empirical evidence, must concede that policymakers already understand quite well what needs to be done to encourage and advance the process of democratization in developing and closed societies. Nevertheless, the current annual budget for NED (including its four core grantees) is only about $16.9 million,[36] and the 1987 (fiscal year) budget for USAID's "Section 116(e)" activities—those specifically designated for the strengthening of civil and political rights—was only $6.2 million.

This is a shamefully inadequate commitment of resources for the largest and wealthiest industrialized democracy, especially now that it claims to have the promotion of democracy and human rights as one of its major foreign-policy goals. Other U.S. government programs (in USAID and the U.S. Information Agency, among others) also expend funds in support of democratic pluralism and change, but the total commitment remains slight in relation to any measure of U.S. resources or national security expenditures. The result is that although USAID and NED do many good works, thousands of worthy efforts around the world go unassisted and badly underfunded and others receive considerably less support than they could effectively use.

Indiscriminate funding will not improve the democratic prospect, but it is disingenuous to presume that funding does not limit what can be done. Building the organizational, informational, and legal infrastructures of democracy—not to mention other aspects of democratic development, such as improving the technical and substantive capacities of legislatures, local governments, and electoral administration—requires financial as well as human resources. Governments and organizations in the established democracies that profess a deep commitment to global democratization must reach much more deeply into their budgets to support it.

The above efforts involve methodically developing social pluralism and the rule of law. When the regime opens sufficiently to permit the existence of opposition parties, financial and technical assistance can also assist them in developing and mobilizing mass support. Reaching that point, however, may be difficult or treacherous, as it requires that the regime tolerate more explicit threats to its own continuation. Before that, a regime (again, if it is not rapidly collapsing) must be persuaded to permit some degree of freedom for groups to organize and alternative sources of information to surface and circulate. This crucial liberalizing step, and others that improve the human rights climate and the rule of law, may result largely from political processes and pressures

243

within the regime or the society, but even in these cases prudent and sometimes forceful diplomatic and economic pressure can help them along.

Even if diplomatic pressure achieves only a grudging reduction in human rights violations by a dictator, such as Mobutu (whose departure from power may be difficult to envisage in the near term), that is important. When circumstances are ripe and societal forces are mobilizing convincingly for a transition to democracy, diplomatic pressure can be elevated to a focus on full democratization. The failure of U.S. sanctions and pressures, however, to force Noriega's departure from Panama (not to mention the full and genuine democratization of power in that military-dominated country) should signal the limits of even superpower influence and the complexities of trying to shape political events in another country. To return to an earlier theme, diplomatic pressure for democratization is much more likely to be effective if it joins with and is responsive to democratic forces inside the country and if it is coordinated with other democratic countries (especially in the region) that have cultural, economic, or political influence.

A fourth international strategy for democratization encompasses economic relations. Although democrats should always be cautious about taking steps that would make the subjects of an authoritarian regime suffer for the sins of their rulers, there are instances in which economic sanctions may constitute a potent form of pressure and an effective component of a larger strategy for isolating and shaming a regime internationally and for weakening its base of domestic support. Constable and Valenzuela concluded that U.S. support for multilateral loans to Chile, totaling $2.2 billion since

1980, helped perpetuate the Pinochet regime, in part by boosting "his claims that he still has important friends in Washington. . . . Yet on the one occasion when substantive pressure was threatened—the 1985 multilateral loan abstentions—the dictator quickly lifted the state of siege."[37]

A more important dimension of economic strategy, however, involves the need for financial assistance to new democratic regimes. Many of these regimes encounter, upon assuming power, a profound economic crisis resulting from the reckless management and even plundering of the economy by the previous authoritarian rulers. Although new democratic regimes may begin with a considerable reservoir of popular legitimacy and goodwill, they must eventually improve economic conditions if they are to survive. Indeed, economic reconstruction is now the most urgent and important challenge facing the new democracies of Latin America and the Philippines, one that seriously threatens their consolidation and survival. With crushing debt burdens that can never be repaid, yet that still sap the resources needed for new investment in economic recovery, these economies are trapped in catastrophic depressions that have seen living standards plunge back in time 10 or 20 years or more. Government policies and mismanagement may contribute to such declines, but huge debt service obligations leave the new democratic governments little room for policy maneuver, and people will only tolerate such depression and misery for so long before they turn to more radical, desperate, and violent solutions.

Nothing the industrialized democracies can do to foster democracy around the world would have as profound and immediate an impact as a far-reaching program of debt relief and development assistance. Such a program must permanently and substantially reduce the foreign debt burdens of economically struggling democracies in the Third World; limit debt service payments to a level consistent with economic growth; and mobilize the substantial new financial resources necessary to rekindle economic growth. Simply providing new loans to roll over existing debts may stave off an international financial panic (and the collapse of individual banks), but it will not renew economic growth in the developing world. New democracies need and deserve the chance to make a new economic beginning for their peoples.

Opening Totalitarian Regimes. Totalitarian regimes are unique in their comprehensive control over individual and group life, but they are not unchanging or invulnerable. Indeed, an important element of the democratic ferment in the world today is the widening cracks in the totalitarian structures of the Soviet Union and China in particular. As Brzezinski recently argued, these cracks will likely continue to widen throughout the communist world because they derive from a fundamental contradiction between the need for participation and individual incentives "to transcend the phase of industrialization" and the need for "highly regimented, disciplined and bureaucratized non-participation" to preserve the hierarchical, centralized control of the Marxist-Leninist-Stalinist state.[38]

Some would regard the changes to date as sufficient to challenge the characterization of these countries as totalitarian any longer.[39] Even with the reduction of terror and repression and the modestly improving climate for dissent, critical expression, and independent organization, however, many totalitarian features remain. There should be no illusion that these will be easily undone, for a distinctive feature of the totalitarian state is that it entrenches such a vast network of party and government apparatchiki whose privileges and power would be gravely threatened by any relaxation of centralized control. As Linz stated, "To be stable, posttotalitarianism can reject the totalitarian heritage only selectively and gradually, if it is not to lead to a revolutionary outbreak that could lead to a radical change of the system, endangering the continuity in power of the elite."[40]

Democracies can do virtually nothing to change the structure of state power and the unaccountability of ruling groups in totalitarian or even posttotalitarian regimes. They can be prepared, however, to encourage political reformers within those regimes when they emerge, and to foster an international climate conducive to reform. In the contemporary world, where international contact and exchange are so fundamental to every dimension of national vitality and progress, the degree of economic, cultural, and political isolation must matter to any regime concerned about national development. To the extent that political and civil liberties in communist countries improve, democracies should be prepared to expand all manner of contacts with them. These contacts will in turn tend to further enhance social pluralism and democratic pressure over time. In this sense, linkage may be an appropriate concept: totalitarian regimes should know that their fuller acceptance into the world's most dynamic orbits of economic, scientific, technical, and cultural exchange depend on their liberalization.[41] There should be tangible rewards for progress, which would generate incentives for further liberalization.

If one assumes, which unfortunately one must, that the major totalitarian regimes in the world are not about to simply collapse, then the transition from totalitarianism will inevitably be a gradual one, although certain phases of it may seem to (and perhaps need to) move with stunning boldness and speed. Hence, democratic nations must plan for a long, subtle struggle of engagement and stick patiently to a coherent strategy. Some obvious features of this strategy will seem familiar:

1. Democratic nations must closely coordinate among themselves their various interactions with totalitarian states, if pressure and incentives are to be effective.

2. Human rights concerns should be regularly and vigorously raised in diplomatic contacts, summits, and international forums. In particular, the Soviet bloc countries should be relentlessly, creatively, and forcefully pressed to honor their treaty obligations with regard to human rights.

3. Democratic countries should focus on initiatives to support the growth of independent associations and scholarship and the freer flow of information, ideas, and opinions. Ways should be found to offer financial and technical support to emergent pluralism in associational, intellectual, and creative life. Institutions in the democratic nations should seek to establish links and exchanges with such emergent groups when they form, and the survival and freedom from repression of those groups should be made a matter of highly visible international concern.

4. The flow of decentralizing technologies should be encouraged. The personal computer and the photocopy machine are serious threats to totalitarian rule because, to the extent that wide access to them exists, centralized control over the flow of information is undermined. More generally, because economic vitality in a highly developed economy requires wide, decentralized access to and rapid flows of information, it is doubtful that a postindustrial level of development and affluence is attainable in a totalitarian (or even highly centralized posttotalitarian) society.[42]

The above principles follow naturally from the preceding analysis, but they also raise a dilemma. Restraining contact and exchange with the industrial democracies enables those democracies to use their economic and scientific advantages as leverage to encourage the opening of totalitarian and posttotalitarian societies. The rapid development of those societies—especially their increasing exposure to the technologies and demands of the information age and the strengthening of autonomous forms of social and economic organization—may prove an even more powerful solvent of totalitarian structures and restraints. Policymakers must be sensitive to the costs and trade-offs involved. When a contradiction does arise, there is something to be said for pushing the development of pluralism forward as fast as possible through the proliferation of contacts, at the same time searching for individual and group recipients of contact that are as independent as possible from the totalitarian state.

Forging a Coherent Strategy

The world is shrinking. As international exchanges of goods, technologies, news, information, ideas, students, tourists, entertainers, athletes, novels, plays, and movies proliferate, people are slowly evolving elements of a common global culture. This is a subtle and diffuse phenomenon that is difficult to measure. It is visible in the spread of democratic values, norms, and aspirations. It is helping to inspire many courageous movements for civil and political liberties, just as the growing density of political and economic ties may limit the options of regimes that would repress these movements.

The global movement for democracy today has momentum, but historically such moments of promise were cyclical swings and did not last. The challenge for committed democratic actors—individuals, institutions, and nations—is to fashion strategies for engaging authoritarian and totalitarian regimes that will be consistent over the long run and coherent and cumulative in their effects. The limits to international pressure for democratization are not only intrinsic but also self-imposed by democratic actors with short attention spans, inflated notions of their individual importance, divergent policies and priorities, and schizophrenic, zigzagging strategies of influence. Established democratic institutions and nations can advance the cause of democracy in other countries, but first they must get their own act together.

Acknowledgement: The author gratefully acknowledges grant support from the National Endowment for Democracy, the United States Agency for International Development, and the MacArthur Foundation for comparative research on democracy in developing countries. However, the views and recommendations in this paper are strictly those of the author and do not represent the above named institutions, the Hoover Institution, or any other agency.

Notes

1. See his annual ratings of political rights and civil liberties by country in Raymond D. Gastil, ed., *Freedom in the World: Political Rights and Civil Liberties, 1987–88* (New York: Freedom House, 1988), pp. 3–89.

2. There were, for example, 53 states rated as "free" in the first year of the survey,

1973, and 54 in 1980, compared with 57 in 1987.

3. The arguments for this approach may be found in the preface to the regional volumes (2–4) of Larry Diamond, Juan J. Linz, and Seymour Martin Lipset, eds., *Democracy in Developing Countries* (Boulder, Colo.: Lynne Rienner Publishers, 1988 and 1989), pp. xvi and xxiii–xxv.

4. Ibid., p. xvi.

5. Linz, "Totalitarian and Authoritarian Regimes," *Handbook of Political Science, Vol. 3: Macropolitical Theory*, Fred I. Greenstein and Nelson W. Polsby, eds. (Reading, Mass.: Addison-Wesley, 1975), pp. 187–192.

6. Ibid., especially pp. 264–274.

7. Some indispensable theoretical and empirical works are Lipset, *Political Man* (Baltimore, Md.: Johns Hopkins University Press, 1981, first published in 1960); Gabriel Almond and Sidney Verba, *The Civic Culture* (Princeton, N.J.: Princeton University Press, 1963); Robert Dahl, *Polyarchy: Participation and Opposition* (New Haven, Conn.: Yale University Press, 1971); Linz, *The Breakdown of Democratic Regimes: Crisis, Breakdown and Reequilibration* (Baltimore, Md.: The Johns Hopkins University Press, 1978); G. Bingham Powell, Jr., *Contemporary Democracies: Participation, Stability and Violence* (Cambridge, Mass.: Harvard University Press, 1982); and Samuel P. Huntington, "Will More Countries Become Democratic?", *Political Science Quarterly* 99:2, pp. 193–218. Much fuller discussions of the evidence and findings from the 26-nation comparative study may be found in Diamond, Linz, and Lipset, *Democracy in Developing Countries*, "Building and Sustaining Democratic Government in Developing Countries: Some Tentative Findings," *World Affairs* 150:1 (Summer 1987), pp. 5–19, and "Democracy in Developing Countries: Facilitating and Obstructing Factors," in Gastil, pp. 229–258.

8. Dahl, p. 36.

9. Ibid., pp. 33–47.

10. Linz, "The Transition from Authoritarian Regimes to Democratic Political Systems and the Problems of Consolidation of Political Democracy," paper presented to the International Political Science Association,

Tokyo Round Table, March 29–April 1, 1982, p. 34.

11. Guillermo O'Donnell and Philippe C. Schmitter, *Transitions from Authoritarian Rule: Tentative Conclusions About Uncertain Democracies* (Baltimore, Md.: The Johns Hopkins University Press, 1986). The quoted passages are from pp. 43 and 11. The book is part of the 4-volume *Transitions from Authoritarian Rule*, O'Donnell, Schmitter, and Laurence Whitehead, eds.

12. O'Donnell and Schmitter, pp. 7–10.

13. Linz, "The Transition from Authoritarian Regimes," p. 38.

14. On their crucial contributions and the process of democratization in Turkey through *reforma* rather than *ruptura*, see Ergun Ozbudun, "Turkey: Crises, Interruptions and Reequilibrations," in Diamond, Linz, and Lipset, *Democracy in Developing Countries: Asia.*

15. O'Donnell and Schmitter, pp. 15–17.

16. Ibid., p. 49.

17. Huntington, *Political Order in Changing Societies* (New Haven: Yale University Press, 1968), p. 41.

18. Ibid., p. 5.

19. On these processes, see also Huntington and Joan M. Nelson, *No Easy Choice: Political Participation in Developing Countries* (Cambridge, Mass.: Harvard University Press, 1976).

20. Linz, "The Transition from Authoritarian Regimes," p. 18.

21. Ibid., p. 19.

22. See Diamond, "Nigeria: Pluralism, Statism and the Struggle for Democracy," in Diamond, Linz, and Lipset, *Democracy in Developing Countries: Africa*, pp. 46–47, 75, 81–82.

23. See in particular O'Donnell and Schmitter.

24. Linz, "Innovative Leadership in the Transition to Democracy and a New Democracy: The Case of Spain," paper prepared for the Conference on Innovative Leadership and International Politics, Hebrew University of Jerusalem, June 8–10, 1987.

25. See Arturo Valenzuela, "Chile: The Origins, Consolidation, and Breakdown of a Democratic Regime," in Diamond, Linz, and Lipset, *Democracy in Developing Countries: Latin America.*

26. On the substantial U.S. role in aiding the "militarization of the state" in Uruguay, see Charles G. Gillespie, "On the Relation Between State and Regime: Authoritarianism and Democratization in Uruguay," prepared for the Symposium on "Democratization and the State in the Southern Cone," 46th International Congress of Americanists, Amsterdam, July 4–8, 1988. For evidence of "a statistically significant and quite strong negative correlation" between U.S. military assistance during 1953–1963 and the subsequent stability (during the Johnson and Nixon administrations) of democracy in 17 developing countries, see Edward N. Muller, "Dependent Economic Development, Aid Dependence on the United States, and Democratic Breakdown in the Third World," *International Studies Quarterly* 29:4 (December 1985), pp. 445–469.

27. Jonathan Hartlyn, "Colombia: The Politics of Violence and Accommodation," and John Booth, "Costa Rica: The Development of Stable Democracy," in Diamond, Linz, and Lipset, *Democracy in Developing Countries: Latin America.*

28. Carlos Waisman, "Argentina: Autarkic Industrialization and Illegitimacy," in Diamond, Linz, and Lipset, *Democracy in Developing Countries: Latin America.* Eloquent testimony to the humanitarian and democratic impact of Carter's human rights policies in Argentina is also given by Guillermo O'Donnell, "Transitions to Democracy: Some Navigation Instruments," paper delivered to the Conference on Reinforcing Democracy in the Americas, Carter Center of Emory University, Atlanta, Georgia, November 17–18, 1986.

29. Howard J. Wiarda, "The Dominican Republic: The Mirror Legacies of Democracy and Authoritarianism," in Diamond, Linz, and Lipset, *Democracy in Developing Countries: Latin America*; and Laurence Whitehead, "International Aspects of Democratization," in O'Donnell, Schmitter, and Whitehead, eds., *Transitions from Authoritarian Rule: Comparative Perspectives*, p. 37.

30. Ibid., pp. 21–23. The EEC's condition is that "only states which guarantee on their territories truly democratic practices and respect for fundamental rights and free-

doms can become members of our Community."

31. Ibid., p. 34.

32. Huntington, "Will More Countries Become Democratic?", p. 194.

33. For an extensive review of the democratization efforts of the SI, see Whitehead, pp. 25–31.

34. An interesting recent development in this direction was the June 1988 conference in Manila of 13 "newly restored democracies" (Argentina, Brazil, the Dominican Republic, Ecuador, Greece, Honduras, Nicaragua, Peru, the Philippines, Portugal, El Salvador, Spain, and Uruguay). The group pledged solidarity on economic issues and mutual support in their struggle to renegotiate their foreign debts. Among other things, they also condemned terrorism, offered asylum for political refugees from dictatorships, and agreed to meet in 1989 in Peru in an effort to transform the conference into a permanent organization ("13 New Democracies Vow Mutual Support," *Los Angeles Times*, June 7, 1988). Although the inclusion of Nicaragua in the conference raises controversial problems about the group's identity, it is possible that this group of new, Third World democracies could join with the seven industrialized democracies whose leaders now confer annually to establish some kind of new international organization of democracies.

35. See the National Endowment for Democracy, "The Challenge of Democracy: Advancing the Cause of Democracy Throughout the World," (Washington, D.C.: National Endowment for Democracy, May 1987); and USAID's annual listing of Human Rights Programs under Section 116(e) of the Foreign Assistance Act of 1961.

36. The four core grantees are the Free Trade Union Institute, the Center for International Private Enterprise, the National Democratic Institute for International Affairs, and the National Republican Institute for International Affairs. Together they were allocated over $11.5 million (over two-thirds) of the $16.875 million congressional appropriation for NED during fiscal year 1988, leaving the endowment only about $5.25 million to fund a wide range of other programs and initiatives.

37. Pamela Constable and Arturo Valenzuela, "Is Chile Next?", *Foreign Policy*, no. 63, Summer 1986, pp. 74–75.

38. Zbigniew Brzezinski, "The Crisis of Communism: The Paradox of Political Participation," *The Washington Quarterly* 10:4 (Autumn 1987), pp. 167, 168.

39. A classic statement of the nature and dilemmas of "posttotalitarian" authoritarian regimes and the dynamics of "detotalitarianization" may be found in Linz, "Totalitarian and Authoritarian Regimes," pp. 336–350.

40. Ibid., p. 342.

41. Linkage of regime behavior (internal or international) to arms-control negotiations is a bad idea, however, because it presumes that arms control is a favor or gift of the democratic West to the Soviet Union and the Warsaw Pact, rather than a matter of mutual security and survival.

42. See Brzezinski, p. 168.